THE SOUL, T
AND THE PSYCH   ALYST

THE SOUL, THE MIND, AND THE PSYCHOANALYST

The Creation of the Psychoanalytic Setting in Patients with Psychotic Aspects

David Rosenfeld

KARNAC

First published in 2006 by
Karnac Books
118 Finchley Road
London NW3 5HT

British Library Cataloguing in Publication Data

A C.I.P. for this book is available from the British Library

ISBN-13: 978-1-85575-470-6
ISBN-10: 1-85575-470-3

Edited, designed, and produced by Communication Crafts

Printed in Great Britain

www.karnacbooks.com

This book is dedicated to my beloved family,
Estela, Deborah, Daniel, Karin, Rolando, Ezequiel, and Tamara;
with my gratitude to Robert Wallerstein, Norbert Freedman,
Paul Williams, and Alain de Mijolla,
and to Thomas Ogden, with whom we also share
our common interest in poetry and Jorge Luis Borges

CONTENTS

ACKNOWLEDGEMENTS

Chapter 1, first published as "Der 11. September: Militärdiktatur und psychotische Episode." *Jahrbuch der Psychoanalyse. Trauma: Neue Entwicklungen in der Psychoanalyse, 50* (2005) (Stuttgart: Fromman-Holzboog Verlag). (Translated by Susan Rogers.) [Also "Dictadura militar i episodi psicotic", *Revista Catalana de Psicoanalisi, 20* (1–2, 2003–04). Publication of the Barcelona Institute of Psychoanalysis, editor and translator, Pere Folch.]

Chapter 2, first published as "Les traumatismes des premiers mois de la vie et leurs rapports avec les troubles de l'alimentation: anorexie, boulimie", *Journal de la Psychanalyse de l'Enfant, 37* (2005): 281–315. (Translated by Susan Rogers.)

Chapter 3, first published as: "Drug abuse, regression, and primitive object relations" (translated by Liliane Hecht, with the assistance of L. Bryce Boyer), in: L. Bryce Boyer & P. Giovacchini (Eds.), *Master Clinicians on Treating the Regressed Patient, Vol. 2* (Northvale, NJ: Jason Aronson, 1993), pp. 205–242.

Chapter 4, first published as: "Psychotic addiction to video games" (translated by Liliane Hecht), in: P. Williams (Ed.), *A Language for Psychosis* (London: Whurr, 2001), pp. 175–198. © John Wiley & Sons Limited.

Chapter 5, first published as: "Listening to and interpreting a psychotic patient", in: J. Reppen (Ed.), *More Analysts at Work* (Northvale, NJ: Jason Aronson, 1997). (Revised version translated by Sylvine G. Campbell.)

Chapter 6: Revised version of "Understanding varieties of autistic encapsulation: A homage to Frances Tustin", in: J. Mitrani & T. Mitrani (Eds.), *Encounters with Autistic States: A Memorial Tribute to Frances Tustin* (Northvale, NJ: Jason Aronson, 1997). (Revised version translated by Sylvine G. Campbell.)

Chapter 7, part of chapter adapted (with order changed) from: "Psychotic body image" (translated by Liliane Hecht), in: L. Bryce Boyer & P. Giovacchini (Eds.), *Master Clinicians on Treating the Regressed Patient, Vol. 1* (Northvale, NJ: Jason Aronson, 1990). Clinical case adapted from D. Rosenfeld, *Psychoanalysis and Groups: History and Dialectics* (London: Karnac, 1988), pp. 65–77.

Chapter 8, first published as: "Freud: An imaginary dialogue" (translated by Liliane Hecht), in: J. Sandler (Ed.), *On Freud's "Analysis Terminable and Interminable"* (International Psychoanalytical Association, Educational Monographs, 1987; reprinted New Haven, CT: Yale University Press, 1991), pp. 142–162.

[Preface, translated by Susan Rogers. All French, Portuguese, and Spanish poems and songs were translated by the author.]

Thomas Ogden

In the course of reading this book, the reader is afforded the unusual opportunity to accompany David Rosenfeld, one of the most inventive minds in psychoanalysis today, as he does his analytic work. In this foreword, I look closely at two chapters that, for me, powerfully capture what is most important and original about the way Rosenfeld thinks and works as a psychoanalyst.

I will begin with Chapter 1, "September 11th: Military Dictatorship and Psychotic Episode". In this chapter, Rosenfeld presents his work with a man whose parents were kidnapped on September 11th by the Pinochet military dictatorship. The patient, "Abelard", who was 18 months old at the time, was cared for by neighbours during the initial years of his parents' "disappearance" and torture. (The date—September 11th—flickers back and forth in this paper between standing as a symbol for an individual's experience, and standing as a symbol for the collapse of the world as it had existed to that point.)

Rosenfeld met Abelard for the first time when the patient was 23 years old. Abelard had recently been discharged from a mental hospital where he had been treated for a chronic psychosis. The initial interview was conducted in a café so that the patient could speak out of the presence of his grandmother, with whom he was living. In doing so, Rosenfeld was showing—not telling—the patient how he works as an analyst: that is, he constructs an analytic frame that reflects who the patient is and what he or she needs in order to make use of an analytic process. The frame, constructed in this way for each patient, is a highly personal statement made by the analyst to the patient.

The initial months of analysis involved the creation of a reliable holding environment for Abelard. By asking the patient why he had not telephoned when he had been awoken by a terrifying nightmare, Rosenfeld communicated to Abelard that in addition to their daily sessions (sometimes two sessions in a day), he was available to Abelard (at that point in the work) whenever the need arose—as a mother does for an infant. This was of great emotional significance to Abelard as reflected in his (psychotic) statement, "How nice! In Buenos Aires there are bookstores open at night."

It must be emphasized that Rosenfeld's approach to working with Abelard involved much more than the provision of holding described above; it also centrally involved the work of putting the patient's psychotic experience into verbally symbolized form. This interpretative work is, for Rosenfeld, guided at every moment by his countertransference experience. For example, when Abelard spoke in a confused, jumbled way of a book that came unbound and about his parents' divorce and the straw that broke the camel's back, Rosenfeld responded by saying, "The straw . . . the divorce . . . unbound the book that is your head, unbound your head, then [there] was the psychosis, the hospitalization." Such interventions capture in words not only the meaning of the patient's fragmented experience, but "the music" of the patient's experience—that is, the inarticulate feeling state that had its origins in a period prior to the patient's development of language. In Rosenfeld's intervention, one set of words and phrases cascades into the next in a way that communicates not only the fact that he understands the way the patient experienced his life, but also that he can render it more comprehensible for the patient. These preverbal feelings were far too painful for Abelard to symbolize verbally—much less to organize by means of secondary-process thinking. The unbearable intensity of that early experience had overpowered Abelard's capacity to think or dream the traumatic early emotional situation.

Rosenfeld describes a session in which Abelard began by saying that when he had left the previous session, he had tried to take the bus back home but had encountered a series of deranged bus drivers who were trying to drive him crazy. Rosenfeld interpreted this experience as an expression of Abelard's fear that Rosenfeld, too, was insane and was misdirecting the analysis to such an extent that the patient would end up back in the psychiatric hospital. (Abelard's communication of his mistrust of Rosenfeld—in the delusional displacement—reflected not only his fear of Rosenfeld, but also his sense of safety and freedom while with Rosenfeld to experience and voice any feeling state, however angry and destructive they may feel to Abelard.) A little later in this session, the patient—completely unexpectedly—began to sing a lullaby. Rosenfeld, without a moment's hesitation, sang the song with the patient for more than ten minutes. They then sang other children's songs together. Each time I read this portion of Rosenfeld's description of his work with this patient, I am impressed with his extraordinary intuitive grasp of what is happening in the analytic relationship. So much was conveyed to the patient—through music—by Rosenfeld's spontaneously entering into that very tender experience with Abelard.

Reflecting on that moment in the analysis, Rosenfeld views the patient's singing—and his own—as a form of bringing to life in the analysis Abelard's very early loving experience with his mother, which had been safeguarded by means of autistic encapsulation. This conceptualization of the function of autistic encapsulation as a sanctuary in which healthy early experiences can be safeguarded from psychotic fragmentation is original to Rosenfeld. This idea, to my mind, represents a major contribution to the psychoanalytic understanding of the role of autistic defences in the psychotic personality.

But it was not creative psychoanalytic thinking alone that allowed Rosenfeld to successfully treat Abelard. As important was his love for the patient: "To tell the truth, it was a luxury to have a patient who, after being hospitalized in a psychiatric hospital, could communicate through emotion, the beauty and aesthetics of poetry and music."

In addition to being an extraordinary clinician and theorist, Rosenfeld is also a gifted teacher. He lucidly and succinctly conveys his ideas concerning the central role in psychoanalysis of the analyst's use of his countertransference experience. He views countertransference as a signal, to be used to think and not to expel or interpret. "[It is] a hypothesis that the therapist creates in the field of work. . . . Countertransference may be a highly useful tool . . . [with which] to discover what the patient makes us feel that he cannot express in words." Rosenfeld's feelings of awe for the power and beauty of the analytic process are conveyed by the beauty of his own use of language: "Some things cannot be translated into words. How can I put the music during the sessions into words? Can states of pain, terror, suffering, and happiness be conveyed only in words? . . . [Quoting Borges:] 'But how can I convey the infinite to others, that my fearful memory can hardly encompass?'"

* * *

The second of the two chapters that I will discuss is Chapter 4, "Psychotic Addiction to Video Games". "Lorenzo", a 17-year-old adolescent, was referred to Rosenfeld because of a history of violence requiring psychiatric hospitalization. Lorenzo was addicted to playing video games depicting characters engaged in ferociously attacking and murdering one another. When the patient's father, in a state of desperation, attempted to take the video games from his son, Lorenzo flew into a rage in which he broke virtually every piece of furniture in the family home. On another occasion, when the patient's parents attempted to get him to leave a video-game arcade before he was able to defeat a menacing character in a game, Lorenzo broke the machine and the window of the arcade.

The hospital psychiatrist forbade Lorenzo the use of video games both in the hospital and after he returned home. Lorenzo's parents were unable to manage him at home and unable to get him to go to school—where he felt under attack by his teachers and classmates. In the initial meeting with Lorenzo and his parents, Rosenfeld invented psychoanalysis—and the analytic frame—anew for Lorenzo: He told the patient that he not only would not attempt to interfere with Lorenzo's playing video games, Rosenfeld "wanted to play [video games] with him in order to understand him better. . . . I also told him that we would be talking together . . . and that when he got a little better, we would go together to a video-game arcade".

Lorenzo, who had been furious at Rosenfeld up to this point in the initial meeting (calling him a madman), calmed down and accepted Rosenfeld as his doctor. Rosenfeld intuited that any attempt to separate Lorenzo from his video games would be experienced by him as a threat to his life and that Rosenfeld must begin analysis by demonstrating that he had no wish to strip Lorenzo of what he required for his survival. Such a capacity to know who one's patient is and to know how to communicate that understanding to the patient—as Rosenfeld did in this encounter—is something that cannot be taught. Each analyst must develop such a capacity on his or her own. But it is a great help to have models such as Rosenfeld to afford us a sense of what it is that we are aspiring to.

The early months of the analysis were marked not only by a psychotic transference, but by physical movements on the part of Lorenzo—such as walking on tiptoe and carrying out a myriad of obsessional rituals—that reminded Rosenfeld of the encapsulating symptomatology of autistic patients. Lorenzo and Rosenfeld played video games during the sessions. In this way, Rosenfeld attempted to gain entry into Lorenzo's terrifying world, which was populated by savage video-game characters.

Things did not go smoothly at the start. Lorenzo raged at Rosenfeld when he—Lorenzo—could not control one of the characters in the video game they were playing. Rosenfeld came to understand that the characters in the video games were as real to Lorenzo as were Rosenfeld himself and the patient's parents, teachers, and classmates. On one occasion, Lorenzo became frankly delusional after playing a laser video game with Rosenfeld. The patient was in a state of panic when he returned home after the session. His mother was able to calm him down by making an aluminium-foil outfit that the patient believed could protect him from the invasive laser beams. Rosenfeld made a pivotal decision not to hospitalize Lorenzo at this point and to see him every day of the week and sometimes twice a day. Rosenfeld explains that he did this "because I was interested in seeing the transferential origins that . . . triggered the delusion". He adds parenthetically, "This is the way I try to reason as a psychoanalyst". I would add, this is the sort of clinical juncture at which the reader learns a good deal about the courage and the belief in one's patient and in the psychoanalytic process that are required if one is to do psychoanalytic work with psychotic patients.

With considerable trepidation on Rosenfeld's part, he and Lorenzo played the video game that had precipitated the acute psychotic breakdown and state of panic. I do not think that it was lost to Lorenzo that Rosenfeld, by not hospitalizing him, was attempting to accompany the patient into the most terrifying corners of the patient's world. After losing a game to Rosenfeld, Lorenzo—still wearing his protective outfit—responded not with persecutory anxiety, but with words used as symbols: "Dr Rosenfeld, when you win, you can be transformed and become other characters, so even if I kill you now, you are still alive and have turned into another character".

Lorenzo was in this way explaining to Rosenfeld the laws of his internal object world: no dangerous person/character is ever killed. Rather, the character becomes transformed into an endless series of dangerous characters/people. Rosenfeld understood for the first time that the characters in the video games transformed themselves into dangerous people/characters in the patient's life outside the games, and vice versa. This was "the Rosetta stone" that allowed Rosenfeld to understand the way in which he and the characters on the screen can metamorphose and fragment into innumerable persecutory objects.

After a period of analytic work based on these understandings of the way Lorenzo's delusional world operates, Rosenfeld and Lorenzo played a 3-D video game at an arcade. The game created the illusion of images flying out of the screen into real life. This experience sent the patient into a state of terror. Lorenzo and Rosenfeld—along with the patient's psychiatrist, who prescribed medications for the patient— went to a nearby café, where they had tea. "Only after that did we ask him to explain to us in greater detail what he had felt." This experience served as the basis for Lorenzo's development—for the first time—of a capacity to differentiate between the two-dimensional characters on the screen and the three-dimensional people outside the screen. In other words, Lorenzo began to be able to create a space between symbol and symbolized, between animate and inanimate, between reality and fantasy.

Rosenfeld's detailed account of this clinical experience affords the reader the opportunity to accompany Rosenfeld step by step in his psychoanalytic work with his psychotic patient: "What is important is to be able to think psychoanalytically about the transference and the patient's inner world, as well as about the countertransference. No one can prevent me from thinking like a psychoanalyst, even when I am walking through the hospital with the patient, or going to a shopping mall and playing video games. Here, what is important is to create a mental space in common that is appropriate for holding and for psychoanalytic work."

Here also is the core of what, for me, is extraordinary about Rosenfeld's way of conducting himself as an analyst: he becomes the analyst that he intuits the patient needs at any given juncture of analysis.

Rosenfeld is never anything but an analyst when with his patients in virtually any setting, and the kind of analyst he is at any given juncture is determined by the analytic situation. In Lorenzo's analysis, at times this meant being an analyst who journeys with his patient into a psychotic, delusional world, involving endlessly transforming characters who move in and out of a video screen; at other times, it meant being a psychoanalyst who, in a café, held the patient—metaphorically—as the patient reconstituted himself after a period of psychotic disintegration; and at still other times, it meant making transference interpretations that addressed the patient's use of projective identification as he emptied his insane mind into Rosenfeld and consequently experienced Rosenfeld—in the form of deranged bus drivers—as attempting to drive him mad. Any single one of these ways of being an analyst for Lorenzo would, in isolation from the other ways of being an analyst, have been inadequate. Rosenfeld demonstrates the way he intuitively moved among a variety of ways of being an analyst in his analytic work with Lorenzo.

To conclude, I have elected to discuss these two chapters from this volume not only because they are, for me, two of the most emotionally and intellectually powerful in this rich collection, but also because, to my mind, they represent two of the most important contributions of the past decade to the understanding of the psychoanalytic treatment of psychotic patients.

PREFACE

lthough I am a classically trained psychoanalyst who has worked for many years, and still works, in the traditional way with neurotic patients, I have also spent the last thirty years working psychoanalytically with severely disturbed patients. As a psychoanalyst, I automatically think psychoanalytically, whether I am treating a neurotic patient or one who is going through a transitory psychotic episode. It is second nature to think about the transference, the internal world, the drives, emotions, feelings, and the internal and external relationships in a psychoanalytic manner. In this book, I wish to share my thoughts and experiences about this deeply fascinating, complicated, demanding work.

The common factor in all the cases is how the psychoanalytic setting is created: the internalization and realization inside the patient's mind with the feeling of fixed hours and the transferential relation with the psychoanalyst. It means that in healthy or neurotic patients the setting also takes a long time to be internalized: this is the dialectic creation, which is built up only after a relatively long time.

My scientific curiosity was aided by the great masters of psychoanalysis whose personal teaching and advice I had the good fortune to receive. They have guided my steps through the mysterious terrain of the mind, especially in its most regressive, primitive, and psychotic aspects. Only with the help of these masters was I able to venture into these mysteries and find the courage to treat, as I describe in this book, and to work the way I think: that psychoanalysis is possible even in the most severe, most acute cases.

There is one important condition for these treatments, which I learned treating neurotic patients, especially children—more specifically, autistic children. The patient must be dealt with at the first sign of illness. If they are not treated in time, they become fixed, rigid, and chronic. My colleagues and masters in France and in London who treat autistic children are in total agreement on this point.

I am grateful that I had the opportunity to live and study in Paris, to supervise with the masters in London for many, many years, and to live, visit, and study on both coasts of the United States. I learned from many master clinicians, and the integration of all these ideas allows me to be flexible with clinical work and with theory.

Of course, this is not to deny the importance of the very good teachers and excellent personal psychoanalysis that I had in Buenos Aires, which gave me a start on a career that began when I was very young.

In one of the psychiatric hospitals, reminiscent of the Middle Ages, where I did part of my psychiatric residency, I learned what one must not do to a human being who is suffering a psychotic episode. Learning what to do and what not to do are equally important.

This book is intended to be felt and thought about. The reader is asked to read between the lines, to imagine and feel beyond the words on the page. I hope that what I have written will become an emotional dialogue between me and my reader.

In a sonnet, Shakespeare wrote: "So are you to my thoughts as food to life . . . Or as sweet-season'd showers are to the ground" (Sonnet 75). I am asking this kind of engagement from the reader because words are not enough to convey what the psychoanalyst and his patient feel when a young man tells for the first time about the tortures suffered by his family in a Latin-American dictatorship.

Written words are not enough to express the emotions recovered by a patient through lullabies, recapturing and recuperating from a lost infancy. Nor are they enough to convey the emotions of a psychoanalyst when, after a long and apparently successful treatment, an addicted patient goes back to drugs. Or what the patient feels—the emotions and sobs of a patient—who systematically draws the face, lips, eyebrows, cheeks, and eyes of a woman and one day, by chance, finds the only photo of his mother who died shortly after he was born, holding him in her arms—a photo of the woman he had drawn over and over again. Words on a page are not enough to express the impact on this patient of the discovery that he had preserved the internal image of his mother and, over the years, had compulsively drawn hundreds of pictures of the bits of her face. What can be experienced in a one-hour session could be years of life. Shakespeare described this better than I ever could: "For in a minute there are many days" (*Romeo and Juliet*, Act III, Scene 5).

As the great poet Jorge Luis Borges used to say in his conferences and writings, written words are not enough to express what the poet wants to say; I quote the difficulties in expressing via the written word: "to translate the spirit is such an enormous and phantasmagorical intention that it might very well become inoffensive" (Borges, 1936).

I want to note my deep conviction about what I also learned about psychoanalysis from poets like Shakespeare and Borges, and from the great philosophers studied at university. My common sense and intuition, however, was not learned from books: this I learned and experienced at home, in childhood.

As you will find throughout the book, I constantly quote Shakespeare and Borges, who capture so beautifully the experience of psychoanalysis. The poet writes that the words never express the whole idea and feeling. Shakespeare wrote about this gap:

> O, let my books be then the eloquence
> . . . of my speaking breast,
>
> . . .
>
> O, learn to read what silence hath writ:
> To hear with eyes belongs to love's fine wit.
>
> Shakespeare, Sonnet 23

2006

ABOUT THE AUTHOR

David Rosenfeld, MD, trained in Buenos Aires, Argentina, and lived and studied for many years in Paris and in London, and also in the United States. He is a Consultant Professor at the Buenos Aires University, Faculty of Medicine, Department of Mental Health and Psychiatry, a Training Analyst at the Buenos Aires Psychoanalytic Society, and an Ex-Vice President of the International Psychoanalytical Association.

His publications in English include *Psychoanalysis and Groups: History and Dialectics* and *The Psychotic: Aspects of the Personality.*

THE SOUL, THE MIND,
AND THE PSYCHOANALYST

CHAPTER ONE

September 11th:
military dictatorship
and psychotic episode—year 1973

> Even in a state so far removed from reality as hallucinatory
> confusion . . . that at one time in some corner of their mind there
> was a normal person hidden.
>
> Freud, 1940a

In this clinical history I describe the story of a young patient who could be considered a paradigmatic case illustrating the effects produced by military dictatorships that were similar in several South American countries.

In the methodological perspective, the therapist is faced with the not always easy task of continuing to think as a psychoanalyst in spite of the real traumatic events suffered by the patient, in terms of the patient's unconscious dynamics in the transference, while also considering his infantile world—and, especially, to be able to bring to a verbal level the terrible traumatic experience of a child under 2 years of age, who was handed over to a neighbour while his parents were being kidnapped by military personnel and then taken to secret centres of detention and torture.

The traumatic stress for a child, unprepared to anticipate danger, faced with the terrible, abrupt disappearance of his mother's and father's familiar voices and faces, is very difficult to work through. This traumatic stress remains forever engraved on the child's receptive mind, which is prone to great sensitivity and suffering in relation to separations and abandonment. For this reason I tried to pay special attention to our leave-taking at the end of each session (see the session in which the patient turns into a butterfly).

The grandmother had taken charge of the child and filled a fundamental role: reconstructing lost internal and external relationships.

The childhood and family history came up in the sessions in a confused, disordered way and was sometimes enacted during the session without words. It was reassembled, reconstructed, taken apart and reorganized again in the patient's mind and in mine as well.

At other times, this history was enacted within the session—he ripped pillows apart, wore dirty clothes, and looked like an 18-month-old baby.

Throughout the interviews I slowly found out how the parents had been persecuted and terribly tortured by the military and secret services of the Pinochet dictatorship.

In time they were able to escape from their country, Chile, and hide in an abbey in Brazil. But there they were harried by the secret services, since the dictatorship in Brazil—like those in Argentina, Uruguay, and Chile—had organized the Condor Plan, with which they persecuted, tortured, and murdered all those who opposed their dictatorships.

Later, the family were able to move secretly to a suburb of Buenos Aires, where they continued to live.

This clinical history begins with the patient's treatment in the city of Buenos Aires, which began after he was released from a psychiatric hospital following a psychotic episode.

The title refers to a historical fact that occurred on 11 September 1973: the day the *coup d'état* began in Chile, when Pinochet ordered the attack and aerial bombardment of the presidential palace, assassinating President Salvador Allende—elected in free elections—and the members of his Cabinet.

This is the other story.

"Abelard"

Methodological problems

My approach to the treatment of this patient included taking into account the real—that is, the reality of his parents' disappearance when Abelard was 18 months old and the consequent real destruction of family relationships. At the other pole, I tried to continue to think as a psychoanalyst, in order to understand his internal world, as well as the transference and the repetition of infantile traumata and psychosis in the transference.

One wonders whether it is possible to keep oneself, as a psychoanalyst, within the strict boundaries of cold scientificism and avoid being moved and abandoning one's role when confronted with the terrible and serious facts of bloody dictatorships that destroy lives and minds. This describes the complexity of this treatment.

I wish to discuss the difficult task, in these extreme situations, of a psychoanalyst who is treating a patient as well as the child within this patient.

Although I cannot omit my intense emotional response to the patient's descriptions, I tried to work with the instruments of psychoanalytic science (Klimovsky, 1971, 1980a).

The clinical and theoretical conclusions and the models used in this clinical work can be applied to other, similar cases.

As for the analytic technique, I tried to be very cautious and not too intrusive, in order to avoid hasty interpretations, given the patient's fragility, and because I assumed that words could be felt as if they were torturers in his ears (see the session when he says: "Don't torture me, Doctor").

I also carefully awaited the appropriate material before interpreting his sexual problem, which was quite mixed up in his internal world with the tortures and sexual abuses suffered by his mother at the hands of the military.

In the final conclusions I include a section on the childhood origins of mental confusion, particularly because of the family's confusing double-binds.

The father's role is also described in the final conclusions, including the oedipal conflict.

The confusions of self-identity with his mother's female body are described, as well as his own fantasies of his internal world. (Example:

at one point, the patient says: "The truth is, sometimes when I wake up and look at myself in the mirror . . . I think I'm seeing my Mum's face. . . . ")

I have selected the material in order to show what happens in the transference between the patient and the analyst, including acting out or enactment in the session, ranging from sobbing to violence, and the therapist's intense countertransferential emotional experiences.

I used some models that were useful to understand the mental dynamics and moments of psychotic confusion.

The patient re-creates in the transference moments of the first months of life and of his psychotic episode.

One of the methods of investigation used is *"autistic encapsulation"*: the encapsulation of aspects of good relationships and good infantile relations in the patient's mind (Rosenfeld, 1992b).

The other basic model is that, in the face of severe real traumata, all introjections or introjective identifications can disappear.

For this reason, I move between two poles of the problem: one, the possibility that everything introjected can disappear; the other, healthier aspects lie "autistically encapsulated" in a different mental space. When the introjects disappear, they can sometimes be recovered. In my experience treating survivors fleeing from the Nazis in Europe, they sometimes remember their own names or their childhood language—German, Italian, and so on—only decades later, while others remember the songs and music of those early years.

This patient ultimately believed that he had also lost his internal and emotional relationships.

Aside from the patient's psychotic moments and mental confusion, we also gradually investigated and discovered the family's systems of communication: double-binds and contradictory messages, as well as a distorted perception of reality, especially by his mother. It was important to detect the confusing double-binds his mother tended to give Abelard, as well as the way she distorted his perception of reality, sometimes with simple anecdotes that, nonetheless, produced intense effects in the young patient's mind. For example, she told him that she had gone to speak to the psychoanalyst because he had asked her to do so, which was not true. This is the family foundation or basis of his psychopathology and mental fragility, in addition to the patient's own dynamics and psychopathology. It is also related to the role of the father, as we shall see in the theoretical conclusions.

We are psychoanalysts and also teachers in a way, since we teach the patient other aspects of the world and reality and, of course, of internal reality as well.

Psychoanalysis, besides interpreting, tries to teach patients to be epistemologists of themselves.

The treatment

The first interview

I had to have the first interview in the house where Abelard lived— the home of his grandmother, with whom he was living.

The patient, a young man of 23, hardly left his bed and was very isolated from his friends.

I went to see him at about 11 am.

He walked into the room as if still asleep and looked untidy and unclean. I thought that he was also over-medicated.

Both the patient and his grandmother—a very kind and affectionate person—said that he couldn't manage to wake up yet, so he went back to bed. He only returned at 2 pm.

Then, when he got up, we talked about a future treatment with me, and he asked me if we could have an "espresso" at the corner café, since he also didn't want his grandmother to listen in. I accepted.

The patient went out with me, untidy and uncombed. He started talking about his psychiatric hospitalization and, later, about his medication. He said that it made him feel "groggy, dizzy, sleepy".

He went on talking about his state of abulia and isolation. He explained that he preferred to live with his grandmother, who was very affectionate towards him, rather than with his mother or father, who were divorced.

He told me he didn't like to go to dances or parties, adding that he had only a few friends—though good ones, with whom he went out to eat.

He expressed interest in knowing what the individual treatment with me would be like, and we talked about it. We agreed to have another interview at 5 pm.

In this interval, I spoke to the psychiatrist medicating him, who was pleasant and correct. I told him that the patient seemed over-medicated to me. The "family therapist" also came in to talk to me, insinuating that she didn't believe young Abelard needed individual therapy, and that "she was already treating the family".

At 5 PM, I met with the patient again. He looked tidier, and said he had taken a shower.

> I told him what I had talked about with the psychiatrist and the family therapist who was treating him and his family. Abelard looked at me with surprise and said, "But ... but I don't go to those family meetings. She only treats my mother and sister, and sometimes calls my father. . . . " I didn't conceal my expression of surprise and annoyance, and told him what the "family therapist" had told me.

> Later, he told me he would be going out to dinner with a friend that evening. He added that he actually went out with friends very seldom.

> We then talked about the treatment he would start with me, which a member of the family had agreed to pay for.

> He and his grandmother decided he would move to the house of an aunt who lived near my office, since the house he was living in was quite far away—in another city south of Buenos Aires.

> I offered him a session every day, and, as in other cases like his, I asked him to come twice a day for the first two or three months. Abelard accepted my offer of treatment.

> I then explained what the treatment with me would be like. I told him that I always start the treatment very intensively in these cases.

The book came unbound (First session)

Abelard came to my office. He is now staying with his aunt, who lives near my office, so that he can have sessions every day.

> The patient's physical appearance is in total disorder: he wears tennis shoes much too large for him, thick socks that fall down

around his ankles, a pair of shorts, socks of different colours, both legs hairy, his T-shirt dirty, and a cowboy hat, with hair falling down all over.

He immediately tells me that he has just come from his aunt's house; I ask him, "How are you? How's it going?" The patient's answer surprises me. He says, "Well, I'm doing well with the alcohol." Then he adds, "I don't know what to do, I wake up at 5 am, I don't know what to do, I don't know what to do. . . . I wander around and I read. I wake up, I wander around, I go out for a walk. At 5 am there is nobody on the streets of the city."

I ask whether he had a nightmare or "saw something" that might have woken him up suddenly. The patient answers tangentially: "I was walking alone." I ask, "Did you think of coming here or calling me at night?" The patient only answers, "I don't know, I don't know, I walked and walked." Then he tells me that he walked all the way to a downtown area where there are several bookstores, and he read a few pages of poetry, adding, "How nice! In Buenos Aires there are bookstores open at night." (I thought about the transference relation: that in this new treatment he had discovered a place where he could go and be received).

Then the patient says that he walked down a very well-known avenue downtown, and although he preferred to talk about the book of poetry he had bought to calm himself down, the therapist thought that this was the narration of a person who was having a nightmare he couldn't shake off. This was only a countertransference feeling. At the end of the session, I tell him that it is a good sign that he has thought about coming in and getting treatment with me, and that if he woke up some time from a nightmare, it would be good for him to come in or phone me. The patient answers, "Yes, I could do that, it's going to help me."

The patient gives some details of aspects of the book he bought, which I consider narrations in the form of poetry, written by people who have suffered. I don't interpret this, as I am trying to be very cautious and unintrusive with this very fragile patient.

Then Abelard says that the book came unbound. And I interpret that it can be fixed and bound again. But that he's also talking about his head, his self, about wanting to put it back together again, to bind the head and the self solidly: "In the book you bring me, what happens to you inside your head, in yourself, unbound and fallen apart, you want me to put you together and bind you." Here, the patient answers directly. He asks, "So then if something gets broken, it can be fixed up?"

Recovering the inside of the mind

Abelard continues [the dates of his history are not clear and are corrected as the treatment advances]: "At age 6, we were already escaping from the military and in the fourth year of high school it was the straw that broke the camel's back. . . . At that point my father filed for divorce."

I intervene, saying: "the straw—divorce—that unbound the book that is your head, unbound your head, then was the psychosis, the hospitalization."

The patient falls into a long and intense silence; he seems moved by my interpretation.

At the end of the session the patient tells me: "You listen to me, but I don't know whether you're interested or if you suffer as I do." And he adds, "You got it right, you came to my city to interview me . . . will I be able to have my independence?"

Then he adds, "I'm afraid of life, Dr Rosenfeld. I hope you can help me at this time, you know? . . . I'm afraid of relationships with people. . . ."

I answer that maybe, since he's just met me, he's afraid of me or distrusts me. . . .

He replies, "You talk in a firm tone of voice, and I talk in a weak tone . . . not very strong . . ."

Near the end of the session he tells anecdotes about his mother; he says that if he tells her a problem, she starts to cry. I tell the patient that I, Dr Rosenfeld, am different.

Abelard says, "My dear grandfather was brutally murdered by the dictatorship. They all disappeared!"

I interpret: "Abelard, the most terrible disappearance is that you believe they also disappeared inside your mind. Inside your mind, not just outside. My job is to try for you to recover Mum, Dad, Granddad, inside you, and for you not to feel completely empty.

(His grandfather, a journalist of an opposition newspaper, was tortured and murdered and his body left inside a car on a downtown avenue in the city of Cordoba, Argentina. This was a warning to opponents of the dictatorship that they would be persecuted the same way in any country they might be living in. This was called the "Condor Plan")

The broken mind—the shredded pillows

In this session at the beginning of the psychoanalytic treatment with me, Abelard arrived precisely at the hour of his appointment. I will show in this session how he re-lives and enacts, during the psycho-analytic setting, something like what happened during the psychotic episode.

I interpret that it is not easy to tolerate what happens in his internal world—and what happened in reality. But that my job of containing him and helping him to put it into words is important. You can read that it is the first time that the patient is able to put into words and describe verbally the terrible tortures his mother has suffered. He is also able to re-act what happened to him in the psychotic episode: breaking objects, violence, eating raw rice. And he even repeats in the session a physical position that reminded me of a schizophrenic patient I used to see.

Breaking objects also expresses how his mind got broken: the container got broken—or, rather, the pillows. He shows me that this is also how his mind got broken and scattered around and fragment-ed into pieces—like the unbound book in the earlier session.

As usually happens with tortured people or Nazi concentration camp survivors, his parents never told Abelard the details of what happened, but he was listening behind a door while his mother was telling about this to some friends.

At some point, my countertransference emotions are so intense that afterwards I can say nothing at first, and only later begin to tell him that the "unspeakable begins to find expression in words".

And then I interpret the internal world and how "this still continues inside, in his mind".

O Lear, Lear, Lear!

> O Lear, Lear, Lear!
> Beat at this gate, that let thy folly in
> And thy dear judgement out!
>
> Shakespeare, King Lear (Act I, Scene 4)

In a session in the first three months, the patient begins the session by saying that he is suffering a great deal. I interpret: "With my help you can talk about what's sad, something not easy for you to tolerate. . . . But you're also going to recover the good moments you have inside and that you also had at times in your life. . . ."

After a silence, the patient answers: "But I can't stand it. I can't stand to know that they made my Mum eat shit, eat excrement, what she shitted they forced her to put into her mouth. I heard her when she told this to other people . . . that's the sad thing. I know that Pinochet's military tortured both of them. I know they had the Doberman dogs rape the women. And then Pinochet's people made them eat the shit they shitted. The Doberman dogs raping, shit in their mouth . . . that's what the Pinochet group did, the Condor Plan."

I can't say anything, have gooseflesh, am paralysed, so deep is the emotional impact, and tears come to my eyes.

Abelard remains silent, as if astounded by the terrible things he said, that he is telling about in detail for the first time. The horror of the unspeakable begins a find expression in words. Long silence.

Analyst [A]: I know this is terrible, and that it's going on even today . . . in your mind, day and night. . . . But listen, I'm a strong person, and I'm going to help you.

The patient gets up, takes a long throw pillow from the couch, turns it around, smashes it on the floor, against the wall, rips the leather and destroys it.

He takes another leather pillow and smashes it on the floor, the couch, and destroys it. He screams out.

Again he destroys another pillow.

I remain silent, trying to take this as a message, a nonverbal communication. The countertransference is very intense.

The patient sits down, agitated and tense.

Patient [P]: I haven't got any more medication, I haven't got any more Meleril [tiorizadine chlorhydrate].

A: It's good for you to get rid of the sadness, the pain, the loneliness, the intolerable, what your mind can't contain, it gets out, it's evacuated by smashing and crying out. But the mental pain is so great that you also asked for medication.

Abelard screams and screams, howls and curses.

He takes another pillow and smashes it against the walls. At that point, I tell him to be careful with the picture, that he almost broke the glass.

Before the end of the session, he says he's thinking about the friends he's going to visit and about another friend, a girl from school.

The mother's clothes; the role of the father

In the first six months, it was common for the patient to wonder about the type of relationship he had with his father—and, especially, he tried to find out what was going on with his mother.

He used an anecdote to describe the model or type of relationship his father had with him: "He phones me, talks fast, and hangs up right away. He's like that . . . he talks fast and hangs up." He added: ". . . I was young and my Dad would leave me little notes with addresses of whores for me to go to. . . . I wasn't ready."

As the treatment went on, he re-examined various other instances during his childhood and adolescence, when his father showed a similar attitude. He rediscovered and reconstructed the role of his father who, in the past, had often suddenly disappeared just when his son needed him most. But at the same time, in adolescence, Abelard had an internal image of his father as full of kindness, taking a protecting and guiding role. As is sometimes the case, the father had abandoned the child: sudden disillusions, when caused by someone we trust, cause especially serious depressions.

In other sessions, I interpreted his confusional states as caused by his inability to achieve a dissociation or a useful splitting that would help him to preserve part of his father, who was also a good person, and at home caused no problems. In other words, the role of the father only existed if the son was on his best behaviour; as soon as this was not the case, the son felt the disappearance not only of the external father role, but also of the internal image, the "father" he carried within his self. This reassessment of his relationship with the internal "father" image was useful to understand those moments of disappearance and loss of his internal objects that he experienced as a total void. This happened again when the father got the divorce.

In regard to his mother, Abelard says, "She told me she threatened to commit suicide if they kept torturing her."

A: This stuck in your mind, that you've got to take good care of her because she could commit suicide, even today. You believe that, even today.

P [very long silence]

A: I think you've been thinking about what I said, the way you stay with your mother to accompany and take care of her, and what you told me a few days ago happens too, that you dress up and put on your mother's clothes.

I remind him in detail of the session when he told me that he dressed up in his mother's clothes, and that I had interpreted that it was a way of not being alone and of living inside the female body and being mixed up with her.

Then I go on to say: "When you're alone, anguished, alone, as you were so often with your parents arrested and tortured, what did you do to find your mother?" At those times of complete abandonment, the way of trying to overcome this and to keep from disappearing yourself was to put on your mother's clothes. It was the way to be inside her, with her."

The patient stares at me with his eyes bulging, surprised at getting back this material he had told me in another session.

P: What a mess!

In another session at that juncture, Abelard tells me that one afternoon he had got together with his schoolmates and friends from high school, but in spite of being happy to see them, he gradually began to get bored. He said, "I got bored."

I interpret that perhaps he called it "bored" because he also re-experienced, while he was with them, some sad things about high school. And instead of saying "I'm sad", some people say "I'm bored".

A: Maybe through them you re-experience so many memories. Because you covered up the sad things, you also covered up the good moments of your life, like that period in Buenos Aires, but the sad part overpowered you yesterday, and that's what you called "I get bored".

After a long silence, the patient gets up and screams, screams and screams, louder and louder.

P: Son of a bitch! Son of a bitch! I'm glad, we went to Dictator Videla's house the other day for an *"escrache"* [an *"escrache"*—a "scratch out" in local slang—refers to an exposé in which people gather at someone's front door to shout insults at that person for a long time, for many hours, as a sign of protest] to expose him. And I went and cursed a woman in one of the apartments who came out to yell at the kids.

And I shouted, "Bitch! They murdered my grandfather here. And you come out to tell us we shouldn't come to protest because the noise bothers you. Bitch!"

You know what, Dr Rosenfeld? I don't remember the date when they murdered my grandfather. How awful what they did to my grandfather! How awful! How awful!

After a silence, Abelard begins to sing a beautiful poem and song by a composer he loves: "The party goes on, the people go on. Here's your ticket to fight . . ." Then the patient sings a beautiful song, a samba about someone who returns.

But then he says that another Chilean composer has written a poem about the political struggle in Chile: "I weep with each memory though I hold it in. . . . I weep with rage on the outside, but very deeply within . . . to remove from my soul the black they left in it . . . they made my soul dark." (The poet is Victor Jara, a Chilean musician and poet, held prisoner in a football stadium with thousands of other political prisoners in the Pinochet dictatorship. His right hand was amputated with a sword in front of all the prisoners in that stadium, so that he could never again play the guitar.)

A: Today you were able to bring in emotion, singing with an aesthetic form of terrible things: the times you had to escape, the torture, when you had to go to your grandmother's, your grandfather murdered, you had to escape to Brazil, then to Buenos Aires, where you were in hiding for a time . . . then to another neighbourhood in Buenos Aires, reunited with your parents . . . and suddenly Dad leaves, abandons you both . . . and you know what happened in your head"? It broke into little pieces.

The patient grabs a piece of paper and tears it to pieces.

A: That's what happened to your head. What you did just now to the piece of paper is what happened to your head, your little head broke apart that way, it couldn't stand so much pain, it broke into little pieces, that piece of paper torn up is what happened inside your mind.

P: It's the past that's coming back now.

The crazy bus driver

During these first months of treatment, distrust of Abelard's therapist was obviously bound to come up.

Perhaps this session clearly expresses the dynamics of the transference. We also began to understand his psychotic episode, which he had just begun to describe.

P: When I left the last session, I went to take the bus, and I told the driver, "a ticket for Belgrano". Then the driver said, "It isn't this bus, take the one that goes in the opposite direction." So I crossed the street and took the bus going the other way. And the next driver said, "No, you're wrong, it's the other way." You know, Dr Rosenfeld? The bus drivers are crazy, crazy. . . . You can't trust anybody, they drive me crazy.

[Long silence.]

A: Maybe you think I'm a crazy driver too, that I'm going to take you just anywhere in this treatment. Maybe you're afraid I'll drive the treatment so badly that you'll have to go back to the hospital where you were hospitalized. This must be your way to express your fear, your distrust of me. Like that crazy bus driver, you don't know whether I'm driving this treatment well or not.

P [laughs]: Well, the truth is, when I was in the hospital, one doctor would talk to me a little bit, another one didn't talk to me at all . . . they had me going from here to there.

A: It's good for you to express your distrust of me.

After a long silence the patient begins to sing and goes on for over ten minutes: *"El mago de Tribilin, el mago de Tiribin . . ."* ["The wizard of Tribilin, the wizard of Tiribin . . . "]

The therapist sings with him for ten minutes—a lovely melody, a song that children sing in Buenos Aires.

Then we sing another song, called *"La Vuelta Manzana"* ["All around the Block"].

P: Hurrah! Hurrah, Dr Rosenfeld! You sing with me, hurrah, Dr Rosenfeld! That's was so good! The other therapist I had was always silent, sometimes for the 50 minutes of the session, totally silent, it was crazy.

A: How long were you with the psychologist?

P: I left right away, he didn't talk.

At another point in the session, the patient's way of being in the session is very strange—odd. His body is totally suspended in the air, held up in the following way: his head and nape of the neck are on the couch, and his feet, the heels, are on the desk. The rest is totally in the air, as if it were a plank supported at one end by the nape of the neck on the couch, and the heels of his feet at the other.

A: This is how you felt yesterday when you didn't have a session—alone and up in the air, with no support.

[The therapist remembered that he once had a schizophrenic patient who took this catatonic position and stayed that way for the entire hour.]

After a silence, Abelard tells me:

P: At the end of high school I had a psychotic episode, and they hospitalized me. My sister was 8 years old at that time. At that crazy time, I used to eat raw, hard rice. What could that mean?

A: You're swallowing the inedible things of life. . . . Not so much raw rice, but rocks, pains, abandonment, grandfather's murder, your parents' torture. . . . What else can you do sometimes but split your head into little pieces and spill it out? Because you can't stand so much pain.

P: The truth is, so much suffering. . . . Then we moved to another neighbourhood the subway got to . . . oh, no, it was another house . . . that was another house. . . . I got confused. You know? It was very hard when my Dad left home. Here again, the confusion of places, spaces and dates can be seen.

A: Dad leaving you after so much suffering was like swallowing rocks, rice, you can't digest that . . . you can't swallow it.

P: Che ["che" in Argentine slang is an informal way of saying "hey" or "you"; it was borrowed from a word used by the original inhabitants—Indians—in whose tongue "che" meant "mister"] [Hey], doctor, you're right. Rocks . . . that's what I swallowed in life."

As he is leaving, the patient says, "This weekend I'd like to have a session. I need you. I need you."

Fear in the transference

During the first year of treatment it tended to happen that Abelard would get frightened at moments of great emotional closeness with the therapist. The following fragment narrates a point during that period, showing these oscillations.

> P: The doorman of this building is a Nazi. He's a son of a bitch, he banged on the door after I went in. That blonde guy with the face of a Nazi. . . . I don't know why, I remembered a masseur in Chile who used to give me massages, like grabbing my neck, that were good for me. But once that masseur told me, "I'm going to give you a back massage." And he pulled down my underpants and I got scared. He touched my ass. . . . I wonder what that masseur wanted to do to me.
>
> A: What did you think?
>
> P: I don't know, I got scared.
>
> A: He makes you drop your underpants, he massages you. Tell me, did you think he was going to have a homosexual relation?
>
> P: Well . . . yes. . . .
>
> A: You're telling me about your fear that if you come here twice a day, and you need me, you need a male psychoanalyst, maybe you think you're going to stop being a boy. Don't you think you're talking about your fears of not being a boy, or homosexual fears about me? Don't confuse feeling affection for me with being homosexual. You're just a little child who needs help.

This clinical material suggests transferential homosexual fantasies. In other words, we may infer the existence of homosexual transference fantasies that the patient uses to relate to the analyst.

It is possible that the emergence and discussion during his treatment of erotic and incestuous fantasies about women are ways to show himself as a male who gets excited about women, thus escaping his feminine homosexual erotic feelings for the therapist (Freud, 1922b).

We can surmise that he searched for his father by playing the role of a woman, believing that this was the only way that he would be loved. We can expand on this theory by thinking in terms of a masculine–feminine confusion or ambivalence.

In this session, his homosexual fantasies in relation to me appeared more clearly.

The music: lullabies

> Philomel, with melody
> Sing in our sweet lullaby,
> Lulla, lulla, lullaby, lulla, lulla, lullaby.
>
> Shakespeare, *A Midsummer Night's Dream* (Act II, Scene 2)

The autistic capsule opens, and what is healthy and preserved that was kept in the autistic encapsulation comes out: the lullabies. This shows how the mechanism of autistic encapsulation is useful for preserving healthy infantile aspects, which appear suddenly in a session. This is the example of the lullabies that come up during a session.

The first songs he sang in the sessions were children's songs. Some were lullabies. He would ask me to sing with him. For example, "El Mago de Tribilin" ["The Wizard of Tribilin"], (which I later relate to myself as if I were a wizard who could cure him).

Another children's song was *"La Vuelta Manzana"* ["All Around the Block"], a very well known song for children.

He recovers the lullabies and remembers and actualizes them with me—he re-creates his infantile world, lost when he was 18 months old.

With some severely disturbed and psychotic patients, the therapist often has to re-create in the transference what has never before existed (Boyer, 1999; Searles, 1979; Volkan, 1997; Wallerstein, 1988, 1993).

The appearance of children's songs and the music of childhood with the analyst is an example of how what is hidden or encapsulated can come out suddenly and be re-lived again. But this does not produce a confusional impact, as often happens when what was dissociated or split off returns abruptly to the self. This time, he does it in a psychoanalytic setting. In this period of lullabies and children's songs, a dual effort was required: (1) to recover and return life to the children's songs, and (2) to recover what had been paralysed in Abelard's development since he was 18 months old. This is the reacquisition of parts of the self (Steiner, 2006).

I think these parts of the self can be re-created only when there is stability and serenity in a relationship that takes care of the patient and contains him—in this case, a psychoanalyst who helps to re-create not only children's songs, but also aspects of the infantile self. Also, in the fusion or symbiosis that is re-created by singing a duet, the patient and I recover the symbiosis with the parents, broken off and shattered when he was 18 months old and disturbing his development towards and through a healthier puberty and adolescence.

The music Abelard sings represents diverse stages in the patient's life. It is possible to think that by singing a duet with his therapist, diverse periods and aspects of his self are brought together.

During the end of the first year of treatment, we had sessions like the following one, where music formed a very strong emotional bond between patient and therapist.

This session has very moving moments, when Abelard expresses his relationship with me through music and songs. I try to include myself in this emotional bond with him through music. He begins to sing "El pasado me condena" ["The past condemns me"] and the tango "Volver" ["Returning"]: "Returning with a withered forehead, the snows of time have silvered my brow", and he goes on singing and invites me to sing. He and I sing. He is much more relaxed.

P: I'm less tied down and rigid from the medication. Dr V, the one who changed the medication, is known all over the world. My psychoanalyst is Dr Rosenfeld. What a difference from the psychologist! The other one didn't talk. What a way to waste years of time!

I'm going to sing one by a Cuban composer, Silvio Rodriguez, and another one by a Venezuelan woman. You know? I had a Venezuelan girlfriend. I'm going to sing a song called "Los Tontos" ["The Fools"]. It's got to do with believing or not believing in somebody.

I'm singing a lot, see? You know, at the soccer match I went to see, I started to sing with the fans? "Dale Boca, dale Boca" ["Come on, Boca, come on, Boca."] And today I'm going to sing the same: "Dale Dr Rosenfeld, Dale Dr Rosenfeld" ["Come on, Dr Rosenfeld, come on, Dr Rosenfeld"]. I feel like singing again. It must be that things come back, right? After so many years.

And he says, in English:

P: I am here, Dr Rosenfeld, I believe in you, I am here and I am crazy with you, but crazy. Crazy [continues in Spanish] was the bus driver. Maybe you're crazy too.

What do you think if, instead of saying this, we sing, "*El Día que me Quieras*" ["The Day You Love Me"]? "The day you love me, the rose that adorns you will dress up for a party in its finest colours. . . . The day you love me there'll be only harmony, the dawn will be bright." This is the most poetic and affectionate tango sung by the all-time idol of Argentine song, Carlos Gardel.] Let's sing a duet, the tango "Volver": "Returning, with a withered forehead, the snows of time have silvered my brow. Feeling that life is a puff of wind, that twenty years is nothing, that my feverish eyes, wandering through the shadows, look for you and call your name. . . ."

How lovely it is to sing a duet, "Che, Dr Rosenfeld." ["hey, Doctor Rosenfeld"]!

A: It's a way of being united, fused. It's a moment of confidence in me.

This whole session, singing a duet together, was an emotional communication such as I have seldom seen in my office: emotional communication through the aesthetics of music and poems. (To tell the truth, it was a luxury to have a patient who, after being hospitalized in a psychiatric hospital, could communicate, through emotion, the beauty and aesthetics of poetry and music.)

An 18-month-old baby in the session

Days and nights passed over that despair in his flesh, but one
morning he woke up, looked at the blurred things around him,
    and felt
inexplicably, as someone who recognizes some music or a voice,
that all this had already happened to him and that he had faced it
with fear, but also with joy, hope, and curiosity. Then he went
    down
into his memory, which seemed to be endless, and managed to
    extricate from
that vertigo the memory he had lost.

Jorge Luis Borges, *El Hacedor* (in Borges, 2001)

This session is an example of regression in the transference, where Abelard re-enacted the traumatic abandoning by his parents when he was 18 months old. But this time he can verbalize it and is contained in the session by the psychoanalyst. We also see his fear of a breakdown (the butterfly) when he is saying good-bye before a journey.

After a year of treatment, towards the end of the year, the patient asked to go back to his city. He had been offered a job that would allow him to help his family economically. In addition to getting up early, he would be able to consider taking up to his studies again.

But the fear of not having treatment for a few months made old terrors return. I describe a moment in a session at that time.

P: I'm afraid I'll turn into a butterfly.

A: Explain it a bit better, because I didn't understand.

The patient explains.

A: Could it be that you're afraid of being a fragile person, that when you take flight you might get blown down by the wind, that you might fall at the first gust and go crazy? I remind you that you told me in the first days of your treatment that in the psychiatric hospital where you were hospitalized, there was a woman who thought she was a transparent butterfly.

P: Ah, yes. She thought she was a transparent and fragile butterfly. As thin and transparent as a butterfly. You're right, I remember, she was the one who never wanted to eat.Che, Doctor Rosenfeld! [Hey, Doctor Rosenfeld], you've got a memory! You really remember!

It is very important for the patient to discover that the analyst has in his memory and contains everything that the patient says and feels. This is the way the patient feels contained in the psychoanalyst's mind.

A: Right now, when you're going to go back for a couple of months to [your city], you're afraid that if I'm not there you could go crazy and have another psychiatric hospitalization. . . . That's why you're afraid of being a fragile butterfly that could fall into another psychosis.

This final decision and leave-taking exemplifies the period when we worked through the intense experiences of what a separation means for Abelard. It is an example of how fragile and sensitive he is to separations, and that he experiences them as irreversible ruptures or deaths. Here, in this example, Abelard is able to verbalize it instead of enacting it in a psychosis, as happened when his father left home. This saying goodbye to me is a rectification of the father's traumatic departure. And of course, it concentrates and represents all the abrupt separations and losses he suffered from 18 months on. It also explains something more about the psychotic episode, as well as his experience of falling into the void, which Tustin (1990b) calls the "black hole".

We can contribute some models referring to experiences of saying goodbye: the emptying of the self is the equivalent of losing introjections in Abelard's internal world. The body is included in this experience of loss. Part of the body departs or "is swept away", together with the real object lost, with which the subject is mingled.

One model can be the following: when the nipple is taken out of the baby's mouth, because of the intense fusion: the baby feels that when the nipple goes away, it takes away his lips, palate, and tongue.

It is important to emphasize that some patients are unable to symbolize (Segal, 1994). Others express it only in body language through a psychosomatic illness. In another paper (Rosenfeld, 1992b), I describe a patient who, whenever she had to say goodbye or before the therapist's holiday, developed bleeding lesions on her lips and palate. This patient had to be placed in intensive therapy (ICU) for her lesions during a long vacation of the therapist.

In these cases, weaning is not normal but is experienced as the loss of parts of the body with each separation.

This is what happens in the transference with me. Abelard also believes that he loses parts of his body and that he is left with only fragile butterfly's wings (cf. session in which he turns into a butterfly). What is striking is that, in this case, it occurs at the level of a fantasy that he was able to verbalize.

When Abelard returned to his sessions after a couple of months, something very moving and important happened:

The session begins with the patient asking for water.

> Then he touches the desk ... runs his hand over it, touching and feeling the furniture carefully. . . . Then he sits down on the floor like a child ... sits on a pillow ... and stares at my face.

In this session, I call upon all my experience as a child analyst and with mother/infant observation.

Many moments in primal transference or psychotic transference and also at those moments when he becomes an 18-month-old baby, my technique is closer to child psychoanalysis, but it is still psychoanalysis and transference analysis.

The initial contacts between mother and baby are re-created in the transference through: (1) eye contact; (2) the repetition of the baby's vocalizations or babbling, which are usually echoed by the parents; (3) singing melodies with the mother or the father; (4) it is interesting to relate this to something I observed in Norway, where the native mothers in Lapland have a special and unique melody for each of their children—a melody without words called a "*jokl*", which is never mixed up with those of her other children; (5) when the patient touches, caresses, and feels the furniture in my office, he is actualizing, acting, enacting the baby's initial skin contact with his mother; (6) the skin contact, together with her familiar odour and voice, create the notion of mother or the psychological skin that envelops and contains him (A. Anzieu, 2000; Bick, 1968; Freud, 1914g; Reid, 1997).

This is the example of what Abelard cannot express—it is the analyst who must put it into words. In every treatment, the patient needs to enact the unnameable—especially this patient, who sends nonverbal messages from a time when he had no language with which to express himself.

Then I interpret:

A: You're recognizing this furniture, each corner of my office. . . . It's as if you were saying: "Where am I?? . . . In what country? Chile, the abbey in Brazil . . . Argentina . . .? . . . And who are you, doctor?"

You're staring at my face to find out who you're with . . . with Dad, Mum. . . . Or am I the neighbour who took you in when you were one and a half? You're re-experiencing your year and a half . . . doing with me what happened when you lost the familiar faces and smiles of Dad, Mum, and Granddad. . . .

Today you're re-experiencing this. . . .

P [lies down on the pillows on the floor. . . . silence]: "I didn't know who the neighbour was either."

[Silence.]

P: All these changes are terrible.

A: This is how you experienced this separation from me of several months. . . . It's as if Abelard goes back home and it's hard for him to recognize the lost faces of Dr David, Dad, Mum. . . . Today you're like when you were one and a half . . . "Whose face is this, that I lost contact with . . . these eyes . . . is it Dr David . . . who is it . . .?"

P: How can I trust a new face if everything before ended up badly?

"*Abelard and Eloise*"

Abelard and Eloise is a most famous love story set in the Paris of 1108, and poets and musicians describe the sexual punishment of this love story.

In this session I interpret what happens in the patient's internal world, as well as the relations with the introjected objects in his infantile world. Working psychoanalytically on what happens in the first introjections and being able to verbalize them is the basis for understanding what happens in his internal world. Up to this time, he had had few possibilities of dreaming or speaking about it. He could neither verbalize nor symbolize it.

This is at the base of the disturbances of normal development, both sexual and of the total personality. This is why I include, at the end of this session, a fragment of another session that centres on sexuality.

Abelard begins the session by saying:

P: I dreamed *I was with a girl—Eloise . . . a friend from high school who was on top of me . . . but dressed, and we danced that way.* . . . It's my first sort of erotic dream.

[Silence.]

Then Abelard goes on to say that he saw a soccer match with friends—he says that he got quite scared when there was a skirmish . . . the fans were throwing things . . . the police, with their dogs, took out their nightsticks to separate the people . . . the fans . . . with the nightsticks and the police dogs barking near the people. . . . I got scared. . . .

A: That happened, it's true—but the most important thing is that you've got that in your inner world . . . inside your mind since you were a child.... That scene you've got all the time, day and night ... that thing that all sex is torture, dogs that bite and rape ... the electric prod, blows with police nightsticks. ...

All these terribly sadistic fantasies, of what a sexual relation is, hold you back ... inhibit you, stop you, paralyse you ... and this belief that fucking is torture, beatings, the electric prod, or bombs that kill is still inside you ... this is your inner world, Abelard ... this is how your fantasies end, inhibiting you from having sexual relations.

[Silence.]

A: Last week I told you something that anguished you and you answered me by screaming, "Come on, Doctor, don't treat me badly!" ... as if you believed I'm a torturer and you, crying out as you surely know your mother cried out when they tortured her ... the military....

P: This is too much, altogether too much. ...

[Silence.]

P: It's easier to go to the stadium to see soccer.... I need some entertainment ... you know?

The internal world and the primal scene

The primal scene is only a fantasy, which can dominate the self. Just as the child imagines that his mind is full of moving objects, so he also imagines the inside of the person before his eyes as being full of objects. He projects what happens in his mind, and believes it happens in his mother's body. This only happens if the child finds a receptive space—in other words, a mother who offers him a space inside her.

If this space is lacking, we enter the newly discovered world of children without projective identification—that is, the world of autism (Tustin, 1986).

Eros

In another session, new material comes up. About a year and a half into his treatment, although he couldn't yet have sexual relations, the patient brought in another sexual dream:

P: Last night I dreamed *a girl was sitting naked on my lap. I was very hot, excited, with an erect penis.*

Is it better to have sex or to masturbate than to have erotic dreams?

I tell him that this dream is a very important sign that, even in the midst of the terror that remains in the child Abelard's mind, sex can appear (Green, 1997).

A: You weren't able to have a healthier adolescence, or a healthy sexuality. It's that you, to cover up the sad things like the tortures, the migrations, the disappearance of your parents, your grandfather's murder, Dad's leaving home, the psychiatric hospitalization. . . . To cover up the sad things, you also covered up the good moments of your life. . . .

P [weeps in silence].

Pinocchio: final stages of the treatment

I consider that the final stages of the treatment began when the patient, together with his grandmother, decided to return to live in their native country. I must explain that his father, as well as his mother and her new companion, had returned to Chile and had found jobs. In the sessions in the following months, the material referred to what Abelard's life, his work, and his studies were going to be like in a different country—but also, very especially, how he was going to manage to stay in contact with me.

When the date had been set for his return Chile, Abelard frequently asked me how many days remained before his departure. We agreed that every few months he would come back to control his medication with Dr V. And to have sessions with me.

What was important in these final stages is that the patient could talk about separation, saying goodbye, the mental and physical wrench, and could express it in words, or even songs.

My countertransference emotions about the leave-taking and the end of his treatment made me think again about Abelard's butterfly-like fragility in former sessions. I thought that he would always need some kind of support and treatment.

After saying goodbye, I remembered and hummed for many days afterwards a beautiful Brazilian song. The lyrics say:

Sadness has no end
Happiness does
Happiness is like a feather
That the wind carries through the air
It goes so lightly
But has a brief life
It needs to have wind all the time
Sadness has no end
Happiness does.]

Vinicius de Moraes & Antonio Carlos Jobim, *A felicidade*

This session represents the final stages of the treatment quite well, describing the structural changes Abelard's his mind and body as well as his body image:

> The patient, like so many other times, is walking and wandering around the office. At one point he goes through my bookcase and takes out an original version of the book *Pinocchio* by Collodi. He looks at the original period drawings and notices that in one of the drawings Pinocchio is sprawled, thrown to the floor, scattered. He points his finger at the drawing without speaking (Rosenfeld, 2001b).

> I interpret: "You want to show me without words what happened to little Abelard when he was 18 months old: they threw him out of a window to a neighbour's house to save him from the military who razed your parents' home. In the drawing you also see when you felt you were thrown down that way and they took you to your grandmother's house."

> Abelard goes on leafing through the Pinocchio book and sees a drawing of when Pinocchio dies and is revived. Again he points his finger at the drawing where the protecting fairy appears, reviving and curing him.

> A: With the drawing and with your silence, you're showing me how terrible it was to feel that aspects of Abelard have been dying since he was 18 months old. It's as if they had killed a normal child's development. This is the part of Abelard, of yourself, that you see in the drawing—all the things of the child Abelard that died throughout his life. But you also show me with your finger

that it's possible to revive and make a wooden body come back to life—a sprawled body thrown to the ground from a neigh-bour's house—and make a real flesh and blood child be reborn, who feels his body, his emotions, his joys, and his erotism.

The patient remains silent, his eyes sad.

A: Abelard, listen to me: when you block out these sad things you've suffered, you end up freezing other happy things in your life. Because you also had other happy things in life.

P: It's like I don't feel my body. It's like my adolescence went on, and I never felt my body—like my body didn't exist.

After some associations from the patient, I interpret:

A: What you're telling me is how you blocked, froze your physical and sexual experiences. And what's worse, it's almost as if you stopped feeling that you had a body—that the flesh-and-blood body had disappeared. What you did with your body was the same thing you did with many happy and lovely things in life, which you also had. Now you have sexual dreams with an erect penis.

   You're like Pinocchio who goes from being a wooden doll and ends up becoming a human being, a flesh-and-blood child.

This is Pinocchio today, in the session.

Conclusions I

I selected sessions that convey what is most intense, terrible, primitive, and uncontrolled in Abelard's internal world during the first months of treatment. This internal world is re-enacted during the psychoanalytic session.

Countertransference

Concerning the countertransference, I have described the moment I was moved to tears when Abelard told me about the tortures his mother had suffered. I also felt intense emotions when, in another ses-sion, he told me how the men—referring, of course, to his father—were tortured with electric prods.

When Abelard left his treatment to return to Chile, I described how, without realizing it consciously, I was humming a beautiful melody for several days, which I then realized was expressing my worries about the patient's future. This song, by Tom Jobim and Vinicius, clearly expressed my countertransferential worries. In other words, even I was finally using melodies and songs to express my own countertransferential feelings, in reference to or thought about in relation to the session in which Abelard believed he felt like a fragile butterfly.

Methodologically, the countertransference is a hypothesis that the therapist creates in his field of work. It is not a certainty but a working hypothesis that should be used to think. Intense feelings are conveyed to us by children, adolescents, neurotic and psychotic patients through mechanisms about which we know very little as yet: projection, projective identification, paradoxical messages, phonology or the music of the voice, broken phrases or syntactic and semantic disturbances, and so on. From the point of view of information, the way in which a patient speaks is as rich a source as memories or dreams are in a neurotic one. I maintain that it is a message to be decoded (D. Anzieu, 1986; De Mijolla, 2001; Laplanche & Pontalis, 1967; Liberman, 1970–72; Ogden, 1994; Rosembaum & Sonne, 1986).

The ideal grandfather

The murdered grandfather is a person who existed as an ideal in the minds of grandmother and grandson. Furthermore, it is as if being remembered and admired by so many people in their country, they had kept his figure alive. This ideal figure also substitutes the figure of the real father and served the ideal as a good model for identification.

The poem at the end of the chapter quotes Don Quixote—the knight who fights all the windmills with his ideals . . . that was Abelard's grandfather.

Aggression and technique

We must be very cautious in analytic technique and not interpret aggression and hate too soon in patients who have experienced terrible, real traumatic events. For example, I don't recall that any analyst ever interpreted "hate and jealousy of his little sister" to a patient whose little sister was murdered in front of him by the Nazis while they were being taken to the concentration camp at Auschwitz (Branik & Rosen-feld-Prusak, 1995; Eickhoff, 1986; Perren-Klinger, 1995)

Winnicott was also interested in the role of the father. In *Through Paediatrics to Psycho-Analysis* (1992) he comments on the role of the father as providing "holding" for the mother, and giving her support, by confronting problems (Painceira Plot, 1997).

Serious disappointments or traumas may blur, erase, and cause the loss of previous introjections or internal object relations.

I will expand on some ideas regarding encapsulated autism. I use the model or hypothesis of "encapsulated autism" to explain why certain patients are able to create mechanisms to preserve infantile relationships. Autism is a mental state that is created in order to have a protective shell against whatever is external that is experienced as being dangerous.

This extreme autistic defence is a survivor's system for not disap-pearing. It is "to be or not to be". These children either construct these defences or they feel that they are annihilated and disappear. This is quite different from the processes of splitting or repression in the hysterias.

The theory of encapsulated autism as a system that is also useful for preserving childhood memories was taken up and accepted by Frances Tustin (2000), who wrote (p. 885): *"Influencée par un article de Rosenfeld, je me suis aperçue que l'autisme avait une fonction de protection et de préservation"* ["Influenced by an article by Rosenfeld, I realized that autism had a function of protection and preservation"].

In the "encapsulation model" there is a shielding of early identifi-cations that are later found to be fairly well preserved—in Abelard's case the music, the lullabies. The first infantile object relations were well "preserved" in his mind; they came forward only at a moment in analysis when he felt contained, in a stable relationship.

This depends on the patient's previous mental structure and the possibility of having a useful substitute for his disappeared parents—in this case, his grandmother, when he was 18 months old—over a long period of time. This is important, especially at an age when expe-rienced time has extreme and intense sensitivity and when minutes of absence can mean long months of absence in the mind of a baby. Short separations or microscopic changes can provoke enormous effects in sensitive children (Corominas, 1998; Ferrari, 1997; Geissmann & Geiss-mann, 2000; Hochmann, 1997).

The following description by Alvarez and Reid (1999) expresses this sensitivity thus:

> There is a delta in south-eastern Alaska where a tiny change in the temperature each spring—from zero to only one degree—melts a huge glacier. The tiny change brings great cascades of ice, sometimes twenty stories tall, crashing down. It brings movement, too: everything is churning. It brings silt down the delta, and seawater back into the bay. The result is a massive wheel of fertility, a huge botanical and biological stew of wildlife and plankton.

Like the glacier, some forms of autism respond to relatively small changes in emotional temperature in the child or in someone else relating to him: this may bring in its train huge cascades of emotion, which the child may find difficult to regulate."

Shakespeare also expresses this special sensitivity in the experience of time when Hamlet goes out at night to seek the ghost that is perhaps his father's spirit. The dialogue with it begins at nightfall when Hamlet cries out: "Angels and ministers of grace defend us!" And then: "I will call thee Hamlet, King, father, Royal Dane, oh, answer me!" (*Hamlet*, Act I, Scene 4).

What is striking is that just a few paragraphs later Shakespeare tells us that it is now dawning. The internal experience of the passing of time is what Shakespeare wants to convey. This shows how Abelard might have felt when he was 18 months old.

Houzel (2000b) describes how a child is sometimes unable to face abrupt losses and separations with the psychic means he possesses at that moment. He points out that when autistic children are able to signify and express these painful experiences of amputation, they nearly always locate them in the mouth.

Houzel also says that, in order to avoid mental catastrophes and breakdowns when there are abrupt separations, a maternal substitute is able to stop what Houzel calls "anxieties of falling". He uses a spatial metaphor to explain that when the baby's communication is successful, it is as if a mountain-climber had secured a foothold in the ice to hang onto and make an ascent, avoiding a fatal fall from atop the mountain.

This also relates to Winnicott's description of what he calls "psychotic depression" (Winnicott, 1958).

Containing the patient in the transference

Containing a patient—holding—means, in the transference, showing him that one remembers what the patient said months earlier. This is how the patient "discovers", in the transference, that he is contained in the other's mind and memory.

That is what I did when I remembered the butterfly lady he had told me about months earlier. Abelard's happy and enthusiastic response is a mixture of happiness at being held in the therapist's mind. This is what I did: make him experience being contained in the therapist's mind.

Conclusions II

Technical handling

Since there is no loss of his sense of reality, there is therefore no delirious idea, no delusion.

At some point in the analysis it became technically important to tell Abelard that I was not a depressed person and that I could receive all his suffering. In other words, during the treatment I allowed him to unfold and repeat in the transference all his infantile history with his father and mother. Based on the transference material, we can say that the patient was a child who always tried to take care of a depressed, weak, and fragile mother and father. Just as Freud tells us (1914f), throughout the treatment I allowed these childhood bonds to unfold in the transference. They were the bonds of a child trying to care for his depressive and fragile parents, represented by the therapist in the transference.

From the technical point of view, I prefer to work with these bonds only within the transference. In other words, during the treatment of some patients I can go for months without mentioning the words "mother" or "father" because I try to have the patient first re-experience these bonds and affects intensely with me in the transference. It was only after some time that I was in a position to interpret for this patient that "I am not a depressed, melancholic, and suicidal person that you have to take care of. . . ." Later on the patient discovered for himself—with the help of my interpretations—that I am not a depressed mother, not someone who is going to commit suicide. Through the analysis of the transference I made him understand that I was there to take care of him by communicating the image of a firm analyst, with a strong voice, providing security and containment.

By using a strong, firm, determined voice, it is possible to communicate, through the music of the voice, an image of security and containment (Liberman, 1970–72).

Probably the voice's melody—or phonology, as it is called in the theory of communication—is the most important element we have for conveying a strong and solid image of the analyst. This is a technical aspect of treatment that I suggest my colleagues should consider.

Theory: The role of the father

A process of creation and learning, what we call "the role of the father" is a dynamic process rather than a static definition.

In Abelard's case, it was also important to analyse the patient's guilt for the father's desertion of the home, as well as his oedipal guilt for taking over the paternal role.

We must highlight the important role the father plays at a very early stage; this subject has been addressed by various authors. Freud was the first to describe the early function of the father in many of his writings (1898a, 1950 [1892–1899], 1900a [Ch. 4], 1905d, 1908c, 1912–13); this concept was also developed by Klein (1945) and her followers.

Klein says that the child searches for aspects of the father in the mother's body. In addition, her theory develops an idea about an early Oedipus complex. She links early anxieties to this complex: very early situations of anxiety and guilt cause an exaggerated fixation at the initial stages of libidinal organization, and, reciprocally, an excessive tendency to regress to those early stages. Thus, oedipal development is hindered and the genital organization cannot be firmly established. In the case we present here as well as in other instances, the Oedipus complex begins to develop normally when the early anxieties subside.

Klein thinks of something more than a relationship with part-objects and suggests that the child associates the perception of those part-objects with his mother and father. She notes that frustration and satisfaction give shape to the relationship between the baby and the good and loved breast and the bad and hated breast, and she adds:

"These two conflicting relationships with the maternal breast are transferred onto the ulterior relationship with the father's penis" (Klein,
1945).

Meltzer thinks that coitus or the primal scene is a scene imagined
within the child's internal world, where the internal objects are in
movement. The self can achieve a projective identification within internal objects.

The pre-oedipal level is developed in the above quotation from
Klein; the early role of the mother is discussed in the following passage from Freud:

> Perhaps it would be safer to say "with the parents"; for before a
> child has arrived at a definite knowledge of the difference between
> the sexes, the lack of a penis, it does not distinguish in value be-
> tween its father and its mother [Freud, 1924b, p. 31; Freud, 1914c]

In order to emphasize the pre-oedipal importance of the mother as
well as identification with the father, I would like to transcribe one of
Freud's best descriptions of the mother's early role, which is so important in the case of Abelard.

In the chapter on identification of his work on "Group Psychology"
(1921c, p. 105), Freud says: "Identification is known to psycho-analysis
as the earliest expression of an emotional tie with another person."

In a description that is fundamental for the creation of the patient's
mental life, Freud also stresses the early importance of the mother in
the following passage (1921c):

> He then exhibits, therefore, two psychologically distinct ties: a
> straightforward sexual object-cathexis towards his mother and an
> identification with his father which takes him as his model. *The two
> subsist side by side for a time without any mutual influence or interference.*
> In consequence of the irresistible advance towards a unification of
> mental life, they come together at last; and the normal Oedipus
> complex originates from their confluence [p. 105, italics added]

The identifications and introjections in the present clinical case are not
the only possible explanation enabling us to understand all psychoses.
Psychoses are not always caused by a disturbance of identifications, or
by an identification with a psychotic father and/or mother.

Freud begins to consider identification as a more important and
vital mechanism for the psychic apparatus—with constitutive and

modifying effects on that apparatus—especially in his paper on narcissism (1914c) when he describes the ego ideal and moral conscience.

In *Mourning and Melancholia* (1917e) he uses the term "identification" for this mechanism. He describes the passage from a narcissistic object choice to the working-through of the loss of that object, and how the pathological working-through of mourning leads to a narcissistic identification. Hence, the object becomes part of the psychic apparatus.

The expression "the shadow of the object fell upon the ego" is a metaphor. The object has entered the psychic apparatus as a part of the ego itself. This part is dissociated and forms a link with the rest of the ego. This is how Freud explains the origin of the superego: through the mourning for oedipal objects. Narcissistic identifications take place through narcissistic object choices. These identifications reinforce primary identifications (Ahumada, 1990; Brudny, 1991; Freud, 1939a).

It is not quite true that secondary identifications have a better prognosis than do primary ones: perturbed identifications are the problem, and the prognosis is not dependent on their being primary or secondary. They are developmental facts.

These identifications, added to introjections resulting from the mourning of oedipal objects, constitute the superego. Primary identifications take place at an earlier stage; secondary identifications are set up later on, as a result of mourning for the object (Bion, 1967; Etchegoyen, 1999; Freud, 1921c, 1924b, 1924d).

In his lectures on Freud's theories, Avenburg (1975) says that the Freudian concepts of primary and secondary identification are sometimes not univocal, and their definition depends on Freud's interest and the level of his analysis in his various works. He adds that in some of Freud's texts pre-oedipal identifications can be understood as primary, whereas in others it is clear that all secondary identifications follow an oedipal identification.

Identifications are mnemonic traces of perceptions, and as such, according to Freud, they are not lost; whereas the relationships among the mnemonic traces are lost (Freud, 1924b).

I believe that all identifications can be lost as a result of a traumatic episode, as I have already described in a paper on identification in the context of Nazism. These patients may lose their introjected fathers, among other problems, because of the pragmatic paradoxes to which they are subjected: if the individual identifies with his father as a man, he is killed because he is a man, and if he identifies with him as a Jew, he is killed because he is a Jew (Rosenfeld, 1986).

The same happens to our patient Abelard, who loses his identifications with his father, even though the loss is not permanent. His father's disappearance when Abelard is 18 months old and, years later, his abandoning them through divorce triggers in him the same pragmatic paradox (typical of psychoses): "This is because he does not love me, it means he has never loved me; therefore I can use nothing of what he has given me. It was all a lie." This is how his self decodes his father's desertion with the divorce.

The oedipal murder—the guilt caused by the fantasy of an oedipal murder—compounds the problem; in the present case, the fact of the desertion and divorce by the father dismantles the structures of the ego. The recovery of those structures is, as far as it is possible to achieve, the function of the psychoanalyst. This can be seen in my work in the transference.

Introjective identifications do not remain immutable. There is ongoing movement and change. Introjections can also be lost, as can the links of relationships between mnemonic traces (Rosenfeld, 1992b).

As a clinician, I am interested in the creation or reconstruction of the father's role in the context of the transference. Order, what is permitted, the limits in time, fixed schedules, the rules of the setting are some of many different ways of creating an order and a rationale of differences and of making it possible for a common semantic universe to exist.

Each family member can fulfil partial aspects of the "role of the father" and even substitute for him in some cases. What is important is the paternal task or role, responsible for clearing up, untangling, and taking apart what is known in the theory of communication as the paradoxical messages or pragmatic paradoxes, and for helping the child out of them.

These are the messages that specialists in the theory of communication define as being capable of causing real, concrete effects, and of modifying the self and the behaviour of the message's receptor (Liberman, 1970–72; Thomä & Kächele, 1988; Watzlawick, Beavin, & Jackson, 1967).

I particularly want to stress double-bind messages, contradictory orders, tangential answers, disqualifying comments, and so on, which are capable of driving the child who receives them literally mad—hence the term "pragmatic" used to identify them, since these messages cause real and concrete effects.

The role of the father could be called the role of the decoder. In psychosis this role is lacking; it does not rectify the paradoxical messages emitted by the mother or by other members of the primary group. It may be sending double-bind messages and thus not help the child to extricate himself from the pragmatic paradoxes in which they are both immersed. Let us note that the essence of paradoxical messages is that nothing the child does or says is considered right or adequate; whatever his answer, it will be considered to be wrong. The child is left with only one way out: to fragment his self, to go mad, or to try to eliminate the source of the message, either outside or inside himself. The role of the father is fulfilled only when the child's primary anxieties find appropriate holding or when the paternal role exists as a psychological presence, not merely a physical one. The father's actual presence within a family does not guarantee the existence of the paternal role: some fathers are present all day long and are still absent psychologically. The true nourishment for the self is affective and psychological caring.

To summarize: the role of the father is particularly important and significant at the pre-oedipal stages. Its absence is at the root of psychosis, and the role of the father at the oedipal stage comes only later. I shall return to this subject later on.

We said before that the role of the father is one of the roles that the small group or primary group within which the child develops must play. It is a role of *holding*, of containing affects, anxieties, and fears. It is complementary to and indissoluble from the maternal role, and both constitute a dialectic process.

The father must be available to receive projective identifications and to modify them before sending them back, and he must also be capable of withstanding projective identifications that are encroaching or parasitical. He must have both time and space available.

One aspect of the father's receptive capacity that must be complemented by the maternal, receptive, feminine role is his capacity to contain, within his internal space, the child's fears, affects, psychotic anxieties, and parasitical projective identifications. Being receptive does not mean being a woman or feminine. Receptivity is indispensable to contain the child, to create a psychological envelope—a sort of protective skin—for him, and this task involves both parents. Some concepts of the interior space, of receptivity, linked to the female body, alone capable of carrying and giving birth to the child, obviously pertain exclusively to the woman–mother.

If there is not a father's and a mother's space, as a whole, available to receive the child's projective identifications, he will not learn to develop these useful identifications, nor the introjective ones. Just as united siblings can substitute for the mother's absence, so the cohesive group can substitute for the absent father's role.

The role of the father is useful only when it fulfils the needs of each of the stages of developmental evolution the child goes through. A constant and dependable role of the father and steadfast affection are indispensable in order to be credible for the child. Inconsistency can cause disappointments. Serious disappointments or traumata may blur or erase and cause the loss of previous introjections or internal object relations. There is a constant need for support, assistance, and help to be given to the internal world, so that it can contain objects possessing functions and roles from which the development of fantasies can emerge.

The primal scene enacts paternal and maternal roles in movement; it is a stage full of characters. The absence of a third party makes it difficult to conceive a three-dimensional space, as I have observed in the course of my work with children.

It is well known that the father role, or the real father, plays the leading role in the Oedipus complex; its structuring and resolution are fundamental for mental structuring. Hence, I emphasize that the father role is the role of a decoder of messages, a facilitator of the primary group.

One facet of the father role consists in imparting an affective coherence to sensations and perceptions in the world of living objects surrounding the child. This role cannot be severed from the role of the mother.

The male person playing the role of the father must allow and foster a masculine sexual identification, make sexual differentiation possible, thus leading to the completion of a long developmental process. This can only be achieved when it becomes possible to differentiate the outside from the inside, "I" from "you", a full mental space from the void, and through the creation of the psychological concept of a skin enveloping and containing, with a known voice, odour, touch, and melody.

Only when pre-oedipal roles are fulfilled does it become possible to enter the world of total objects and the Oedipus complex described by Freud. It is only then that depressive anxieties and introjective identification of the total object can be experienced. In some societies, social codes assign the man–father the role of confronting outside reality. But through my experience with seriously ill patients—drug addicts, psychotic patients, and so on—I have become increasingly aware of the existence of micro-cultures that have their own particular codes.

Obviously, a structure and a set of relationships and links are involved, and the son or daughter is included within this global whole. The child has his or her own fantasies and ways of managing schizoid, paranoid, and depressive anxieties. The child may have his own disorders, affecting the reception of introjections within his internal world; he may also have his own particular manner of using projective identifications, either through normal communication or else in an exaggerated, massive, or omnipotent style. There is also envy and hate.

The role of the father can also sometimes be assigned by the child. An infant turning his head away, refusing the breast, and rejecting his mother's care is a child who does not allow his mother to be a mother. The same happens with children who do not allow their father to be a father.

The role of the father does not exist as a thing-in-itself. Quite the opposite: this role is a long and probably never-ending dialectic process of creation and learning.

*Abandonment and separations in childhood
and their relation to sexual difficulties:
sexual difficulties and castration fantasies*

Let us now examine the subject of castration: we can also speak of oedipal or pre-oedipal—more primitive—castration. Primitive castration is perceived as the loss or disintegration of parts of the body. McDougall (1990) describes it as follows:

> Separation anxiety is the prototype of castration anxiety, and the presence and absence of the mother are the factors around which

the first oedipal structuring will be built. . . . The trauma of primal castration, expressed as fear of disintegration of the body and loss of identity, unfailingly leaves its traces in sexual disturbances.

Jones (1962) defines a certain type of primal castration and describes it as an utter loss of libido and of stimulation through sexual contact: he calls it *aphanisis* (in Greek).

On the subject of the father's role, I would like to quote Freud's *Leonardo* (1910c), where he describes different situations:

1. the role the father plays in the son's erotic development;
2. fathers who are absent from the very beginning: "I was . . . strongly impressed by cases in which the father was absent from the beginning . . .", says Freud;
3. the function of the father in the choice of the opposite sex. I quote Freud: "Indeed, it almost seems as though the presence of a strong father would ensure that the son made the correct decision in his choice of object, namely someone of the opposite sex". In this dialectic interplay, feminine as well as masculine figures are necessary.

In *Leonardo* (1910c) Freud describes the model of the traumatic rupture that causes early alterations of the ego. It is important to underscore Freud's interest in the early alterations of the ego, not only in this work on Leonardo, but also in "Analysis Terminable and Interminable" (Freud, 1937a; see also Sandler, 1991).

In the clinical material I describe here, I would like to emphasize the importance of pre-oedipal material in the case of the patient Abelard, as well as the importance of the mother's early role.

The clinical material suggests transferential homosexual fantasies— in other words, we may infer the existence of homosexual transference fantasies that the patient uses to relate to the therapist, both *wanting* and *fearing* to succeed.

It is possible that the emergence and discussion during his treatment of erotic and incestuous fantasies are a way he can show himself as a male who gets excited about women, thus escaping his feminine homosexual erotic feelings for the therapist.

We can surmise that he searched for his father by playing the role of a woman, believing that this was the only way he would be loved. We can expand on this theory by thinking in terms of masculine–feminine confusion or ambivalence.

Final words

In short: autistic encapsulation, which preserves the most valuable elements of the self in the face of a terrifying external world, may sometimes preserve many of the introjections and identifications and avoid total loss. There are children whose internal wounds are always open and painful. One of the aims of autistic encapsulation is to preserve the previous introjection of a personality that has been integrated hastily.

A model may be created, on the basis of experience, showing that many children, in the process of autistic encapsulation, have become isolated in a "pocket" of functioning, so that the developmental process seems to continue normally. This is my hypothesis transferred to adult patients.

I shall leave to the readers the task of drawing their own conclusions from these theoretical discussions, after examining the clinical case I present here.

However, sometimes theory alone cannot entirely encompass the richness and dialectics of clinical psychoanalysis. Clinical practice, with its interplay of projective identifications, introjections, and the dialectic exchange of transference/countertransference, is often much richer, more dynamic and more dialectic than most theories.

In concluding this paper, I reflect that some things cannot be translated into words. How can I put the music during the sessions into words? Can states of pain, terror, suffering, and happiness be conveyed only in words?

What I want to say is expressed better by the poet, Jorge Luis Borges:

> I've come now to the centre of my story, and my desperation as a writer begins. All language is an alphabet of symbols whose exercise presumes a past shared by its interlocutors. But how can I convey the infinite to others, which my fear-filled memory can hardly encompass?

> Jorge Luis Borges, *El Aleph* (in Borges, 2001)

We have seen, in this case history, Abelard bringing forward many things, among these the music of his childhood. As the poet says:

> He thought he was done for, alone and poor
> not knowing what music he mastered,
> crossing the deepest floor of some dream,
> where Don Quixote and Sancho were already riding.

Jorge Luis Borges, Un soldado de Urbina (in Borges, 2001)

CHAPTER TWO

Eating disorders:
psychoanalytic technique

Who wanteth food, and will not say he wants it,
Or can conceal his hunger till he famish?
Our tongues and sorrows do sound deep
Our woes into the air; our eyes do weep
Till tongues fetch breath that may proclaim them
Louder.

Shakespeare, *Pericles* (Act II, Scene 4)

In this presentation, I describe the psychopathology of a female adolescent with eating disorders oscillating between bulimia and anorexia. I emphasize and highlight particularly the technical handling, based especially on transference interpretations.

I discuss the importance for her of having been abruptly separated from her mother, who was critically ill. The material of a dream shows how she now experiences and how she experienced this separation as a baby: the patient narrates a dream in which she says, *"my mother dies and then I die too"*. In this way, she expresses, symbolically and absolutely clearly, how she experiences having been abruptly abandoned.

43

This traumatic model, which is reactivated with each separation or loss of an object relation, shows that she is a young woman with the kind of hypersensitivity we find in autistics, for whom the rupture of a relationship is experienced as "annihilation" and loss of parts of the body (Tustin, 1990b). This is why I considered it especially important to pay particular attention to ends of sessions and missed sessions.

In the course of my discussion of the clinical work, I suggest theoretical models (summarized at the end), which show how bulimia, anorexia, and vomiting have different subjacent explanations: there is no unitary or lineal explanation, since it depends on the point in the transference and the patient's psychopathological state.

I wish to underscore that it is not important that the patient's vomiting, bulimia and anorexia had existed before starting treatment, because I consider that, in my role as psychoanalyst, "everything must acquire experienced meaning in the transference". Therefore, the clinical material shows how her psychopathology slowly acquires transference meaning with me.

The disorders mentioned are also handled in the transference as a deficit of introjection that is manifested in difficulty for listening, which means to be fed through the ears and hearing. It is my words that nourish her.

This discussion is not limited only to eating disorders: it is the analysis of a severe subjacent psychopathology, consisting, for example, in aggressive and self-destructive behaviour.

Part of this material comes up after several months of treatment in dreams that give words to the patient's deepest fears of madness, suicide, violence, and revenge (see "revenge" dream). In several dreams, as in fairy tales, there are snakes and dogs' teeth that attack. This helps to bring to light the darkest, most primitive and terrible fantasies of babies.

Thus, through dreams and clinical material, I begin to understand the patient's delusional relationship with her mother, which allows me to create hypotheses concerning her relation with her internal objects.

I systematically focus special attention on asking her whether she has heard and understood each of my interpretations, for fear that she could evacuate, expel, and vomit them from her mind.

Finally, I illustrate the intense transference relation with the description of some key sessions.

For the purposes of showing the psychoanalytic technique, I only discuss the first two years of treatment. The entire treatment lasted for five years.

"Julie"

Clinical history

The family requests an interview for themselves and for Julie, their 16-year-old daughter, and I accept. The mother is talks about her daughter's impulsive and violent behaviour towards her; she says that she has realized that she induces vomiting, which is another of the reasons she is consulting me. The mother speaks the most, while the girl answers her mother sharply and bitterly and does not accept treatment with me willingly. The father intervenes rarely. Her father was sent when very young by a large Scottish fishing industry to organize and set up a factory for packing and exporting high-quality fish and seafood from the Patagonian coast of the Argentine Atlantic. While he was there, he met his wife, a member of the large Welsh community in the South of Argentina. She was a teacher in one of the cities where most of the inhabitants were descendents of Welsh immigrants, and she was also the director of the Museum of Welsh Culture. The patient's mother lived with all her family, and her father soon sent tickets for his parents to come over from Europe.

I suggested to the girl that she come to see me for a series of interviews, but she broke these off at some point and stopped coming.

A year later, I received a telephone call asking me for treatment, and at that time the girl accepted to come for four sessions a week.

After the first interview she tells me, quite anguished, that after a certain episode she had to be hospitalized in a psychiatric clinic. She says that it happened after the fellow she calls her boyfriend, Adam, left her on the pavement and told her he didn't want to see her any more.

It was her mother who, during a joint interview, explained what had happened just before the psychiatric hospitalization, since Julie had partly erased and partly dissociated this memory.

What had happened was that she had arrived at home, had the broken the furniture and shattered the windows, and had attacked her father physically, fracturing one of his bones, while she was seized with an unstoppable flow of words. All this was so impossible to control that they decided to hospitalize her.

The patient reconstructed all these events only later.

During the first few interviews, there is clearly a recurrent fantasy of suicide (which she already had while she was hospitalized). At that point, I insisted that during the first months the treatment take place every day, from Monday through Saturday, in view of the patient's anxiety and suicidal fantasies.

In the initial sessions, she also tells me about her crises of bulimia followed by vomiting.

I will narrate parts of the first year and especially of the second year of treatment—the period of most frequent dreams.

The linguistic shell

In the first sessions Julie uses such rapid, unstoppable language that it is impossible to get in a word to ask questions or interpret anything. This tremendous flow of words creates an impenetrable wall—a shell that makes it impossible for the analyst to get through by means of words or interpretations.

I approached this fact from the linguistic perspective and told her that she was keeping me from intervening, that she refused to listen to me, and that this was an equivalent of not lending her ears to words or food. In the session, feeding is done through the ear rather than the mouth.

On another occasion her mother called because she was very worried about the violent relationship with her daughter. In an interview, she related the real story of the patient's first weeks of life. Having given birth to her daughter by Caesarean section, the mother had had a severe haemorrhage while walking on the pavement with her baby. She fell into a deep coma that left her hospitalized and unable to take care of her baby for eight months.

A neighbour lady recognized her and took the baby to her grandmother's, who took care of her very lovingly and affectionately for the first eight months of her life. Her two grandmothers and one grandfather are still extremely important people for her.

During the beginning weeks of treatment, the patient often told me that she had skipped school, that she made herself vomit, and also that she remained silent for long periods of time, after which she would say that she was tired of it all and wanted to die.

She spent many minutes showing me stickers of some cartoon characters called "The Power Puff Girls": very small girls who can fly and have powers like Superman. She usually stuck these stickers onto her fingernails, and she gorged on candy from a box that had a picture of the Power Puff Girls.

At the beginning of the treatment, Julie told me about her great crises of bulimia or eating binges, especially after leaving her sessions. I systematically interpreted this as not being able to listen to me, not being able to introject me. This is why she tried to eat outside what she couldn't receive or eat through hearing.

I also interpreted her narrations of vomiting in the morning or at night as the transference relation, where she vomits me, vomits a person, or vomits an interpretation. As the reader can see, I try to handle psychoanalytic transference in a strict way: what it means to eat and vomit the psychoanalyst and the interpretations.

At the beginning of her treatment, the patient moved to an apartment in the city, since her parents work in the fishing industry in another large port city. During that time, there were frequent descriptions of fights and violence with her mother, as well as drug consumption with her classmates.

She frequently missed sessions without giving notice—something that is quite common in anorexic patients (Wilson, Hogan, & Mintz, 1992).

I systematically interpreted this fact as vomiting me.

Although the patient was quite thin, she said she was too fat—a typical disturbance of the body image in this type of patient.

I interpreted that she had many pounds of madness in her head, and she preferred to see them in her body as pounds of weight. This interpretation of pounds of madness in her head caused intense emotional reactions in the patient, as well as nightmares.

In the course of the first year she told me about the many boys with whom she chatted on the Internet; and over the months, bit by bit, I began to learn of her precocious and intense sexuality, which had started when she was 13.

Over the months, she also told me about her dates with men, usually young but some also older, with whom she had sexual relations.

Her description of the one she called " my boyfriend Adam"—who had told her in a coffee shop he didn't love her any more and had then, on the pavement, said, "Go away, I don't want to see you any more"—was told more and more clearly in the following sessions, as well as the impact provoked by the break-down episode that had led to her psychiatric hospitalization.

The following is an extract taken from a session in the first year of treatment, which shows how episodes of abandonment reactivated having been abandoned in the first weeks of her infancy.

In this session, Julie talks about a book by Spitz, with photos of babies who are depressed when abandoned after birth in hospitals and nurseries. It shows how the babies, abandoned in the nurseries, left there by their parents for many hours of the day, became depressed when the nurses changed, and that they suffered after-effects in the form of physical and mental disturbances as well as feeding problems. I tell her she is still talking about herself.

The patient shouts, "No, no, that has nothing to do with me!" She screams, "No! No! No!"

I tell her, "What you're talking about has to do with what happened back then, when, after you were born, your mother was gravely ill; unfortunately, she was on the brink of death and was forced to leave you and be hospitalized. And this was left engraved on your mind, as if it were chiselled into stone. But you deny it. You do the same thing with my words. You vomit them and expel them."

Then she tells me a dream: *she is in the kitchen washing knives.* Does she want to kill her mother? Or is she afraid her mother would kill her? In any case, these are associations to the dream of the fact of killing or being killed by her mother. In the same dream, she says that, at another point, *her father appears, with a knife in his hand.* She again says that, in the dream, what she most fears (because she was afraid in the dream) was that her mother might come up from behind with a knife and stab her.

Knives, in the sink, covered with blood: I ask her for associations and ask about her menstruation. Surprised, she looks me in the eye and says, "Yes, right. I had the dream after my period started."

She has sexual relations without any protection.

She says, "The only thing I can think of to talk about is that guy Adam, the only one I consider my boyfriend. And who left me in the coffee shop, left me alone; I ran after him on the pavement, but he yelled at me and left me. On the pavement I felt it was the end of the world."

He was leaving and she was left all alone and he shouted that he was leaving her; it was the end of the world. That day, when she arrived home, she smashed everything.

Later on in the session we are able to listen and talk a bit more calmly. I tell her that what she re-lived in that scene in the coffee shop when the guy Adam left her abandoned on the pavement and shouted that he was leaving her . . . was what is still engraved on her mind, from her first months of life: a Mamma who had a nearly fatal haemorrhage and left her abandoned on the pavement. For her, that was the end of the world, because she never again saw that face, heard that voice, or recovered that Mamma until several months later (the months when her grandmothers took care of her) (Ferrari, 1987; Hochmann, 1994).

The patient doesn't answer this and changes the subject.

I repeat that what she felt was having been abandoned in early childhood through her mother's sudden haemorrhage on the pavement. And that she re-lived this experience again, which for her was the end of the world, annihilation, abandonment, and that she had unfortunately expressed, with shouting, violence, and madness, what had remained engraved in a month-old baby girl abandoned on the pavement.

I add: "In your mind or psyche, your inner world, that guy Adam repeated on the pavement exactly what your mother did when you were a baby. Look, you're trying to put into words the story of the first month of life with your mother. You're trying to give it words for the first time." I tell her that this is important. The past is never the past."

At the end of this first year of treatment, her vomiting, bulimia, and drug consumption intensified and the relationship with her mother worsened, to the point that the patient wouldn't allow her into her apartment in the city.

The dream of the dirty kitchen

A month later Julie tells me about the quantity of interchanges (chat) she has by computer with people she doesn't know, through ICQ; they ask for her photo, and she sends it to them.

Her monotonous and formal—almost intellectual—way of speaking provokes a very distant, far-away countertransference. She goes on to say that she has met a very sad young man who told her about his father's death and his mother's psychotic depression.

In the course of the session I show her that she is perhaps taking care of a part of herself—when she is going through severe depressions—projected onto another, as if she were in front of a mirror.

Finally, I interpret that she prefers to take care of someone else and see herself projected in another person: it's better to see the straw in the other's eye rather than the beam in her own.

At the beginning of another session that week, she tells me a dream: *her kitchen is dirty, with dirty food and unwashed dishes . . . strewn all over the table and the floor of her house. . . .* I ask whether this dream dovetails with physical experiences of diarrhoea or menstruation. Yes, she says, she is menstruating and she vomits every day. Then she says that she doesn't want to go to visit her grandparents; on the basis of material from previous sessions, I tell her that she is very frightened, is suffering and feels anguished by the grave illness of her granny who brought her up, and that this awakens her fear of seeing her die.

In the following two weeks she skips several sessions, of course without giving notice. This behaviour is typical of individuals who vomit: they vomit the therapist. Because of her sadness and grief about her sick granny, she cannot tolerate her own sad and ill aspects. This is what she does: not coming to her session is equivalent to not thinking. She believes that by vomiting she eliminates thoughts, pain, grief, sadness and madness. She vomits and expels aspects of her mind. There is no mental space to contain her pain.

She repeats that the food she has just chewed already seems like something dirty; I tell her that this is because she thinks this food turns into faeces. I think about the relationship between the baby and the mother's milk: in her fantasy, the baby defecates onto the mother's breast, which is thus invaded by faeces. Therefore, she drinks in the return of the projected: excrement instead of milk.

In her dreams too, when she projects hate onto the mother's breast; therefore, instead of receiving milk, she believes she is getting knives and snakes.

Since she comments that she is menstruating, I go back to the interpretation of the dream and point out that she also believes that her body is full of blood, poop, dirty food, and vomit, which form the excess pounds that make her too fat. The interpretations centre on the fact that the more she deludes on this subject, which expresses her hypochondriac fantasies of dirtiness, the more vomiting she provokes.

I repeat again that not coming to a session is equivalent to vomiting.

Omnipotence and its relation to anorexia

Julie begins by saying that she had a dream in which *she is an older, adult woman, but goes out with a 12-year-old boy.*

I ask her to help me to understand her dream. To my great surprise, the patient says, "I don't know, perhaps I am mentally 12 years old, as you said."

I tell her, "You disguise yourself as a grown-up woman, and you project your childish aspect onto a little 12-year-old girl. But in the dream a masculine aspect of you appears. You know that this is the childhood history of your life: I show you two aspects in your inner world. You appear here as a little boy, as if you had always been afraid to be a feminine little girl, a woman." I remind her then of a dream she had in which *she is in bed with a transvestite.* "It was a transvestite, and you didn't know whether it was a man dressed up like a woman. Perhaps your dream today is the continuation of the other one, where you didn't know whether it was a man or a woman in bed with you. But I think that it's you, with your identity problems, not knowing whether you were a girl or a boy when you were 10 or 12 years old.

Then I explain my ideas to her: I make the connection between the anorexia and the childhood omnipotence that pushes her to want to be an adult—or, rather, a pseudo-adult: then she would have no need of the breast or food. It is the same omnipotence that makes her have a penis in her dream, so that she would have no need of a man. This is the same as saying: "I am the breast and I feed myself all by myself, and I also have a penis and I don't depend on a man."

After a long silence, to my surprise, she gets us, picks up her handbag, takes out a large photo album, and says that she wants to show it to me. These are photos of her childhood, extremely beautiful photos; she shows me what she was like when she was a child. In one photo, she shows me her little cousin, with whom she used to play; they would play at getting married: they were a couple. They can be seen in photos when she was two, smiling, and in another she looks very sad, at the same age. . . .

In several photos her father hugs her affectionately.

She went without food for four days, then swung to the opposite extreme, with episodes of eating binges, bulimia, because she couldn't listen to me and be nourished by my interpretations.

In the perspective of psychoanalytic theory, I think that what the patient absorbs is not introjected and her psyche vomits it, which provokes a severe disturbance of her capacity to think and consequently of her conception of the theory of thinking. For example, she cannot study and pass her courses and exams successfully.

Dream of a woman with a penis — problems of sexual identity

In this material, my purpose is to illustrate the disturbances of the patient's sexual identity.

In this dream there is *a nightclub dancer, very daring and well dressed, but with a huge penis: she is a woman, but she has a penis.* Julie adds that it is perhaps a vibrator.

When I ask her to give me some details, she adds that she had this dream after a date with a man. She says, "Yes, it's true that John bought a vibrator, and we used it and I had some orgasms with it."

The following week, there is a variation on this dream: she is in her apartment with her partner, but she has a real penis. She believes that she has sexual relations with her penis, and that her partner is passive.

I ask her whether, after all, in her dream, her partner is a man, or whether he belongs to a different gender. She says that she only remembers that she had a penis.

Then she talks about the little childhood cousin who lived in the same house with her. She remembers many outings together and anecdotes from their childhood, and that he used to get quite jealous if she played with other children.

I ask her whether she believes that all this is related to the sexual games she might have played with her little cousin. The patient says yes, they used to show each other their sexual organs, she would ask him why he had a penis when she didn't have one; she would touch it and let herself be touched by him (A. Anzieu, 2000, Green, 1997; Meltzer, 1975).

I tell her that the dream of having a penis was and always is the fantasy of Superwoman, that she could have her own breasts, her own penis, that she had no need for men or her mother, for food or breasts, thereby reminding her of my interpretations of her infantile omnipotence that enable her to not depend on anyone.

Re-emergence of suicidal ideas—
manic-depressive oscillations

Julie tells me that she went to the baptism of the baby of a friend her own age, a schoolmate, which made her think that there are

classmates her age who are already mothers. She changes the subject and tells me that she was alone on Friday night and Saturday
morning, and that she was so desperate that she dreamt of killing
herself (Klein, 1935).

In my countertransference, the re-emergence of these suicidal fantasies provokes serious worry, both emotionally and as a man of
science (Boyer, 1999; Searles, 1979; Wallerstein, 1994).

I try to translate her very grave fantasy of suicide into words; it had
already come up at the beginning of the treatment, and again after
her hospitalization—at least, this is what her mother told me, that
Julie had such thoughts when she was hospitalized. The patient, in
a kind of repudiation, says, "Well, for me, it was more important
to get angry at home with my family, who gave me a lot to eat,
because they forced me to eat, then I would go off and vomit."

I tell her that I intend to prescribe her some medication, and that
I am going to call her parents to talk to them about her ideas of
suicide. I even call my team of colleagues, thinking in terms of
hospitalization. I tell her that she must come to see me twice a day
for the whole week.

The mother's psychopathology

In view of the danger of suicide, I asked her mother to come to see
me urgently so that I could tell her about the danger her daughter was
in, considering her ideas of suicide, the need to intensify her treatment
to two sessions a day, and the probability of hospitalization.

Her response was surprising: "I can't pay for that many sessions."
I explained the seriousness of the case and the dangers of suicide. She
replied, "I will send her to a public service, to a hospital."

I answered that she would not receive the care she needs, that she
would have to wait for a long time, and that they will see her only
once a week.

I told her, "If a patient needs to take an antibiotic three times a day,
you cannot decide to give her only one dose a week. This is what you
are doing."

This was a wealthy family, who owned several factories and therefore had no money problems. She seemed distant from the situation

of urgency and danger that I conveyed to her. In this interview, I discovered much more about this mother than the patient was able to tell me. Just as she now avoided contact with her daughter's fantasies of suicide and the danger involved, she had been unable to make contact with her daughter's emotions, grief, nightmares, or terrors during her daughter's childhood.

This was gradually confirmed by the patient's clinical material. Her mother was incapable of getting into her daughter's mind to understand her emotions.

In the theoretical perspective, I would stress that she didn't have a "useful projective identification", as described by Herbert Rosenfeld (1987).

Vomiting and disturbances of thought

Two weeks later, the vomiting started again and increased, which made it more difficult for the patient to listen and to think during the sessions; vomiting is equivalent to not listening to me, not being able to absorb the words with which to think: it means not understanding.

After a few days, she went to the opposite extreme and had crises of bulimia. Each instance of bulimia is acting out that consisted of going on an eating binge and gorging compulsively when she left the session, precisely because she was not able to listen to me and be nourished by my interpretations.

In ten days she came to four sessions, and each time, when she returned home at night, she made herself vomit.

I systematically told her, "Try to think with me: what did you vomit? Did you vomit what I tell you? Think of the person you vomited, or perhaps you vomited an aspect of yourself."

On the theoretical level, I think that what she absorbed was not introjected and was vomited from her mental apparatus, causing a severe disturbance of the capacity for introjection and the ability to think. This is why she was unable to study and pass her exams.

The most important dream in her life:
"when her mother dies, she feels that she herself dies"

In the second year of treatment, the patient had very intense experiences of separation from the analyst, following vacations. This material was fundamental for her to achieve better insight, which would consequently help to produce positive modifications in the patient's life (Painceira Plot, 1997).

> After the therapist's absence for a ten-day vacation, Julie began the session by saying that she had two dreams.

Dream 1:

> This one made the greatest impact, both on her and on me. In it, *her mother dies and immediately afterwards, she also dies.* She says that she was very shocked, and adds that she think that it's the most important dream in her life. Towards the end, I am able to interpret that today she is able to translate what happened to her since her early infancy into dreams—that is, to symbolize it in dreams. When I left for ten days, I disappeared, just as her mother had disappeared. The baby experienced death, and she felt that she died too, disappeared, stopped existing, felt annihilated, and she cannot conceive the idea in her mind that she will recover me.

> I repeat my interpretations, in which the disappearance of the figure she knows so well, the familiar voice, the well-known odour, for the infant that inhabits her, is the same as seeing her mamma, gravely ill, disappear when she was hospitalized when she was born, and then the little girl, Julie, disappeared too. I insist again, telling her that she finally has the chance to express all this in a dream, all this that is always engraved in her; this is why she says that it is the most important dream in her life (Houzel, 1988).

Dream 2:

> Here, she dreams about *the young man she calls "Adam, the first boyfriend I fell in love with"*. It is not by chance that he appears after the dream where her mother and she die.

> I interpret: she is now bringing in the second part of the dream, in which her mother leaves her on the pavement.

> I complete the interpretation by saying that this experience is repeated when this boyfriend leaves her on the pavement and tells her that he doesn't love her any more; we must bear in mind that she had to be hospitalized after this. But today she expresses it in a dream, while before she couldn't do that, so she had a psychotic

crisis. I insist particularly on the transference: this dream also reflects her experience of my absence.

Dream 3:

To my surprise, she brings another dream about *"boyfriend Adam"* to the following session. *They are in bed naked, but she doesn't think they had sexual relations.*

She says that she was terribly afraid of losing him, and that she wished very much that he would come to see her, but when he came to see her, she locked the door. She adds: "That way, he couldn't go away for the whole weekend, I had him trapped, closed inside my house under lock and key. . . . When I suspected that he would leave me to be with other girls, I would cheat on him too, going to bed with two classmates and another guy I knew."

Since she was very young, she has engaged in a manic sexual hyperactivity in the belief that this is the way to recover lost ties; she attacked or destroyed whoever abandoned her. She used this method as a weapon against being left alone. But in spite of all her manic sexual activity, her experience of "the end of the world" caused by having been abandoned could not be worked through, so that it always persisted in her.

This material is interesting, because it offers a theory on parasitical projective identification (H. Rosenfeld, 1987).

We see again in the following dream how separations cause the patient to re-live her infantile losses. A notable element in this dream is her attempt to understand the voices of her infancy:

Julie says: "I dream that *I hear my grandmother's voice; I was immersed in a muddy swamp, and she comes to save me."*

I reply: "I think that in this dream you show how you sought my voice when I was away, just as you sought your grandmother, who rocked you and sang you lullabies."

We see more clearly than ever how she sought me and her need for my voice, just as she needed her grandmother's voice.

Then I tell her that for her, just one day's absence is like a year of abandonment; if I go away for a week, she feels that she will never find me again. The concept of meeting again seems to be inconceivable for her.

The balcony dream

The dream that is the key to understanding the origin of her terror and revenge, which allows the revelation of her delusion of taking revenge on her mother, which we call the balcony dream, is a very important moment in the second year of treatment. In this dream, *she is on a balcony, and then finds that she is on the ground, on the pavement.* This dream provided the key to understanding the appearance of her transference with me, her fear of my revenge, because she missed sessions without giving notice. She is afraid of me when she declares that Doctor Rosenfeld will not say "hi" any more. She tells me her dream:

She is on the pavement, with one of her young male friends; she doesn't know whether it's this Adam who abandoned her, when she had to be hospitalized, or if it's another male friend.

She says: *"In my dream, this boy passed me on the pavement, but he didn't say hi to me anymore."*

I ask her whether she doesn't think that this dream perhaps evokes the fact that I was going to see her today, after she missed four sessions without giving me notice.

The patient stays silent.

Here, in the transference, the origin of the revenge that she fears from me today is revealed, a revenge that she feared after birth from her mother. This dream allows me to see in the transference the delusion of revenge and the struggles in her inner world (her psyche). Now this can be worked on in the transference (Freud, 1912–14).

The struggle between the healthy parts and the sick parts in her inner world

In her dream, Julie *is napping, and there are two persons: the first is herself, who says "I'm not going there, I'm not going there." The other says "Okay, okay, go there, go there."*

I tell her that perhaps her dream refers to a Julie who wants to come to her session and be trusting, and a second Julie who is suspicious and is afraid to tell what is happening with her feelings and her emotions. But in any case, it's a dream that concerns me, that concerns the transference. I explain to her that it is about two parts of herself—one that is trusting and another that is suspicious. This is her inner world, her psyche, I emphasize.

This dream was highly important for showing her that there are two aspects in her: one that is afraid and suspicious, that doesn't want to come, and the other, the healthier aspect, that says yes. Perhaps in this dream she explains why she misses sessions without giving notice. It's because there is a struggle inside her inner world, inside her psyche.

She tells a surprising dream: she is with her mother, who is very friendly, almost as if they were two girlfriends, classmates or friends, not at all like a mother and a daughter. The two go for a walk with the same man. She says that in her dream, she is the adult, while the mother is a weak little girl, and she lets her share the father with her. I interpret that she is omnipotent, while the mother is the poor weak, fragile, impotent Julie. This is the projective identification of her weak and infantile part onto her mother.

I have the impression that this interpretation makes an emotional impact on her. But she replies as usual, with manic comments, telling me how many young people she chats with on Internet.

Second year of treatment

The recovery of internal objects: the songs of her childhood

> If music be the food of love, play on;
> Give me excess of it, that, surfeiting,
> The appetite may sicken, and so die.
>
> Shakespeare *Twelfth-Night* (Act I, Scene 1)

At the end of a session in the second year, after a long silence, Julie says that she heard some music, a tango titled *"Quejas del*

Bandoneon" ["Laments of the Bandoneon"], that she was moved to tears, she doesn't quite know why. I ask her to help me to discover the cause of her emotion. She wants to tell me something else: she says that she heard this tango when she was at her grandparents' house, and she adds: "I've just remembered, it's the tango my grandfather used to play, and he used to sing it to me when I was a child; I often lived with them at that time."

What the patient recovered through this music are the lullabies and songs of her infancy: it is a tango made into a lullaby by her grandfather, who took care of her with her grandmother while her mother was in hospital, until she was 8 months old. This grandfather died when Julie was 12. She spoke of the death of this very dear grandfather.

The countertransference is one of intense emotion and great emotional contact with the patient (Ogden, 2001).

When talking about her precocious and intense sex life starting at the age of 13, I pointed out that all her sexual relations could perhaps be an intense search for objects—especially a loved and lost object, her grandfather, who was very close to her when she was 12. And he died. He had brought her up, and we worked intensely on this emotional shock, the sadness and the mourning. She tried to find her lost objects—her dead grandfather—through sexuality and her crises of bulimia. Karl Abraham (1911a) offers us a marvellous description of oral sadism and cannibalistic introjection.

During this period, we were able to talk about and analyse her father's psychotic depression. I asked her a lot about her father's illness; in spite of my insistence and interventions, pointing out that this subject was very important for the patient and that it frightened and saddened her, her response was always silence.

In my experience with anorexic disorders, I find that detained eating is due to a mechanism of symbolic equation (Segal, 1994).

In this case, there is confusion between a father who suffers from a psychiatric disorder and food that cannot be swallowed. It is as if the patient were saying: "I don't want to swallow my father's madness" or "I don't want to swallow my family's madness." In my experience with anorexic patients who have a psychotic parent, these expressions often emerge.

She is able to ask for help.
the appearance of useful infantile dependence

I think that when the patient recovers bonds through childhood songs, she is able to get closer to me: in this material, she asks for more frequent sessions—that is, more food. On the phone, the patient told me, "I want an extra session."

This session was to tell me a dream that anguished Julie very deeply: *She was in her father's bed. It was her father's bed, but she was there with John, a friend. But in the dream she was afraid she might be seen by her mother.*

This dream is immediately followed by another, in which *she lies down naked between Daddy and Mamma;* but what is important is that she had this dream after a whole week when she missed her sessions without giving me notice.

This dream shows us how she looks for defences, in sexualized oedipal seeking, against the loneliness that she herself provokes by not coming to her sessions.

My interpretation provokes a deep silence and has a great impact on the patient. I tell her that, when she found that she was alone, she tried to get into my bed; she thought that the only way of not being alone and recovering me would be to get sexually into my bed, between me and my wife.

Tears and sobs

During the following session a very intense event occurs for the first time: Julie weeps, she sobs, she talks about forming a stable relationship with this very affectionate and serene fiancé, and she talks about pregnancy.

She says that she cried a lot the night before and that, in the midst of a crisis of weeping, she called her mother and said, "Mamma, come over, I need you." Nothing so intense had ever happened to her.

The interpretations suggest that the patient recognizes that there is a powerless little girl who is finally trying to admit that she needs to be taken care of, and that she recognizes it.

She can show me that she cried and that she's afraid: she is not Superwoman.

Guilt emerges: the depressive position

The patient decided to live in her apartment with her stable partner, but her pathology returned. She fought with her boyfriend and threw him out. After this episode of verbal violence and shouting, her fiancé, John, called me by phone, quite frightened, and told me that Julie had had a crisis of violence at her parents' house, that she lost control and threw him out screaming, told him to leave, and that he's afraid that this loss of control might be bordering on madness.

I calmed him down and told him that I was going to try to understand, but that he must also help me to calm her down. He gave me the impression of being a very calm, quiet person.

After the four following sessions the patient decided to call John and ask him to come back to live with her. During the session she was very sensitive, very impressed above all by the quiet and serene attitude of her fiancé, who didn't get angry or react violently. She had never had a partner like him. She cried and sobbed during the session and told me something she had rarely said: that she felt very guilty for having treated her current partner so badly.

I theoretically understood what happened in her: the beginning of a perception of grief and reparation, it is the start of the depressive position (Geissmann & Geissmann, 2000; Houzel, 2000a; Klein, 1968).

After a weekend Julie says that she dreamed that *her fiancé, John, was with a girlfriend who was trying to seduce him in bed. But she came in and screamed and he got out of bed, all frightened. All of a sudden, her fiancé had white hair.*

The patient comments: "a bit fanciful".

He catches several mice in the bedroom, and immediately a snake appears and wants to eat the mice; John throws some mice to the snake. But the snake, wanting to catch a mouse that John is holding in his hand, bites him. And "she bites him with her canines".

Obviously, it is also a model of the patient's oral-sadistic relation with the mother's breast in the first months of life.

Then I tell her: You attack him with your canines like a snake, because he went to a party and left you alone. It is a vicious circle that exists in your psyche.

Today, she can symbolize all this in a dream. And this capacity is something new that she has acquired in recent months (Grotstein, 2000; see also Folch & Eskelinen, 1989).

Reflections

Recapitulating, it is evident that this patient presents a severe pathology, marked by great emotional instability, fluctuations of her state of mind, eating disorders, sometimes severe alterations of her body image, unbridled sexual activity, premature eroticization of relationships, polymorphous sexuality, in which we presume that the most important aspect is the search for bonds, skin-to-skin contact, and a certain excitation as a defence against loneliness. We have also described the disorganized, aggressive explosions—the first one during her hospitalization and a second when her boyfriend abandoned her on the pavement. Also, she has suicidal ideas and a feeling of inner emptiness, which she is, of course, unable to fill with concrete objects such as food. Guilt feelings and the depressive position emerge only after a long period of treatment (as described in the fist part of the case example). We thus highlight her imperious need of closeness and intimacy, which her inability to generate stable and solid relationships keeps her from satisfying.

We have described this young woman's enormous sensitivity when she is faced with anything she might experience as being abandoned by her significant objects (see, for example, the session after my return from holiday).

The autistic-like seeking of sensorial stimuli (Tustin, 2000) and many autistic type mannerisms and hand movements, as well as the constant search for "bodily sensations" through stimulation of the oral and vaginal mucous membrane (as in the case of some autistic girls) led me to think that this patient had, during her first weeks of life, used autistic defence mechanisms in order to survive.

* * *

Ogden's theory of "the autistic-contiguous position" enables us to better understand and elucidate the mechanisms of search for contiguity that this patient uses in her relationships. Ogden (1994) defines it in the following way:

> The contiguous-autistic position is conceived as a psychological organization that is more primitive than the positions designed by Klein. This position represents an elaboration on and an extension of the work of Bick (1968), Meltzer (1975), and Tustin (1986).
>
> The contiguous-autistic position is associated with a way of generating experiences characterized by proto-symbolic impressions of sensorial experiences that, associated, contribute to constitute an experience of joined surfaces.
>
> The rhythmicality and the experiences of sensorial contiguity (particularly on the surface of the skin) contribute to an elementary sense of continuity of being over time. These experiences are generated in the invisible matrix of the environmental mother. The relations with objects (that are not felt as objects) are produced in the form of experiences of "auto-sensual forms" and auto-sensual objects (Tustin, 1990a).
>
> These idiosyncratic uses, though organized and organizers of sensitive experiences of softness and hardness, represent two of the facets of the process by which the sensorial base of all experience is organized.

And he adds that

> the contiguous-autistic mode provides a large part of the "sensorial base" of experience . . .; the paranoid–schizoid mode generates an important part of the immediate and vital nature of the concrete experience that is symbolized; the depressive mode permits the creation of a historical self that is capable of interpreting.
>
> These three positions are related to each other, both diachronically and synchronically. In other words, there is a chronological, sequential relation between these three positions (a developmental progression that runs from the primitive to maturity, from the pre-symbolic to the symbolic, from the pre-subjective to the subjective, from the a-historical to the historical, etc.)" [pp. 36–38]

Another part of the patient's psyche, with neurotic aspects, was able to adapt to reality, which enabled her to use certain mechanisms of projective identification. The concept of useful projective identification (H. Rosenfeld, 1987) for communication appears only at the end of the second year of treatment, when she begins to understand the suffering she causes others and when guilt feelings emerge.

This group of symptoms and pathologies could also be interpreted conceptually through the fundamental theories of Kernberg (1984) concerning borderline cases. This description does not exclude all the theories that I describe at the end of my discussion, when I develop the theoretical concepts.

The other important element for the treatment of patients suffering from severe pathologies is to be able to decode and understand the experiences of the countertransference.

* * *

I highlight the importance of the work done in the transference and countertransference. The careful analysis of countertransference feelings becomes an essential technical element: the analyst must be able to decode and to translate into words, if possible, and to contain them. This is an indispensable instrument. I am extremely careful when verbalizing transference interpretations. I allow time for the unfolding of the internal world and for listening (understanding) the messages of the child through drawings, games, and troubles. Psychoanalytic treatment centres on the interpretation, in the transference, and the importance of the handling of the countertransference, of the internal world, of the interpretation of dreams and nightmares. We do all this without forgetting the importance of the setting. The analytic cures of children help me more and more to better understand and penetrate into the infantile world of my adult patients.

Early psychoanalytic diagnosis and treatment are the basis of better diagnoses and prevention of mental illness in adults.

The study of the mother–child relationship in the first years of life has enriched the therapist's contact with child and adult patients. The psychoanalysis of children leads us to create new models that enable us to improve our understanding of the most primitive levels of mental functioning. The notion of the "autistic pocket" or that of "encapsulated autism" can remain isolated or coexist with the healthy or neurotic aspects of the personality; they also permit a different approach to the severe pathologies.

In my position in the Chair of Psychiatry in the Medical School, I teach the importance of prevention. For this reason, the introductory subjects deal with the mother–child relationship and the first years of life. I consider early diagnosis essential (de Mijolla, 2001; Rosenfeld, 1991, 1992b, 2000, 2001a, 2001b).

* * *

During the second year of treatment, the possibility emerged for the patient to express symbolically in dreams what she had previously expressed only via acting out or actions. Naturally, it was important that she remembered her dreams so she could bring them to the sessions.

The words the patient used to describe a dream that she considered "the most striking, the most important in her life" are very important. This is the dream where her mother dies and then the patient also dies. This is a short and simple dream, but precisely for that reason it is tragic in its unadorned simplicity. Here we see, as we rarely have occasion to see, the role of the mother who gives life and identity to a baby and a little girl, and how her absence provokes states of "non-life". These states, as Painceira Plot (1997) stresses, can perturb the creation of the transitional space and the transitional object. The real external object is what contributes to keeping the inner object alive. I would add that catastrophic traumata may also transform this object into emptiness, or else—as I describe in my paper on the "Nazi phenomenon" (Rosenfeld, 1986, 1991, 1992b, 2001a, 2001b)—any introjected object can disappear following traumata of the magnitude of those of a Nazi concentration camp.

This patient's aggressiveness is a defence that serves as a temporary way to avoid fragmentation and to unify the fragments of her self, as described by Winnicott (1962). It is important to underscore that the aim is perhaps the unification of the self (Volkan, 1996; Williams, 2001).

* * *

The concepts of the omnipotence of the ego and its importance in numerous pathological symptoms are described and discussed throughout the case example.

It is convenient to remember that, for the treatment of patients suffering from severe pathologies, beyond applying psychoanalytic technique, the psychoanalyst becomes a screen for the reception and projection of the patient's primitive experiences. These projections are not always expressed verbally, since during the first weeks of life there is no language. Through diverse detours and labyrinths connected with syntax, the phonology of the voice, absence and presence in the sessions, the psychoanalyst is obliged to receive the primitive experiences that the patient cannot express in words.

This is part of the concept of countertransference; constant supervision by colleagues and teachers is necessary, and the first countertransference emotions should not be interpreted too soon, before they have been decoded and submitted to supervision.

Following Freud, we could assume that this patient has remained in the stages of oral and anal functioning. The abrupt and traumatic separation from her mother generated a state bordering on a narcissistic state, and after many, many sessions she seems to go farther than what Freud called a "psychoneurosis of defence" (Freud, 1894). This patient was unable to develop the stages of oral sadism and anal sadism, which seem to have been disturbed. The return of the aggression of oral and anal sadism is turned against herself and then becomes melancholia, which emerges in the form of suicidal fantasies, as Freud describes in "Mourning and Melancholia" (1917e). We also observe the return of oral sadism in the dream of the knives and again in the dream of the snake's teeth. The return of these aggressions is transformed into the feared object, which she calls "mother". (I describe this complex relationship with her mother throughout the case example.)

Towards the end of the second year of treatment great changes are stirring when the patient is able to sob and to weep and mentions the word guilt. Below, I discuss the modifications (the change) in my models of interpretation after the interview with the mother. The patient draws a "symbolic equation", as Segal described it (1994), between the space of her psyche and the space of her apartment.

* * *

The theories we have described may not contradict the description of autistic mechanisms, which are much more primitive. They emerge in different levels of the clinical material. Just as she has autistic mechanisms, she also presents more highly developed and neurotic aspects, where projective identification functions.

The seeking of sensoriality in the mucous membrane of the mouth closes the patient in and traps her in this world of "bodily sensations", so that she lives as if inside an oyster shell, with no possibility of making contact with projection and introjection, mechanisms that consequently remain blocked. This is quite previous to the notions of a mental sphincter or an anal sphincter or anal masturbation, as mentioned by Meltzer (1986).

The protective barrier against the stimuli that the conscious can receive depends on each individual in particular: it permits the passage of stimuli in quantities adapted to each individual.

Another conceptualization for understanding the patient's delusion regarding the internal mother object from a different vantage point is Freud's, when he says that the delusion is an attempt to re-connect with the world of objects (Freud, 1915e).

Methodology

On the methodological level, this chapter proposes that there may be several subjacent explanations for the same clinical phenomenon. I would like to underscore that one sole theory or linear explanation is not enough to explain all the clinical phenomena that we describe in this patient.

I propose several models of interpretation: (1) the linguistic; (2) the ways of "vomiting" the analyst; (3) the difficulties for development of the mind and thought, associated with an inability to receive and introject words in order to symbolize and to think; (4) the bulimia, manifested by the act of leaving her session to eat a concrete object, since the patient cannot absorb the words and thoughts on the symbolic level.

Experiences of catastrophe in the face of brutal abandonment

As I said above, there is an eclosion of experiences of the most primitive aspects of the patient's psyche. This occurs, for example, following my holiday. It is then that the patient, instead of reacting with violence or with crises of bulimia, is able to contribute these aspects in a dream that she calls "the most important dream in my life": "I dreamed that Mamma died, and I also died."

This dream reflects, in condensed form, how a little girl receives the concept of identity through containment, affect, and bodily contact with her mother. When this relation is introjected, a stable bond is created that provides containment in the internal world. This process is the origin of the creation of mental space.

The patient, who cannot contain her anxieties, terrors, and hatred in her limited mental space, can only expel what is intolerable in concrete acts—for example, the vomiting and the fights.

The creation of a mental space is a long and unceasing dialectic process. As Winnicott says, the stable and constant presence of a mother or an object able to contain is needed to make it possible to maintain the preceding introjections.

My concepts (Rosenfeld, 1992a, 1992b) demonstrate how all the introjections can disappear when there is severe trauma, as in the case of the Nazi extermination camps; it is true that these situations are traumatic, while Winnicott's account referred to normal development.

The discovery of new hypotheses: an example

In the course of an interview with her mother, I discovered aspects concerning her mother that Julie had never expressed in the clinical material. I am referring to the moment when the mother, emotionally distant, feels no interest in the risk of suicide her daughter is facing (see the session of the interview with the mother).

At this point, the ideas of Boyer (1999) and Searles (1979) were very useful for me.

After this interview, I changed the interpretive model in my interpretations, insisting more on pointing out that she misses her sessions because she believes that I cannot contain her, listen to her, and receive her fears with the affection and serenity of a therapist—that is, I must differentiate myself explicitly from the internal mother object. I must therefore show her that I am different from her mother, who was never able to make contact with the danger of her suicidal fantasies. I begin to work and to interpret along these lines: her mother had this lack of empathy during her entire childhood and adolescent life; her mother was not a stable element in her real life. Not all her problems stem from the abrupt separation in the first weeks of life.

This approach enables me to carry on with the treatment from a new perspective. Julie's search for hugs, caresses, and skin contact since her precocious initiation to sexual relations at 12 or 13 years of age was a pseudo-sexuality in which she was seeking containment and holding.

She also sought sensory stimulation of the mucous membrane of the vagina and the mouth through her food, as autistic children do. For them, bodily sensations are the most primitive way to feel that they exist and do not disappear.

I proposed new models to explain the vomiting. At the beginning, I interpreted how she vomited my words, my interpretations.

Following the dream in which a girl-friend vomited on her and she on her friend, I modify my theory on the vomiting, including the model of projective identification and the return of the projected—that is, I use a different perspective to understand the vomiting.

After the dreams in which she is afraid that her mother will attack her with *bloody* knives, I include in my interpretations that vomiting is a concrete way to express her hate and her wish to kill her mother.

At this time, material emerges concerning the baby children that her mother couldn't have when her uterus was removed after Julie's birth. She believes that she is to blame for this, and the persecutory strength of a primitive and cruel superego grows.

The vomiting acquires different meanings: it helps her to expel parts of her psyche and her self, since she cannot tolerate the existence inside herself of a little, fragile girl who needs help from the therapist (see the dream in which a part of her says "come to session" and the other says "don't go").

When I discover the alterations of her body image, especially during her menstruation, I add a new *ad hoc* hypothesis. In the clinical material, I described the increase in the patient's vomiting when she imagines her body full of faeces and blood.

These fantasies concerning her body image enable me to create new theoretical models with which to understand her psychopathology and to observe her clinical picture of vomiting, which increased during her menstrual period, from a new perspective.

In reference to the theories on violence, this patient was often disorganized and chaotic, with no notion of guilt. Only at the end of the second year of treatment, when the concept of guilt emerges for the first time in a verbalized and experienced form, does the depressive position (Klein, 1968) begin.

I would like to add that I have formulated my theories on violence in schizophrenics on the basis of my experience in treating psychotic patients (Rosenfeld, 1992a, 1992b).

Another theoretical model I use, which complements those described above, is the one in which I describe the omnipotence of the ego and its relation to anorexia, since the patient believes that she is, like a cartoon character, the all-powerful "superwoman".

At other times, I interpret her omnipotence on the basis of her dreams: in some, there are transvestites with a penis, in others, women with a penis, and, finally, in another, she herself possesses her own penis, while she is having sexual relations with her boyfriend.

My theories are modified dialectically and are enriched with new points of view on her omnipotence. My interpretations centre more on her lack of need to need a penis, breasts, food, or therapist.

Thus, we see that one sole theory is not enough to explain the general behaviour of this patient.

The different hypotheses are not mutually contradictory, and the models I propose do not exclude each other. In effect, there are sometimes diverse unconscious motivations for identical behaviour. For this reason, I propose no general theory but prefer to suggest that all these medium-range models or hypotheses have a place in the frame of the great psychoanalytic theory.

Some may suggest that everything is included in the great theory of the pleasure principle, while others can also be explained by the death instinct. These are general theories of psychoanalysis that we can apply, which include most of the material presented.

However, the models I use are closer to clinical practice.

I emphasize that the models I use are medium-range and that some are more stable than others. In other words, certain models are useful because they help to explain a fact, whether in clinical psychoanalysis or even as it occurs in nuclear physics, with the model invented by Niels Bohr of the electrons that spin around the atom. Models are invented by creative minds and are useful as long as they explain facts.

The hypotheses I propose are "preponderant" and can be tested or corroborated by means of their usefulness for psychotherapy.

It is also good to point out that, at the methodological level, the defence mechanisms change depending on their context and the moment of the transference. Thus, we see how the therapist modifies his models to understand and interpret, on the road to the discovery of new labyrinths of the mind.

As I have said, although the symptom may be just one, it may have different explanations and motivations. Being able to unravel it depends on the therapist's creative capacity for inventing new models.

* * *

During the second year of treatment, great changes were set in motion when the patient was able to sob and to weep and when she mentioned the word guilt. Below, I discuss the modifications (changes) in my models of interpretation following the interview with the mother. I also pointed out and interpreted how important her acting out was, when the patient threw her mother out of her apartment and did not allow her to return. The interpretations were connected to the "symbolic equation" (Segal, 1994) the patient made: she equals her own space in her mind to the space of the apartment.

Bulimia and sexuality: "Josephine"

There are other types of eating disorders that, unlike the clinical case discussed in depth in this chapter, are quite clearly related to substitutes for sexual satisfaction. I present a clinical vignette to show the example of a female patient whom I will name "Josephine". She was short and smiley, although her laughter was loud and had a manic tinge to it. Her clothes were very unkempt and her hair generally uncombed. When she started the treatment, she weighed 162 kilos [356.4 pounds]. She was 37.

The patient asked for treatment with me after breaking up with her partner, with whom she had been living for four years. She supported this man and even gave him pocket money.

Josephine talked very fast. Her crises of bulimia were repeated in the transference communication. For many months, in my interpretations, I pointed out how, before I could finish speaking, she would interrupt me and would go on talking fast. My interpretations were aimed at showing her how she was unable to finish chewing and eating what I was giving her with my words and that in this way "she couldn't absorb what I tell her in the session". She couldn't digest and absorb what I was saying to her, and therefore she was always hungry at the end of the session. For months, the interpretations centred on pointing out how her hearing functioned like a mouth, but that she didn't finish the session, so that, at the end of the session, she was often angry, saying that she was going away without solving all her problems. I told her that these ends of sessions, which ended the same way for months, were due to her not listening to everything that I was telling her, that she interrupted me avidly, hungrily, asking for more and more solutions. My interpretations centred on showing her that she behaved in the session as she did with food. She went fast, but didn't finish listening and therefore didn't finish introjecting. We worked on the deficit of introjection constantly.

The levels of sexuality in relation to the bulimia became clearer when it was hard for Josephine to find transitory sexual partners. One of her many sexual partners was a Paraguayan taxi driver who frequently picked her up at work. The sexual relations were like her crises of bulimia: she suddenly felt sexual hunger and had sexual relations right there and then in the taxi, rapidly and abruptly. It was quite common for her to tell him to leave afterwards: she seemed to vomit him after a fast binge of sex.

But when this partner and two others with whom she was looking for this type of rapid sexual relation left her, she began to replace the missing sexual relations with enormous ingestions of food whenever she was frustrated by not having sexual relations. The details of her huge eating binges were very interesting: if she was sexually excited and was missing the taxi driver, she substituted the lack of sex with the Paraguayan by a binge on typical Paraguayan food. Another time, she was masturbating, thinking about the good sex she had had with a Brazilian partner one summer—but she filled it out with great ingestions of Brazilian dishes and desserts in restaurants that serve typical Brazilian food. Other moments of intense sexual excitation were substituted by dinners in the most luxurious restaurants in Buenos Aires.

This brief vignette is meant to show that there are other events that lead to eating crises or bulimia; the substitution of sexuality with eating binges was already described in the early years of psychoanalysis (see Otto Fenichel, 1945).

The scientific method

The scientific method is not limited to formulating great explicative theories: it attempts to find explanations that enable us to detect what is present in the phenomena being studied. Therefore, we can create *ad hoc* explanations, since the general theory is often insufficient for understanding what occurs in clinical work.

Everything depends on the creative talent of the investigator. In general methodology, we try to understand what has happened at each specific moment. Even in the hypothetical–deductive method, *ad hoc* hypotheses are accepted only when they permit an independent investigation.

I wish to stress that the models I use are closer to what happens in a certain, limited context.

The general theory of psychoanalysis and ad hoc hypotheses

The general theories of psychoanalysis, such as the pleasure principle and the death instinct, are not invalidated by medium-range hypotheses or models that explain better (more comprehensively) the work done in the transference.

Ad hoc hypotheses are applied when the general theory is insufficient to explain the fact, whether in physics, chemistry, or psychoanalysis. In this case, an *ad hoc* hypothesis is created to add to general theory. If in the course of a chemical experiment a reaction does not tally with the general theory, the researcher can take various attitudes: He may think (1) that the general theory is erroneous; (2) that it is his fault, that he is stupid or that he doesn't know how to do it properly; or (3) that there are residues that intervene with their impurities. In the latter case, he will create an *ad hoc* hypothesis when he decides to investigate residues and impurities. And this attitude is useful for research (Klimovsky, 1980a).

Some may ask what happens in psychoanalysis. I think that here, too, "residues and impurities" can emerge: for example, when the therapist is unable to handle his difficulties and emotions in the countertransference, or when he has personal problems. In the countertransference, if the therapist is unable to decode and detect his own countertransference, this provokes impurities in the field of observation and treatment. This is why it is important for every psychoanalyst to take supervision in order to decode his own countertransference, and to return to psychoanalytic treatment from time to time.

The decoding of the countertransference is the central element for future investigations. It is like the use of the cyclotron in nuclear physics for the production of colour images in place of the old black-and-white images.

Summary

The theories that we have described do not actually contradict the description of autistic mechanisms, since the latter are much more primitive. They also emerge at different levels in the clinical material. While the patient has autistic mechanisms, she also presents more highly developed and neurotic aspects, in which projective identification is able to function.

The seeking of sensoriality in the mucous membrane of the mouth shuts the patient into and leaves her trapped in this world of "bodily sensation"; thus, she lives as if inside an oyster shell, where there is no way to make contact with projection or introjection; consequently, these mechanisms could also remain blocked. This situation is much earlier than the acquisition of any notion of a mental sphincter or anal sphincter or anal masturbation.

The protective barrier against the stimuli that the conscious can receive depends on each individual in particular.

Another conceptualization for understanding the patient's delusion in relation to the internal mother object in a different perspective is Freud's explanation that the delusion attempts to re-establish the connection with the world of objects (Freud, 1915e).

This case example highlights the importance of microscopic work in the transference and the need to create hypotheses and models that improve access to certain specific psychopathologies, as well as of decoding the countertransference, especially with patients whose primitive psychotic transference perturbs the psychoanalytic field.

CHAPTER THREE

Drug abuse, regression, and primitive object relations

> And here we are mingled to each other,
> She is half alive, and I am half dead.
>
> Victor Hugo, Booz Endormi

In this chapter I develop a conceptualization of the dynamics and psychopathology of the structures of drug addicts. I propose a theoretical classification and present a detailed history, complete with clinical material and dreams. I also introduce concepts related to the technical use of countertransference.

My objective here is to underline my view that many drug-addicted patients have different underlying psychopathological structures, and that we must therefore approach them through a different implementation of psychoanalytical technique, depending on their specific dynamics. Because of my clinical experience with such patients, I can conceptualize these ideas and classify different types of patients according to a series of models.

This proposed classification should be considered a research model. When a model is invented, it acquires strength from the explanatory perspective. This does not mean that the model represents the ultimate truth, but, rather, that it is useful for a specific stage of the research. The model is not an entity that can be observed at the concrete level. For example, nuclear physicists see the effects of atoms, but they do not see the atoms themselves. In the case of psychoanalysis, we can observe the clinical effects, the manifestations of the model, in various types of patients. Science is the ability to discover the facts behind the observations. The power of science rests precisely on the theoretical models of what lies behind observation, and on the possibility of then observing those models on the empirical plane.

Categories of drug abuse

We propose a classification of different types of drug addicts that will be useful for the evaluation of the clinical and prognostic status of these patients, as well as the therapeutic approach.

Type A

This group is composed of patients who need to feel enfolded by the sensations the drug produces in them; they are in search of an envelope or a skin substitute. In these patients we generally find less pathological mourning than in other cases, and, provided they are in therapy, their prognosis is generally more favourable.

Type A patients bring their dreams to sessions more readily than do other drug addicts. Some of their dreams are actually related to skin substitutes: clothes, overcoats, animal skins, or furs.

They usually take the drug orally and rarely inject themselves. In their fantasies, the drug is associated with an impression of warmth and glow on their skins, so that the substance seems to provide them with the sensation of being held. Naturally, in the transference, this turns into aggression against the therapist, since the patients want to manage on their own, feeling omnipotent thanks to the drug, and refuse the nurturing or the treatment the therapist offers them.

Patients we classify as Type A usually have a more neurotic adaptation to reality than do other types. Many of these cases are triggered by internal factors reinforced by real situations of mourning. They generally accept analytic treatment.

Type B

This type is composed of patients in whom we find a pathological mourning process, because they identify with a dead object from whom they cannot differentiate. These patients have no concept of danger; they have no perception of risk. Their minds lack this concept because they feel dead. They therefore expose themselves to high-risk situations in which their lives are in danger. They may drive at 90 miles an hour on a city street or at 120 on a highway, or they may cross a busy avenue when the light is red. At the most perilous point they defy death; if they survive, they feel as if they have been remarkably resuscitated. On occasion, a test of life or death may be represented by drug consumption to the verge of an overdose, as in the case of my patient "Philippe", who identified with his father and his brother who had died in car accidents while driving at 90 miles an hour, and also with a daughter who had died when she was 4 years old. This patient used to subject himself deliberately to life-threatening situations that sound preposterous, such as driving at exactly the same speed at which his father and brother had been killed, or walking on the ledge of a high-rise apartment. (For details of Philippe's case see Rosenfeld, 1992b.)

It is very difficult for us, as psychoanalysts, to realize that we are faced with a dead person, an individual who feels dead—a patient totally identified and blended to a dead object, because of a pathological mourning process—and sometimes it is hard for us to understand that everything the patient does when he defies death is really aimed at feeling alive for a short while. In such cases, the whole interpretation technique needs to be reconsidered.

Within Type B is a subtype, in which there is an added presence of a cruel and persecuting superego, that accuses the patient, generating intense guilt and not allowing a normal working through of mourning. Often, these subtype patients use drugs as a means to evade their terrifying guilt feelings and the persecution of their merciless superego. Nevertheless, it is important to note that we can find in this type a more integrated psychic structure (such as we see in melancholic patients), through which patients experience depressive guilt, especially when they are hospitalized. (Hospitalization means containment.)

In this regard, it is important to elucidate if a patient accepts hospitalization because he is convinced it is necessary, or if he only complies to please someone else (a family member or the analyst himself). In the latter instance, hospitalization will prove useless. This is a significant risk in such patients, since drug abusers are habitual liars.

Unlike hysterical patients, who try to impress the analyst with their mythomania, drug abusers erect a world of their own and want the analyst to believe them. But, if the analyst believes them, he is confirming to the patients that reality is whatever they have constructed. Therefore, the patients come to assume that they share the same drug with the analyst, which makes them both see the same reality.

Thus, for Type B addicts, consumption of drugs has two objectives: (1) it stimulates them and provides them with very intense sensations when they are feeling dead, because of their identification with a dead object; (2) it allows them to evade their cruel and persecuting superego, which generates in them an intense and unendurable sense of guilt.

This is the group in which we find more promiscuous sexual acting out, where the combination of sexual orgies and drug consumption is more frequent. This is also the group of patients among whom I have had the highest rate of treatment termination and/or failure, especially in the case of individuals living in groups, whose members are all drug addicts. They prefer living, or establishing links, with those groups rather than suffering from isolation and loneliness. Fighting against these group structures is sometimes impossible. Many of these failures have taught me lessons that I have applied successfully to other patients, since failure is also a source of knowledge.

Type C

In this category of addicts I find patients who had, as children, some autistic features and survived by creating their own world of sensations and feelings. In agreement with Frances Tustin, I consider such feelings typical of autistic children. These adult patients function within an autistic encapsulation (Dupetit, 1985; Green, 1986; López, 1983; Resnik, 1987; Searles, 1990; Tustin, 1986). My own hypothesis differs somewhat from Tustin's. In 1985 I postulated that encapsulation also plays a role in protecting and preserving a part of the self. My theory was accepted by Tustin (1990b). This mechanism is completely unrelated to repression and dissociation (or splitting), and very different at the clinical and theoretical levels.

Autistic "sensations" are self-generated sensations that are of pre-eminent importance to such children. Tustin (1990b) says:

> Their excessive concentration on sensations engendered by their own body makes them unaware of sensations with more normal objective relevance. For example, many of these children are unaware of being hurt if they fall down or hurt themselves. [p. 17]

To return to our adult addicts: Type C patients are confined within a paradox, because if they do not achieve those autistic "sensations", they believe they will disappear or die, and if they resort to drugs to achieve them, they may actually die of an overdose. These are extremely serious cases, with scant probability of a cure.

These patients differ from Type-B cases, in that they often are reticent to express themselves. They are rarely involved in promiscuous sex or actings-out, and their everyday behaviour displays little violence or exuberance.

I would like to digress for a moment, to emphasize that patients who use drugs intravenously have a mental functioning based on a psychotic body image—an unconscious fantasy in which their bodies have no skin or muscles and are made up only of vital fluids or blood (Rosenfeld, 1990b, 1992b). In my view, the extreme notion of what can be conceived of as psychotic body image is the thought that the body contains only liquid, one or another derivative of blood, and that it is coated by an arterial or venous wall or walls. These vascular sheaths take over the functions that normally are fulfilled psychologically by the actual skin, the muscles, and the skeleton. There is only a vague notion of a wall that contains blood or vital liquids.

In turn, as can be seen mainly in crises associated with acute psychosis, this membrane containing the blood may be perceived to have broken or to have been otherwise damaged, resulting in a loss of bodily contents, leaving the body empty, without either internal or external containment and/or support. Sometimes the experience of becoming empty is expressed linguistically through a sudden and incessant verbal flow: the patient cannot stop talking.

The notion of a psychotic body image is not limited to clinical cases that are phenomenologically psychotic. It may be present in people who are neurotically adjusted to reality; I would even say that the psychotic body image prevails in personalities that may be very well adjusted to reality—as, for example, in some psychosomatic cases. This psychotic conception of the body breaks through and invades what had up to that moment been a different kind of mental functioning, and this may be expressed either through words or nonverbally through body language, in the psychosomatic disturbances.

At this point, I would like to add a comment about countertransference in the treatment of drug-addicted patients. In these cases, the most serious difficulty the therapist has to face in his countertransference is to avoid becoming a drug or an inanimate object, since this is the role these patients constantly force him to play, through projection. When a therapist begins to feel countertransferentially that he responds in a mechanical manner, or feels like an inanimate object, or discovers that he speaks and responds whenever a patient wants him to, he is confronting countertransferential signs that he must be capable of using to avoid this mistake and save himself, both as an intelligent analyst and as a sensitive human being. If the therapist detects these feelings in time, he may be able to rescue the treatment from the monotony, the role rigidity, and the lack of interpretations of regressive and psychotic aspects that lead to years of ineffective pseudotreatments.

In the following section I present clinical and therapeutic aspects from the case of a 34-year-old drug-addicted patient whom I will call "George".

"George"

In December, when the patient initially appeared at a private clinic, he told us that he came to comply with the wishes of his parents: he had problems at home and violent quarrels with his stepmother. He barely mentioned that he used drugs from time to time. He appeared only twice and did not take the prescribed medication. A year later, his parents requested an appointment at my private office.

First stage of treatment

George's father accompanied him to the initial interview. An amiable person, he showed affection and grave concern for his son. He said that his wife, George's mother, had died when the boy was 2. Later he had married George's stepmother.

The father, who appeared very worried, said: "Look at [George's] eyes, reddened by all that drug. He does nothing, he doesn't work, doesn't use his degree . . . he's already been arrested twice for drug possession . . . he brings objectionable friends to the house, and they take drugs and drink, and he gets very upset if I ask them to leave." He added mournfully: "Some time ago he threatened to kill me and then kill himself. . . . This is all I can take. . . . I bring you my son to see if he accepts help, I can't . . . this is more than I can bear. . . ."

During the same interview, the patient gave his own version of recent years of his life. In his comments he disclaimed the importance of his drug consumption, saying that he used very little of it, that he had been detained during a police roundup when he had only one cocaine dose on him. Another time a friend had falsely accused him to the police. He said: "My mother constantly harries me to know where I go and whom I see."

His attitude and remarks were very similar to those of most drug abusers, who always try to minimize, to distort, or to misrepresent reality: in short, I did not think he was being truthful. On this occasion he also remarked that he only came to see me in order to pacify his father, because "I love him and I don't want to break his heart." When I suggested that this time he should come for treatment, he said that he would do it, just for his father. I recommended that he seek therapy so that I might help him with problems about which he could not speak to his parents.

When I said "stepmother", George immediately reacted and said, "my mother". I took the occasion to comment: "Your mother died when you were a little boy." This statement mobilized very old and primitive emotions and affects in the patient. I remarked that with his reaction to the word "stepmother" he was showing me that he was still a small child who had not accepted his mother's death: "I think you are a 2-year-old orphan, and you refuse to realize it."

His father's reaction to my remark was also very significant: he shed a tear and slightly moved his chair away. It was obvious he did not want his son to see he was so moved. Finally, I told them both that they had an unresolved mourning process, and that it would be a good thing if they could both come to the next interview.

They did not return. Three months later, both parents called, very distressed, saying that George had lost control: he had threatened his father with a knife during a violent brawl. After this I visited them and decided to send a group of highly specialized members of my team to the patient's house. The patient submissively accepted hospitalization.

The first time I saw him at the clinic, George was sloppy, messy, dishevelled, and overweight. In spite of his attitude of violent rejection towards me and all those who surrounded him, I firmly and calmly insisted on keeping him hospitalized in order to perform a complete check-up, and I instituted a rehabilitation program to wean him from the drug he had been abusing for years. Despite his negativity, George seemed to comply willingly with my decision to treat him on an inpatient basis with intensive psychoanalytical therapy. For the first month we had one daily session, often two, either because I thought it necessary or because he himself asked for the extra session. Moreover, George started to integrate with the patients within the therapeutic groups in the clinic, accepted the specific medication he was given, and began dieting to lose weight.

At the clinic staff meetings I discussed the case and commented on my impressions of the patient. I said I felt that the patient sometimes rejected me, just as at the beginning of the treatment. On the other hand, during that month there were moments when the patient seemed to be too well adapted. This over-adapting seemed phoney to me, merely formal, and I said so at the staff meetings. I used to collect information from those meetings. I also received information about the therapy group in which George participated with the other patients, as well as from the music and drawing lessons he was taking. As already stated, I felt the typical countertransference with a drug-addicted patient, when one tends to feel as if one is a drug or an inanimate object, and one also feels sometimes like a machine being manoeuvred. As a therapist, I could never be sure whether the patient was trying to propitiate me by complying with all the clinic's rules and regulations, by behaving formally "well."

This was not the first time I had experienced these countertransference feelings with a drug-addicted patient. During the first months of their treatment, such patients sometimes masquerade as over-adapted, for a variety of reasons: sometimes to placate the therapist, at other times to hide the drug consumption or sexual perversions they had kept secret.

It should be noted that the hospitalization had to be enforced with a medical and court order. My firm attitude had a very positive impact on George, who later confirmed this during a conference he gave to other patients (details of this conference are reported below).

During the first week of treatment, the main issue was George's apparent adaptation to hospitalization. At a meeting with therapists, social workers, and others, I remarked on his overly good adaptation, which seemed artificial, just meant to please us. His cooperation seemed a sham.

It was necessary to show George the real goal of his hospitalization. When I hospitalize a patient of this type, my objective is to treat his mad and addicted facets, which may sometimes lead him to suicide. Hospitalization ensures proper care for the patient 24 hours a day, especially for the psychotic aspects of his personality. But it also allows his developed and normal part to express itself, as we will see later on in this case. Thus hospitalization comes to mean containment and holding, because it becomes necessary for the therapist to protect the patient and keep him company when he is feeling guilt, sorrow, pain, or catastrophic anxiety. In summary, hospitalization makes it possible to contain the healthy component when it expresses itself, and to protect the patient from the psychotic and drug-addicted facet that enslaves him. Moreover, in this case, my firm decision to hospitalize the patient proved that I was stronger than the drug (Rosenfeld, 1992b).

In the course of this period of treatment George asked repeatedly to have two sessions a day, because of anxiety crises.

George had lived for the last years in an atmosphere of untidiness, neglect, drugs, and alcohol—in a mental space he called "the sewer". That physical place was a shanty-town where he abused drugs and lived with prostitutes, junkies, and all kinds of criminals. During one session he requested at the clinic, I tried to show him that he had actually tried to entomb himself in the "sewer" with the dead, that he was committing suicide through his use of drugs in order to bury himself with his dead mother. Thus I was able to show him that he wanted or was trying to die as his mother had died, in an attempt to come together with her. I worked on two levels of his psychotic aspect: his identification with his dead mother in his use of drugs to feel alive and his attempt at suicide to meet his mother in the grave.

Discovering this identification aspect was very important for the treatment. George began showing interest in drawing and painting classes at the clinic.

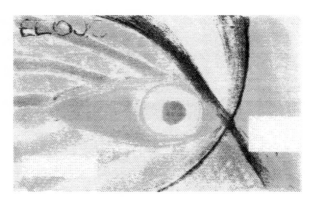

Drawing 1: The eye.

That week we began working on the mistrust George felt towards me. We also tried to delve into his history as a child, of which he remembered only nebulous facts. For instance, he remarked that he had never seen a picture of his mother, not even pictures of his parents' wedding. He suspected that his stepmother had destroyed any photos.

At this point, when George said that he thought his stepmother had destroyed his mother's pictures, pictures of himself when he was 1 or 2 years old, and pictures of his parents' wedding, I confess I felt in my countertransference that perhaps this was an exaggeration or mythomaniac fantasy. Mythomanias are typical of drug-addicted patients, so I thought it was probably this kind of fantasy, of some sort of malignant, all-destroying stepmother.

At the present time, long after that period of the treatment, I want to state that these were not fantasies conceived by the patient but a reality that was subsequently confirmed, so that what George had said was true. The reader may wonder how I can know this. During an interview I had with George's father, stepmother, and George, the following slip took place: I asked whether they had a picture of George's mother, because I was very surprised to see the drawings George had made of her eyes and lips. I had the impression that he was drawing exactly his mother's lips and eyes, which was later confirmed when, in the only picture that could be obtained, she had the same eyes and the same smile. (This can be seen in Drawings 1 and 2.) During the interview I am describing, George's father said to his wife, "But you tore up all the pictures", and she answered "No, I didn't tear anything up." Then the father, in his usual weak response, placatingly said, "No,

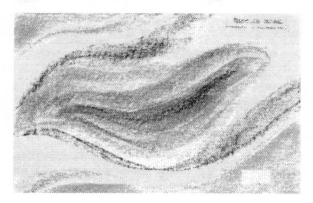

Drawing 2: The lips.

no, of course, they probably were lost. . . ." George looked from one to the other with his eyes popping out, and it was only at this point that I had a confirmation of the facts. (As an aside, let me mention that the only picture that could finally be obtained was found in the archives of a famous photographer in Argentina.)

Second stage of treatment

At one of the art classes George attended, he drew a picture that showed meteorites falling from right to left. He entitled the drawing "Meteorites Falling from the Sky". The picture conveyed a great sense of movement (as can be seen in Drawing 3). At one of our sessions

Drawing 3: Meteorites Falling from the Sky

George said the meteorites were coming from the sky. Simultaneously, he remembered that when he was a child, he often thought that his dead mother was in heaven. These two elements, his drawing linked to his memory, led me to interpret that he must have thought he was being persecuted from heaven, found guilty, and accused by his dead mother. The drawing was a sort of X-ray or picture of his own mind. This is how he had thought that the meteorites or his mother persecuted him from heaven.

Now, it is important to emphasize that two defensive processes are associated in this patient's self: there seems to be a profound and early mourning, which has led him to identify with a dead object, and the presence of a cruel superego (the meteorites) that harasses him and accuses him, generating intense guilt and preventing the normal working-through of his mourning.

In another picture George drew round objects and said that they were "eyes" that looked at him. I asked him: "They look at you or they pursue you?" The images of the painting evoked shapes that the patient had associated with eyes and breasts, the outstanding elements in the visual space of a baby (Bick, 1968; Pérez-Sánchez, 1986). I told him that perhaps this drawing showed his mental image or his most primitive fantasy of his mother, which he kept in his mind.

These drawings seemed to show an aspect of the most primitive structure of George's inner world: something that persecuted him from heaven, falling on his head, or eyes that he looked at or that stared at him.

Third stage of treatment

In the course of this period with George as an inpatient, I had the opportunity of watching, without being seen, how he tried to calm down another patient who, in an aggressive outburst, had badly hurt his wife with his verbal insults. During the session we had after this incident I was able to show him his projective identification to that patient who had lost control and become aggressive, enraged, and frenzied, hurting everyone around him. George saw in this scene someone dominated by drugs, which could hurt and destroy other people. I interpreted that he had seen himself reflected in the other patient, when he was under the influence of drugs and went mad. When he became aware of all this, he started to sob and tremble, feeling anguished. Thus his armour of lies and pretences broke down, and he admitted that when he was drugged, he did exactly the same to his father, whom he loved so dearly. It was then that I remarked that perhaps he thought he had done the same to his mother; perhaps he thought he had destroyed her when he was a child. George's tears expressed the authentic depressive guilt he felt then.

I avoided hiding from him or assuaging his hateful and destructive aspects. On the contrary, I believe it is always useful for the patient to bring them to the sessions, and for the therapist to interpret them in the transference. I think that accepting and containing these aspects—and, even more importantly, of interpreting them if possible—will allow the patient to lose most of his omnipotence by seeing how the therapist can interpret his destructive elements and not die.

Probably it is only by working with severely disturbed patients, hospitalized psychotics, or drug addicts that the therapist can observe and really feel the impact of these elements that are out of the realm of rational, normal, and verbal neurotic communication.

In the course of the psychoanalytical treatment of psychotic patients, the countertransferential feelings that emerge are of such magnitude that they can only be experienced consciously. Practitioners who are not used to treating severely disturbed patients may find it difficult to understand such countertransference feelings, because they themselves have not experienced their emotional intensity.

On occasion I am very moved after an individual session with a patient. With this particular patient, this was especially the case when I saw him sobbing, trembling, and communicating his grief.

What I am trying to underline is the enormous effort the therapist must make when confronted with extreme situations of violence, grief, and disintegration—the effort that is necessary to decode countertransference in order to interpret it effectively psychoanalytically.

Psychoanalytical work with seriously disturbed patients is not an easy task: it can, on occasion, invade the therapist's mind and even his family life. I want to stress the importance of being able to share these matters with and have them supervised by a colleague. The emotions the patient forces us to experience are very intense—no one has ever contained them for him, and he has never found anyone who was capable of receiving them: he projects on the mind of the therapist many of the feelings he could never express. Consider George, who could never cry or show his tremendous grief and guilt because he did not have a mother who could put up with him, or a grandmother, since she had died when he was 5.

The mother's picture

> Mine eye hath play'd the painter and hath stell'd
> Thy beauty's form in table of my heart;
> My body is the frame wherein 'tis held.
> Now see what good turns eyes for eyes have done:
> Mine eyes have drawn thy shape, and thine for me
> Are windows to my breast, where through the sun
> Delights to peep, to gaze therein on thee;
> Yet eyes this cunning want to grace their art,
> They draw but what they see, know not the heart.

Shakespeare, Sonnet 24

I asked George if his father could try to find a picture of his mother and him, since there were none in the house.

In his art classes, George painted really beautiful watercolours, but it was obvious that he always tried to paint eyes of a specific colour and lips with a very special smile. We must remember that he began by drawing meteorites that persecuted him from the sky, or clouds that became monsters and tormented him. He was recovering images, some sort of mental pictures of his mother, that he had almost forgotten and erased.

It is important to note that when I asked him for a photo of his mother and him, it was because my countertransference coincided with what he and I were observing in the pictures. When I say "observing in the pictures", I mean that we would sometimes spend an hour or two discussing one of his paintings.

At this point, I would like to express what I felt when George brought me a photo. It was such an intense emotion that I got goose bumps. I think he was feeling the same way when he saw the picture and when he showed it to me: his eyes were wet, he was on the verge of tears. I was immensely moved, first of all at seeing him as a small child—he looked very much like he does now. His mother's smile, her eyes, her lips, her eyebrows, her loving way of looking and smiling at him, the way he looked into his mother's eyes, all this had an aesthetic and emotional impact on me that I find difficult to describe. Perhaps my personal sensitivity made me feel all this, but I believe I was the receptor of George's feelings, which he projected onto me. Many readers may find it hard to understand why, when this patient asked me to go with him to get a photocopy of a picture he wanted to give me, I complied. It is not just a simple photocopy he wanted to give me: he wanted to deposit in me the picture and the most precious memory he had in his mind—that of his mother. In other words, analytical technique is very important, and so is the setting, but even if I go with a patient to get a photocopy, and even if I think as a psychoanalyst in transference, I am still a psychoanalyst.

At the next session, George broke down and cried. He could not express in words what he felt, he just gestured with his hand over his chest, trying to convey that his feelings were very genuine and profound. He suggested we go out to have a cup of coffee, but I replied that it would be better to keep on with our session, because I could provide holding and containment for his grief and his emotion. After a while, I told him he had drawn the picture of his mother before this, with her cheeks, her eyes, and her smiling mouth. He pointed to many details in the photograph, and I could feel how his anguish relieved him.

He felt anguished, but this relieved him because he discovered his mother's smile, with her big lips, fleshily sweet, incredibly similar to the picture he had drawn in beautiful colours. The patient himself began to discover how he saw himself reflected in the photograph, how happy he looked, held in his mother's arms, and the inner joy his mother's half-smile suggested, like the Gioconda's, because she was holding him. I then asked him what else he felt, saw, or thought of when he looked at the photograph. He pointed with his finger to her lips and to her eyes. I realized he could not speak, because he could not hold back his tears. I remarked that he was very stirred at seeing for the first time this picture of his mother and himself, and I added: "I think we are both very moved at seeing that her lips and her large eyes are so much like the ones you painted." He nodded his agreement, still unable to speak. Then he said that his mother's eyes looked as clear in the photo as in his drawing.

This meant he was beginning to place his trust and his affection in me, and this change of role in the transference proved to be extremely important: I stopped being the stepmother the patient could not trust and became the mother who nurtured and protected him.

* * *

In another session I told George that we would try to recapture the peaceful and serene child that was within him, and he replied: "We radiate such serenity, my mother and I. . . ." For a long while he kept silent, staring at the white wall. Then I said: "This you are see-ing now, the void, the white wall, this is how a child would feel the disappearance of such a smiling and happy mother. Perhaps you felt that instead of your mother's face you would see a white wall and never again the smiling and peaceful expression." George's face became tense and grim, and I interpreted: "When you looked at the emptiness and thought of your mother vanishing, perhaps your face became tense and grim, as it did just now." He asked me to repeat the interpretation, and I repeated: "It is as if that smiling child had disappeared with his mother's death, and this is what he has been reliving since then: the death of a smiling child."

At the next session, George told me that he had been questioning, for the first time, his father and a cousin about his childhood history, something about which no one had informed him previously.

What I describe below took several weeks to reconstruct. We had to assemble it like a puzzle, as follows: to begin with, George was not sure whether his mother had died when he was 2 or 3. His father told him that his grandmother had cooked every day. She seems to have been an extraordinary person, who, in turn, died when George was 5.

At these sessions he told me the following: "Remembering the deaths of my grandmother and my aunt, who died some years later, was like the explosion of a volcano". He had thought he had been 13 or 14 at his aunt's death, but he then found out this was not the case. He remembered being a child, and looking at the sky in school, thinking that his grandmother was there. All through elementary school he had wished his grandmother would come back from heaven. I interpreted that he could now remember and reassemble a history because he felt contained and supported by me.

Explosion of the mind—explosion of the water heater

The following Monday George told me that he had learned that his mother had died in a gas-water-heater explosion: she had been severely burned and had been in agony for two weeks. He said, "It must have been terrible. . . ." and added, "I told my cousin that the first dead person I ever saw was my aunt, whom I loved so much." I interpreted for him: "That is the first time you could really bury your dead mother, your grandmother, and your aunt." It was only with his aunt's death that he was able to bring everything together: the wake, the burial, and the mourning for his mother and grandmother.

He then told me about another patient in the clinic, who had gone for a walk escorted by a member of the staff and had asked to go to a tea-room to have a snack. That patient, Luis, had recognized in the place a girl who was a drug-dealer, had been able to sneak into the bathroom to meet her, and had gotten some cocaine. He had been so fast that the psychologist who was with Luis had seen nothing. George added that he had had the fantasy of asking for permission to go out in order to go to the same place. I interpreted: "Note that you feel like going to the snack bar to get some cocaine, as if you were escaping into drugs from the things we have been talking about. We have just been saying how you were able to bury your aunt, your grandmother, and your mother, all together. And you felt such grief and anguish that you thought your head was going to burst from the pain. You must realize that it is precisely when you are in that mental state of suffering that you run looking for drugs. It is as if you had just become a child, crushed by grief, and you were trying to conceal it by taking drugs."

Near the end of the session some new material came up that gave me the opportunity to interpret another aspect of George's search for drugs. I told him that perhaps it was a revenge, a way to disparage me because I had not come at the weekend and had left him alone. It was like showing he did not need me any longer, that he could get along fine with the drug (Garzoli, 1991; Resnik, 1987; H. Rosenfeld, 1987).

George denied this, saying his wanting to go to the cafe to buy cocaine had nothing to do with revenge. The session was about to end when I said: "You cannot tolerate waiting, you do not understand what it means to say goodbye or to meet again. You think saying goodbye is final, like death. Something of this kind happened to you yesterday, on Sunday, when we missed a session."

At this point, I would like to comment on my countertransference when the patient brings material about another patient in the clinic. It is very important to communicate here what I felt and thought when I discovered in this material a part of the patient's self projected into someone else. I thought of it as an attack on the therapist because I had abandoned him for a couple of days without session. The patient takes revenge by using drugs. It is an omnipotent and manic form of defence, which in his fantasy allows him to look after himself, to need no one. In this case, he repeated in the transference, as an adult, the more infantile and primitive forms of his earlier years, to defend himself with a system based on narcissistic omnipotence in which he is the omnipotent breast that nurses itself and needs no other external nourishment.

This fantasy, which has characteristics of a murderous assault on the therapist, with the patient fantasizing the search for drugs, generates countertransferential affects. A relatively sensitive therapist—such as I believe I am—comes out of such a session with a certain hopelessness, seeing that because of only one session that had to be cancelled, everything crumbles down. It is as if all the previous work had been for nothing: the patient had gone back to his primitive defence or survival systems. The despair felt by the therapist is the patient's own projected despair caused by his losses and deaths.

It is important to decode this despair by disentangling it from personal situations. The patient felt my absence as a catastrophic abandonment, since for him all partings are experienced as a mother who dies and abandons him forever. He lacks the mental concept of a reunion, of the future recovery of an object. The concept of the future itself is perturbed at the symbolic level.

My abandoning him and his retaliatory reaction can be seen in another perspective, or on the basis of another hypothesis. His hate, his revenge, the attack on the therapist through the search for drugs, all seem to be based on a delusive conception of his mother's death. This delusive conception was to come up in the material many years later.

And—as is always the case in any study on countertransference—one only writes about it when one realizes it has happened.

Session of the impact and the insight:
the place of time, the place of mournings, the place of grief

At the next day's session, George began to speak about the weeks of agony his mother had to go through. He said that he could imagine her in pain. I interpreted: "Does this make you think of what you have been doing these last years, abusing drugs, on the verge of agony, but never quite dying?" Then I said: "You were trying to repeat the moments of agony, but you never finished dying", and added: "I think you were mixed up with your mother and identified to her in her death throes; you were trying to become a mother who is on the verge of death."

George was facing me, sitting on a revolving chair; he came closer and asked me to explain, as if surprised, like someone who understands and feels the impact. I reinterpreted: "Exactly, these last years you became a mother in her death throes, agonizing, but not dead." I continued: "At other times you tried to commit suicide so that they would bury you with your mother. These were your two ways of looking for your mother: first, by playing the role of your dying mother and, second, with your suicidal fantasies, by wanting to be buried with your mother."

George was silent, thoughtful, and motionless for a long time, with his arms resting on the desk. He said: "You know, Doctor, I was trying to sort out the dates, and I realized that my aunt, who was the first dead person I ever touched and buried, really died many years after what I had always thought. I touched her when she was dead, and this happened when I was 25 years old. One sure does get confused with dates, doesn't one?"

I interpreted that what is really difficult is to reconstruct a history, a puzzle encompassing so much pain, grief, and death, with a child who suffers because of his loved ones' deaths. Then I added a transferential interpretation, saying that perhaps he would be able to assemble his history because he felt I contained him and provided him with holding, and because I was not afraid of the things he told me. I could be strong and withstand so much sadness.

George went on to wonder how he could have made such a mistake about the dates and the events in his life.

I admit that countertransferentially I remained absorbed, trying to sort out the dates of the mournings and the onset of his drug abuse habit. Then I said: "But, George, I am thinking that you started taking drugs nine years ago. Do you realize that you started to be on drugs when your aunt died and you buried her, exactly at 25, the age your mother was at her death?"

George practically fell backwards from his chair. He collapsed on its back; he was pale and speechless for the remaining minutes of our session.

I also felt countertransferentially a strong emotional impact, and I respected George's silence and insight. It was only when I told him that his time was up that George said to me, very softly, while he shook my hand: "Yes, I started on drugs after my aunt's death", and I answered: "It is quite understandable for you to mix up dates and periods, since you really did not know whether you were burying your aunt, your grandmother, or your mother. You did not know whether you were 2, 5, or 17 . . . it was all a muddle in your head."

Today, after reviewing my notes and the ensuing evolution of the patient, I can affirm that this session was a very important milestone in the analysis: first, because we experienced together his collapsing in the chair; and, second, because I helped him to differentiate among his mournings and assign precise dates to them. This was like helping him find a broken-down and fragmented 2-year-old boy; it meant locating a child he had been trying to keep blurred in time and in space.

George transcribed this session in his pocket-diary, which gradually became a diary, where he took notes and wrote down his fantasies, as well as some stories and poems.

For the rest of the week the analysis was focused on this session. He read to me what he had written, small stories he thought of. He also told me he was reading some of it at the group therapy sessions with other clinic patients. I told him that I liked what he wrote and how he wrote it. To my surprise, he showed me a very old book of poems that had belonged to his mother and made me read one of the poems. I told him my opinion: that I thought it was beautiful, very moving and dramatic, and he answered: "These poems were written by my father under a pseudonym. My father never wrote poems again after my mother died."

He then read to me a story he had written the night before: a combination of verse, emotion, drama, and fear. I said that he was recovering and reviving something of his father that had disappeared, that had been paralysed by his mother's death. It meant giving life back to something that was vital for his father, the father who used to write poems and stories. Then George said: "My father is very happy when I read my stories and poems to him."

The clock of time: the inner journey,
the voyage into childhood

On another day, we left the clinic. He had asked me to go with him to get his drawings and a photograph of his mother photocopied. He had two reasons: the first was to actually get the photocopies, and the second because he wanted to show me the house where he had lived until he was 8.

During our walk, we talked about many things. I took the occasion to interpret that he had lost that child (the one who smiles in the picture with his mother), and that when we had the photocopies made, we were looking for someone to take care of that child, so that when he gave me a copy of that picture, he was asking me to look after that child and provide him with holding.

George listened attentively and thoughtfully. I added: "To avoid the grief you felt when your mother disappeared, you finally ejected from your mind the child who suffered, but you also ejected the child who smiled." George felt the impact; he understood, felt, and experienced (lived) the interpretation with an emotional impact he had rarely felt.

George took me to the building where he had lived with his mother and for the first years of his life, until he was 8. While we were there, he said, "You know, I really remember that clock and that statue, and also the garden." Then he added that he would like to live there again, and said he was going to find out if there was an apartment up for rent.

I remarked that the real journey took place within his mind—a journey into his past and his childhood, and this was more important than living again where he had lived as a child. I said the clock and the garden were indicating the journey we were taking through time: "The important thing is the inner journey."

At the next session, George read two lovely short stories related to his childhood. Then he told me a dream:

He was taking a non-stop train from Rome to Egypt's pyramids. The journey was somewhat fantastic, he said, because there was no need for transfers. It was as if the track had been all in one piece, going directly and with no obstacles through the mountains, the seas, and the deserts.

We saw that this was a journey he made to his past, trying to trace his family's history. In real life, his family is related to the geographical region of the pyramids.

We both agreed that this dream was like dreaming with the journey to his inner world, to the world of his childhood. It also meant bringing back the session we had had on our walk to see the house where he had lived as a child. In his dream, George was bringing all these things he had discovered in his analysis with me: it represented the journey we took into his childhood and his past, to the history of the pyramids, now the tombs of his mother, aunt, and grandmother.

I also interpreted for him: "You can make this journey and have this dream because, as the dream shows, there is a passenger car in a strong and solid train, supported by steel tracks, showing my role as a therapist. Because you feel contained and enveloped in this treatment, you dare make the long journey from Rome to Egypt."

Fourth stage of treatment

On days when he could receive his parents' visit, George made his stepmother the butt of violent verbal abuse. On one occasion, he did the same with his father.

During these months, I was unable to understand all the mechanisms generating so much violence. For several weeks, I interpreted in the transference. I told him that his violent hate and aggression against me probably stemmed from the fact that I had hospitalized him against his will. I interpreted his violence against his stepmother and his father as an acting out; in other words, a transferential feeling towards me was enacted and evacuated onto another person.

I could begin to understand all the violence somewhat when George started going out on a special pass to take walks, during which he went home. I was able to understand the reactions elicited in the stepmother by the progress made by George (and especially by his release from the clinic) in a quite direct and straightforward way, since they were directed against me.

I will explain this now.

Countertransference and release from the clinic

When George was released after several months as an inpatient, his stepmother began to harass me on the phone, since she made me responsible for the fact that George was "bothering around the house"—in spite of the fact that she used to beg me to cure him in order for him to return home. The things the stepmother said did not justify her complaints. George continued with his treatment with me in my office and attended the therapeutic groups at the clinic.

Faced with this accusation, I told her that if George was at home, it was because he was feeling better. She replied: "Sure, you are angry at me." I said, "No, I am not angry at you." She went on using double-bind messages and pragmatic paradoxes to tell me that "I was hurting her." She changed everything, and now she was accusing me.

I must admit that in my countertransference I felt a strong emotional impact, because I was discovering the hidden face of her mind. The things she said allowed me to realize that many things had changed: first, she was angry because George was better; second, she had invented the idea that I was angry at her (a delusion she did not verify);

and third, she accused me of being guilty of hurting her through my anger. This, I thought, was an inoculation of guilt and was difficult to stop, because the receptor was confused by the double-bind message (Liberman, 1978; Pichon-Rivière, 1970).

Nevertheless, this episode allowed me to understand, from the standpoint of my countertransference, the effects of the maddening messages that left the recipient feeling confused and trapped. I confess to having felt some of these emotions, which I was able to escape when I recovered my distance. Then I understood that these were the types of messages George received daily at home—in other words, I was the object of maddening messages and guilt-generating accusations: the stepmother was doing to me what she did to George every single day. The technical use of the countertransference was very effective in helping me to discover the family structure and the sick communication system in which George was ensnared. Each time he told me some family anecdote about his stepmother, I tried to show him and interpret for him what I had discovered from the vantage point of my countertransference. At this level, interpreting consisted in decoding the maddening double-bind and guilt-generating messages his stepmother kept sending him and whose object he was without having realized it.

On another occasion, I pointed out that when he resorted to drugs and alcohol, it was after his stepmother had inoculated him with guilt. I added something on which we went on working: the stepmother was an actual, current representation of the dead mother of his childhood. Since the age of 2, George's fantasy and his mind were full of meteorites, or a mother who persecuted him and accused him from heaven. That is why his stepmother's accusations evoked the accusations of his childhood, the severe and cruel superego his mother became in his fantastic infantile world (meteorites persecuting him from heaven).

The therapeutic effect of an adequate technical use of countertransference was of the utmost importance, because it allowed me to clear away and sort out the stepmother's double-bind messages and the familial communication system. Those messages were the final straw, and many times George felt the impulse to leave the house and start taking drugs in an attempt to dilute, to dissolve, and to fragment the delusive guilt he felt at the accusations coming from his stepmother on the outside and his superego inside himself (Freud, 1917e; Green, 1986; Ogden, 1986).

This psychoanalytical work allowed me to understand what had been the triggering causes of his enactings. Moreover, during the whole treatment I interpreted all his emotions and transferential fantasies as potential triggers for the impulsive acts he used as drugs. The patient was capable of generating emotions in my countertransference.

Technical use of the countertransference

As I say in my book (Rosenfeld, 1992b):

Methodologically, countertransference is a hypothesis the therapist creates in his field of work. It is not a certainty, but a working hypothesis that should be used to think. Intense feelings are conveyed to us by psychotic patients through mechanisms about which we know very little as yet (projection, projective identification, paradoxical messages, phonology or the music of the voice, broken phrases or syntactic and semantic disturbances, etc.). [p. 79]

Sometimes the theory does not comprise and explain the richness, dynamics, and dialectics of the clinical practice. For instance, while Freud was theorizing about countertransference as a problem—perhaps objecting to Ferenczi, who used it inappropriately: he kissed his patients, and so on—at the same time he used it with his patients and made notes of it, as he did in the case of the "Rat Man", when he wrote down some notes on his own countertransference (Boyer, 1982b, 1990; Rosenfeld, 1980, 1991).

Some readers will insist that countertransference is disturbing. I would say they are right, but only if the therapist does not perceive what countertransference means, and if he does not know what to do technically or how to use it. Papers on countertransference are usually written once we have already understood almost everything.

But countertransference may be a highly useful tool if we try to discover what it is the patient makes us feel that he cannot express in words—words that never existed to express his chaotic infantile world (Boyer, 1989; Racker, 1968).

His father's hospitalization

At the time George was released from the clinic, his father had an accident: he fell and fractured his hip. George felt intense anxiety until his father was taken to the private hospital where he would undergo surgery and the doctor and the anaesthesiologist were chosen. He then felt real pain and grief that, as he remarked himself, "I was never able to feel or to tolerate before."

George had to choose the surgeon and make arrangements for his father at the hospital. He still came on time to all his sessions and even phoned me to tell me how his father and he were doing. George was being treated on an outpatient basis, but he still attended the therapeutic group at the clinic, where he discovered how affectionate and caring all the other patients were with him. He found out that many of those "mad" patients were actually more affectionate than some members of his family, who had left him alone during that difficult period. At several sessions during this time, I suspected that he had been taking drugs the night before, when he had stayed up to take care of his father: more than once he came to our sessions with reddened eyes and alcohol on his breath.

The loudspeakers dream

While his father was in the hospital, George had this dream: *"Two loudspeakers are on fire; I am in another room. Then a figure appears; perhaps it is my father, or my therapist."*

What is important in this dream is that there are loudspeakers, or amplifiers, or some devices of that sort, and that they are burning. George associated and said that the previous night he had left the house after berating his stepmother.

During this session I perceived that he felt overwhelmed, that he could not withstand the pressure of having to see his ill father. He then told me about the episode with his stepmother: she had told him not to leave the house at night, or she would "burn him alive". George had turned on her and screamed all kinds of abuse at her, so that she had shut up for the first time in her life.

I respond: "But this is significant, because your mother did burn alive. . . . I think you are bringing an explanation of the loudspeakers dream. . . . Where did your mother die?"

George pointed at the Rivadavia Hospital across the street from where we were.

I took him to the window and asked him whether he knew which ward. He said no.

I said: "That building on the right, right across from my office, is more than 100 years old. It is the morgue. Your mother went in and out of that door."

George was very impressed. His eyes were red (I thought that he had been taking drugs). "So my mother went through that door", he repeated.

"Yes", I said, "so at least now you know where the morgue is, where she went in and where she came out."

George stared again through the window, stood up, then sat down again.

I interpreted: "I think the dream has something to do with the amplification of your father's noises." George had just told me that he had not slept all night because when his father groaned, even if he was several rooms away, he could not sleep. I said that he wanted to burn the amplification in his head of his father's groans, because he thought his father was dying. Just like the moans he had in his head from a mother who was in agony and was dying; this was amplified and returned from the past under the guise of his father, who, he thought, was dying now. For George, it was like his mother dying all over again, and both things got mixed up in his mind.

"When my father groans in pain", he said, "I imagine my mother must have gone through the same thing."

"There is more", I continued. "Your screams and your tears when you were a small child, all alone, not finding your mother's face, her voice, her smile. How did your mother die?"

"Of burns. . . ."

". . . it must also be the voice of your mother, burning and disappearing; those loudspeakers, carrying the music, the melody, and the voice that burned and disappeared forever. Yesterday you were frightened by the amplification of your father's moans and groans; you were afraid he would die, like your mother died of her burns." And I added: "Perhaps that is why yesterday you were talking so much about music, about Mahler, Mahler's symphony, about the dead mother."

"After all", I said, "a mother's emotion is not made of verbal words: it is music, it is a feeling; perhaps that is why some melodies and some voices move you and have an impact on you."

Dream of the bull and the horse

George brought a dream about *a race between a horse and a bull*. He said: "*The bull was leading, he was winning. The track was square, with right angles, which seemed strange. I was at one end of the track, inside a house, watching the race.*"

When he drew a diagram of the racetrack, I asked him why he guessed it had right angles. Then I thought the angles might represent the abrupt changes in his states of mind, in this analytic race.

George then remembered another part of the dream: "*No, I think it was different. They were not racing, they were pulling a stagecoach, the horse and the bull together.*"

The dream then shifted to another scene: "*The horse had bolted, it ran out of control, like a wild animal; it ran madly until a horseman jumped on his back and tried to subdue it. It was like a scene from a Tom Mix western or a Zorro movie.*"

We worked and reflected together on the dream. I interpreted that a part of himself was like a wild animal on the loose; another part tries to get hold of the reins to control that wild part. The scene where the rider controls the horse represents a rational and orderly aspect trying to bring under control his impulsive and mad aspects. I told him: "It is the first time in a dream that you appear yourself as an observer [an observing ego], watching the race from the outside, the treatment race, your life's race, your inner world's race. It is the first time a sane aspect of yourself appears, trying to control, to restrain, to take care of something. It is the beginning of insight. It is also important that it is not just any cart, but a stagecoach. A stagecoach is a means of transportation with a purpose, an aim, and a goal it has to attain, a place it must reach. This shows there is a perspective for the future."

Later I added: "Another important element is that the bull, the horse, and the rider all end up pulling in the same direction."

This dream reappeared and we worked on it at other sessions, especially on the role of the therapist in the analytic race.

The dream of the Magnum revolver

George recounted another dream. *He was travelling on a bus. In the bus, one group of persons started a fight with another group. One of the individuals took out a rifle with a cut-off barrel and shot a man. The dead man, who fell to the floor, seemed to be someone George knew. Then the man who had the rifle took aim and shot at George himself.*

First George said that he was killed, but he immediately added, "No, he didn't really kill me, because another person on the same bus shot him with a Magnum revolver; he killed him and ran away."

The dream continued with a scene in which *George escaped in a car. In his flight, he discovered that the police were following him.* He added: "*I was with a patient at the clinic, Marcos, the one who had a car accident when he was under drugs, and had a neurological sequel; he was almost decerebrated.*"

In another scene, 15 police officers walked by him, and George recognized one of them. "Then", he said, "I took a gun and shot myself in the mouth." I asked him whether his dream had ended there, and he said that it had. As for the shot in the mouth, I asked him whether this could be a suicide fantasy, and he said: "Committing suicide with a Magnum is like taking cocaine." He added: "The Magnum gun reminds me of the model one of the policemen used."

It is important that in the dream George did not die after shooting himself. He just had a hole in his palate and his nose. So I asked him whether it was not like the hole or the perforation those who are on cocaine get in their nostrils. He nodded his assent, and I added: "You are together with Marcos, the inpatient who is 'almost decerebrated,' because in the dream Marcos seems to represent a part of yourself (a part of your own self), a mad part that was trying to commit suicide through drug abuse."

As we analysed the dream, we began to understand better the first scenes: in this dream there is a war, a conflict, taking place in George's mind. The bus seems to represent the inside of his mind.

Then I asked him about the person who shot and killed, and he said: "The strange thing is he shoots, and it seems he kills me, but he doesn't, because someone else shoots him first."

I tried to interpret and told him that inside the bus, inside his mind, there was a part of his self that shot and wanted to murder another part of himself. It is as if the madman was trying to kill the sad and orphaned little boy who is inside him, a little like trying to make the sadness within him disappear.

I interpreted that the dream could be seen as a war between a sane part and a part that is mad and murderous, an ever-present conflict within him (Bion, 1967; Eickhoff, 1986; Kernberg, 1979, 1984, 1985; Rosenfeld, 1992a; Schacht, 1988; Segal, 1950, 1986; Steiner, 1990; Wilson, 1989). The confusion of situations and characters was expressing the confusion in his inner world.

George spontaneously remembered an anecdote in which a policeman showed him a gun. I asked him if in this memory the officer was chasing him, and he said no, they were helping each other. I remarked that, nonetheless, in this dream, there were many officers chasing him. Then I added something that generated a strong emotional impact in him: "The policemen chasing you in the dream seem to be similar to the meteorites persecuting you, the famous meteorites in your drawing we already analysed. Both are expressions of what is going on inside you, in your mind, people pursuing you, meteorites, the police, or perhaps a mother you think pursues and accuses you."

We worked for an hour analysing this dream. Near the end of the session, George asked me whether I would be coming the next day. I said that he was probably worried because I could not come to the last two sessions for personal reasons (he found out through the doctors at the clinic that a relative of mine had died). So I said: "I believe the dream also expresses something that is going on with me, or better still, against me, because I stood you up for two sessions [I had not seen him for one and a half days]. Your reaction against me seems to come from an aggressive and mad child who feels abandoned; perhaps you felt furious, you felt like shooting me."

He then associated this dream with a later one, in which *he threw food out the window of a bus he was riding.* I thought that this material was indicating the analytic food he vomits, spits out, or throws out the window. I thought that throwing food away meant throwing away the analytic food—in other words, the therapist's interpretations. I also felt, without saying it, that throwing food away showed his object relations during the early oral stage in his childhood. I associated this with the dream about the shooting in the bus, especially the part where he shot himself in the mouth. This led me to the hypothesis that instead of shooting me because I abandoned him for two sessions, he mixed up the self and the object.

I then suggested an interpretation: "There seems to be another reading to this dream. You felt very angry in it; you felt hate and the wish to shoot me, Rosenfeld, because I abandoned you for two sessions."

I went on: "Because you do not understand and cannot bear farewells or partings, since you believe that all partings are a decisive and final death, neither can you withstand waiting, you cannot tolerate delay." I added: "I became a mother who abandons you and dies, and you became a child who wants to shoot me. But you got mixed up, and instead of shooting Rosenfeld, you shot yourself."

I interpreted: "You hate me so much that you are afraid I will take some horrible revenge. And that is why, in your dream, I become the policemen who are chasing you. It is as if I, by persecuting you, became the meteorites and the mother that persecute you and accuse you inside your mind."

Last stage of treatment

At the clinic where George had been an inpatient, conferences and talks are held for the patients. On one occasion, both the patients and the staff agreed on inviting a former patient to tell about his experience. Patients suggested that George should be invited, and everyone agreed on the choice.

George narrated the occasion himself about seven months after his hospitalization, when he was an outpatient. He brought me his conference in writing, and I am transcribing below some parts of it.

I consider this narrative as very valuable: in a way, it is as if the patient is cooperating in a scientific work, giving his own version of his disease, his treatment, and his hospitalization. Here is his report:

"Well, I shall be telling you about my personal experience. And you may or may not relate my experience to yours. I hope it can be useful to you. I am not going to give you any advice or bring you any solutions, either to general or specific problems. I will just tell you about my experience in this clinic.

"Generally speaking, I saw that there were three kinds of patients: those who had been forced to come—as in my case, since I was brought against my will, and without my consent; those who come of their own free will, but just to please others; and those who come because they really want to get cured, and not just to humour someone else, be it their parents, a brother, or a wife.

"I think the type I am included in is the most complex. It took me about 25 days just to begin the treatment.

"In my case, for the first week I was in total and absolute revolt, all I wanted was to run away, I was surrounded by enemies, I was extremely angry, and I accepted nothing: I did not want them to tell me anything or explain anything; I understood nothing, and nothing was right. . . .

"In the second week, I began "masquerading"; I realized the best solution was to pretend I was getting better, in order to scram from here.

"And then, after the second week, I began to feel some changes, which made me think something was happening, that some information was getting across to me and was being processed in my head and was making me understand things that I had never understood. For instance, very, very slowly, my anxiety was lessening. My eating habits were changing, because my anxiety had decreased. I could begin to think.

"I began feeling pleasure when the day was sunny, which would have seemed impossible to me. I started keeping a semblance of order in my things: I have always been terribly slovenly. After the third week, I slowly began to feel at ease, without even knowing why. The fundamental thing is that I started to feel I wanted to communicate, both with the doctors and the patients, to tell them something about my feelings; this was an aspect of my personality which had been totally dormant.

"Together with all these new signs I began to discover in myself, I started assembling a puzzle, the puzzle of things that had happened to me, which I knew had happened to me but I could not acknowledge as important; in my case, they were my mother's death and the impact it had on my life.

"I was sleeping too well, and I started remembering my dreams; this was about 25 days after I had been hospitalized, and I could not recall having remembered a dream since age 7 or 8. Then I began a sort of study of myself, at a quite deep level, which encompassed my drawings, my dreams, my writings, and the things I said during therapy, both in private sessions, where I brought very personal and painful things, and at group therapy.

"What I want to comment here is that I entered analysis without realizing it. One day I found I was talking to my therapist, and feeling that I was communicating, that someone was listening and what I was saying was helping me. I felt I was not under so much pressure any longer.

"At that time, together with the analysis and the subtler changes I began to feel, the different feelings, such as being able to feel melancholia or sadness, or grief, which I could never feel before, because I had always been either euphoric or full of anxiety, gradually the obsession about cocaine began to decrease slowly, the constant need to speak about it and the temptation to use it. This surprised me because I could remember that for the first days we spoke of nothing but drugs. It was like being on drugs without drugs.

"I had the whole puzzle sorted out, but I could not really feel it. I wondered if one day I would be able to cry for my mother's death:

it was hard to believe. But it happened: in the course of a session, I wept for 40 minutes watching my mother's picture with my therapist, it was such a feeling of decompression that I could not ... it is very difficult to explain what I felt in my chest, *as if my chest was about to burst*, I wanted to feel what my therapist later told me was psychic pain. I explained the feeling to him, and he told me about psychic pain. It really hurt, as if somebody had bitten me on the chest. The pain lasted for four or five days. I think that was the first step of really getting well.

"Well, the final thing I wanted to tell you is that, although one phase of my treatment is over, I feel it is just a change in habitat, I am now living out of the fishbowl where I learned to swim in the sea, so now they have let me loose on the streets outside. I am back on an orderly schedule, skilled people are taking care of me, and now I have to start taking care of myself, aware of the dangers around me. Because I think I am at the threshold of my cure, everything is now easier than it was when I started here. I believe that when I was hospitalized, I was going mad, and now I have the chance of not going mad. I think that everyone ... well, at least I have two Georges in my head, *the madman was Goliath, and George was David,* and now David is growing and Goliath is losing strength, so that now everything is easier, and in the end I can win. I intend to go on with my analysis, I will come here to group therapy once a week, and from Monday to Saturday I will have the sessions with my analyst. I am building an important continent of affects for myself. I am planning a schedule for my next job that will help me have an order, so as not to disperse myself. I am very aware of certain fears, for instance, which I thought were over last week, but now I realize there are some fears that, well, can be managed. But my release really means just that, a continuation of my treatment as an outpatient."

Addendum to the subject of countertransference

Recovery, family reactions,
and their impact on countertransference

In this addendum I would like to discuss the frequency with which therapists receive attacks and complaints from the family just at the moment when psychotic patients are discharged from the hospital and return to their homes. Although it does not happen always, it is a frequent occurrence. Of course, there are also families that are thankful for the recovery.

After his discharge, George continued to come to my office for treatment every day, from Monday to Saturday, for several months.

It is important to stress that after three months of this treatment period he found a job, although the economic recession made it very difficult to find work at the time. He made obvious efforts and showed a great sense of responsibility in order to accomplish his work and comply with his working hours and his sessions. However, when he left the clinic, his stepmother began to complain. She either called me on the phone or took the opportunity when she came to my office to pay me to complain about George: in the beginning, because he was not working, and when he found a job, because "he didn't make enough money." I used to receive these complaints and criticisms. George told me she also constantly nagged him at home.

At staff meetings, where with my team I evaluated George's evolution in the therapeutic group he still attended, one of my colleagues noted that the stepmother's reaction showed a significant contradiction: when the patient was hospitalized, she used to implore me to cure him, yet once he recovered and was discharged, she phoned me herself to tell me she could not stand him at home.

She seemed to function towards George as a primitive and cruel superego, and as an ego ideal that was so demanding that nothing he might do could satisfy it. Moreover, these demands became accusations in his unconscious. In George's primitive unconscious, his stepmother's accusations were related to a very specific criticism: if everything he did was wrong, he also stood accused of his mother's death.

Of course, as a psychoanalyst experienced with seriously disturbed patients, I supposed that these might be aggressive reactions, or a negative therapeutic reaction, reflected in his transference with me.

But the reader should remember that the family's reaction was real and concrete. In countertransference it is important not to assume the role and the reactions of the patient's self.

Let me underline that this type of attack coming from the family of some severely disturbed psychotic patients is very common at a time when these patients show a favourable evolution, generally at the point when they are discharged from the clinic and return to their family group.

In these cases, I always remember what I learned from one of my mentors, Pichon Rivière, who said that when the therapist returns a recovered psychotic patient to the family group, the family is afraid of receiving back a psychotic part of themselves that had been projected onto the patient (Pichon-Rivière, 1959). Other authors have very similar ideas on this subject (H. Rosenfeld, 1987; Searles, 1990).

Based on my own experiences, I can add some different elements to these views. The recovery of a socially adapted psychotic patient and his return to the family group can be perceived by the family as an accusation. The reader may wonder why. On occasion, the parents of these patients feel accused for not having been able to care for the patient or to cure him, and they see the therapeutic success as something they themselves could not achieve. In other words, in their minds the important thing is not that the therapist has cured the patient but, rather, that having achieved what they could not achieve themselves, he accuses them: they perceive the therapeutic success as an accusation of ineptitude.

Conclusions

In this chapter I give a detailed presentation, from a large quantity of clinical material, of my work with a very regressive patient, first while he was hospitalized, and later while he was in private sessions at my office.

From a methodological standpoint, I think psychoanalysis is, among other things, a method of observation, in which we try to carry out a meticulous and microscopic observation of the small variations that take place in transference and to observe during the next session how the patient has received, transformed, expelled, or dreamed the previous session's interpretations.

There is also a general theory of psychoanalysis, which helps us to explain many different clinical situations.

The reader will become aware that I use what is known in methodology as *ad hoc* hypotheses or theories, such as the concept that there is one part of the self that is more regressive, or more ill, or more destructive, that attacks, destroys, or inhibits the healthier part of the patient's self. This concept is at the root of many of my interpretations.

Here another *ad hoc* hypothesis involves working with the infantile part of a child arrested in time and space as a 2- or 3-year-old, at the death of his mother. The reader will see how I try to rescue that child, so that he can express himself through his emotions and experiences, such as paintings and nonverbal language, until that aspect of his childhood can be expressed in his dreams and intensely lived in his transference with me—as in the case of the session on his mother's picture.

My technique consists of providing the patient with strength, containment, holding, and firmness so that those aspects may emerge without causing fear. The psychoanalyst provides strength through a fixed analytic framework a precise schedule for sessions, a composed and calm voice, conveying warmth, affection, and containment.

The reader will also see how I constantly interpret, in the transference, the fear of the patient—or, rather, the scared child who lives within the patient—about his therapist's dying or disappearing each time he goes away after a session.

Note how many months elapse before a patient comes to believe in his therapist's stable containment (the dream about the train journey).

The chief secret of psychoanalysis is that the work can be done in the transference. I consider a psychoanalyst as someone who thinks that everything his patient tells him is a message about his relationship to the therapist. This does not mean that interpretation must be going on all the time, at a breakneck speed, or that everything has to be interpreted. But the message the patient is sending must usually be decoded with the right timing, in the here-and-now, including its known or strongly suspected genetic antecedents.

The psychoanalyst also has the task of working with the patient's inner world. The reader will note with what meticulous care I explore and interpret what goes on in patient's inner self (I refer the reader to the detailed interpretation of the different parts of the self in the dream about the shooting in the bus)—in other words, the various aspects of his self: the smiling child, or the sad child, or the mad child inside him, or the broken-down and grieving child.

I interpret the aspects of the self either in the patient's dreams as a part of himself, or in his transference to me, or else the interpretation comes up when I show him, for instance, that he is trying to commit suicide and bury himself in an attempt to find his dead mother.

The reader will note that I stay alert to any suicide fantasy or to things that are typical in drug abusers, such as habitual lies. I want to stress here that in addicts, lying is a way to force the therapist to participate in an invented, hallucinatory, delusive world.

If the therapist does not detect the lies, the patient considers he shares his drug consumption and his new invented reality: his neo-reality (McDougall, 1990).

The mourning process and its vicissitudes must be the object of constant work and interpretation; this is necessary in patients whom I classify as Type B, where mourning and melancholia are a central theme.

The reader will note that from a methodological standpoint I con-sider every interpretation as a hypothesis or a model to be pondered. For this reason, many of my interpretations are suggestions, models, or hypotheses that I propose to the patient, on which we work together to understand a dream—such as the dream of the bull and the horse—and the interpretations are really made jointly with the patient.

As stated in this chapter's title, I detect and interpret primitive ob-ject relations only when they emerge (i.e. the Magnum revolver's shot in the mouth is a model of the infantile relation to the breast and the nipple in his mouth—Sandler, 1988).

The aim of psychoanalysis is to relive (or re-enact) in the transfer-ence those early object relations. It is only through the intense emo-tional experience of transference that an enduring modification of the patient's deep psychic structures can be achieved.

At other times, the hypotheses of early object relations are suggest-ed by me—such as when the patient sits silently, facing a white wall.

Constructions and reconstructions (Freud, 1937d) are made jointly by the patient and the therapist. In this case, the construction of the his-tory, the dates, years, periods, and spaces, is of paramount importance. To situate past times means that one is able to face the fact that those times are gone forever. For this patient, acknowledging the passage of time means recognizing dead or vanished objects.

The concept of the passage of time is very important in regressive patients; denying it is the equivalent of denying mourning and of living in an ongoing present, which, in turn, means maintaining a psychotic identification to a dead or dying mother. It is a past that never stops being the past.

I also work with the model on drugs, which is often a way of preferring the drug over the therapist's words. As to my frequent resorting to the theory of communication and pragmatic paradoxes, I propose that these are extremely important in this type of patient.

Countertransference is the field I consider most promising and fruitful for acquiring knowledge about psychotic and regressive patients. The impulsive search for drugs—generally cocaine, never intravenous drugs—can be triggered by a dominant fantasy, by the external world, or by an element in the transference.

Concerning projective identification, the reader can observe its technical application in clinical practice when I interpret to the patient how a part of his self is projected on another person. My interpretation allows him to reintroject aspects of his self that he had projected outwards.

The model of the early, primitive superego, sadistic and cruel, can be seen in clinical practice when the patient feels the internal demands it imposes on him.

Another model I propose is that many drug abusers (especially Type B) are identified to dead objects and persons and mixed up with them. This means that we are actually treating a dead person, not a live one. This is not only a useful theoretical model but an influence on our technical approach to drug-addicted patients.

I have suggested several alternative hypotheses, according to the stage of the transference, on how to make the patient understand the impulses that led him to drug abuse. One theory alone would not be capable of explaining the fantasies that trigger his drug consumption.

In summary, I have transcribed here an actual vital experience, complemented by theoretical and clinical conceptualizations. I hope they may be useful for those who work with this type of patient. I can only add that the study of psychotic and very regressive patients is an unknown field into which we are only beginning to venture.

Of course, new fields imply difficulties, and no one can express that better than Shakespeare:

> If to do were as easy as to know what were good to do,
> chapels had been churches and poor men's cottages princes'
> palaces.
>
> Shakespeare, *The Merchant of Venice* (Act I, Scene 2)

Epilogue

At the time the final corrections to this volume were being completed, on the occasion of an International Congress on the Education of Children some years ago, a participant at the Congress—a young man impeccably dressed in a grey suit with tie, gold-rimmed glasses, and short hair—walked up to me and said, "Hello, I'm George."

My surprise and emotion were very great, and as we looked at each other and greeted each other with a handshake, we both spontaneously gave each other a big and heart-felt hug, he with tears in his eyes and I with eyes also moist with emotion.

He was a teacher, specialized in teaching young people, and was working very happily in this activity.

CHAPTER FOUR

Psychotic addiction to video games

The term "addiction", from the Latin *addictus*, means "slave of his debts". We speak metaphorically of addictive behaviour when referring to a strong dependence on something—for example, a drug. Sometimes substance addiction is substituted by addiction to an activity. In this chapter, which illustrates the case of Lorenzo, who is addicted to video games and computers, I shall present theoretical hypotheses concerning these types of addiction and their treatment.

"Lorenzo"

First contact

Lorenzo's mother's first contact with me was over the phone: we arranged a meeting, and when I asked her whether her son would attend, she explained that Lorenzo, 17, had been hospitalized in a psychiatric clinic following an episode of violence. "They have diagnosed schizophrenia", she specified. She wanted to know whether the father should also come; I said yes and added that I would prefer to see Lorenzo, too. At the first interview I met them in my office. They sat facing me: the boy to my left, the father further back, a little distant, to my right, and the mother between them. She began to tell me Lorenzo's history: he had a lot of problems in his relations with people: behavioural problems, he was very violent, and, she added, "We took him out of the hospital a month ago, because we wanted to change the treatment and the doctor."

Lorenzo was a 17-year-old young man, of medium height and slim but athletic build and with dark brown hair. He walked in a rather strange manner. It was only after beginning treatment that I realized that he sometimes entered my office on tiptoes, which accounted for the strange gait. Lorenzo's eyes were constantly shifting and fluctuating. I think that he was tense and hyperkinetic, perhaps because of the psychiatric medication he was receiving. The mother said: "Lorenzo has had communication problems since he was 12 or 13 years old. He has almost no friends, but he relates quite well with his two sisters, who are two and four years younger than him. He had to repeat one year at school because he has problems concentrating on his studies. These problems stem from playing video games day and night for the whole year." The father, who was not very communicative, said, "Lorenzo gets so involved in these games, it is impossible to get him to stop". They explained that Lorenzo chose very violent games, with characters that attack and beat each other: the games are full of blows, murders, and karate fights. I asked them why he was hospitalized, and the father said, "Yes, yes, I authorized the hospitalization because one night when I tried to make him stop, he broke all the furniture in the house." The mother added: "In the evening we had violent quarrels; he would break the windows, pound on the doors and wardrobes. Once, in a video-game arcade, Lorenzo could not beat a video character that was attacking him, and there was no way they could drag him from the screen. Finally he broke the machine and the arcade's window, and we had to restrain him with the help of other people. The owners of the shop wanted to call the police. The father added: "A boy with so many learning problems and such violence is incurable: it must be genetic." I think that the father, in front of his son and on the first interview, was conveying a sense of his hopelessness. As we shall see, in the course of the treatment the mother did her best to help her son, to escort him to his sessions, to take him to school, and so on.

I tried to talk to the boy, but he could not fix his gaze on anything. He reminded me of a frightened, terrified child—the kind of picture we can sometimes observe in babies during their first year of life. I asked him what goes on in the video games, what he feels, and whether they arouse him. The patient became enraged, stood up, and screamed at me: "This psychoanalyst is crazy! Look what he's telling me, he's talking about sex, he's mad, mad!" My intervention provoked this reaction: the fact that the patient stood up and reacted so violently against me suggested to me some sort of differential diagnosis. I asked him what he could tell me about his hospitalization, and he answered: "I'm angry at you, I don't trust you at all! You are mad!" At that point I remembered that it is very common for psychotic patients to undertake powerful projective identification of their madness into the therapist, and it drives them crazy to believe that when he speaks, the therapist is returning to them their own madness. It is their own madness, projected onto the mind of the therapist, that creates the anxiety.

Lorenzo told me one version of his hospitalization: "I was playing in a video-game arcade, and they wanted to make me leave. I screamed because they had no right to make me go. I hadn't finished playing. I hadn't won or lost. And then they took me out of there, they took me to the clinic, and they didn't let me play any more." I asked again if they hadn't let him play again, and Lorenzo answered: "The psychiatrists confiscated the video-game machine I have at home, and they forbade me to go near any video game." The parents explained that this was a strict order from the psychiatrist. After a few months of treatment, it transpired that the patient remembered that one of the psychiatrists went to his home accompanied by a legal official, and, just so that there would be no doubts about how serious they were about the prohibition, they wrote a notarized document in which it was stated that all video games and video cassettes were to be confiscated.

From then on, I realized that all the characters of Lorenzo's inner world were present on the screen, but they were projected onto an outside stage where he could murder them, or they could pursue him. When he heard that I was not going to forbid him to play with his video games and that, moreover, I wanted to play with him in order to understand him better, Lorenzo stopped looking angry, while his parents asked him whether he accepted me as his doctor. I told him that I was looking forward to treating him and that I would do my utmost to help him feel better in a relatively short time. I also told him we would be talking together, that I would gradually explain to him what was the matter with him, and that when he got a little better, we would go together to a video-game arcade. These were apparently the key words to enter the patient's private world, because he said: "This doctor is mad, but I accept his treatment because at least he promises to go to the video games with me." After a week of daily interviews, I considered that he did not need to be hospitalized for a second time, and we started working with my team, where a psychiatrist is in charge of the medication and a psychologist takes care of emergencies when I am temporarily absent. All the team members are also psychoanalysts. Lorenzo's family lives in a town a few hours' drive from Buenos Aires, so we arranged a schedule for sessions, and they decided they would stay at Lorenzo's grandmother's, who lives close to my office, when they had to be in Buenos Aires. Lorenzo stayed at his grandmother's house for the first four months of treatment and had four sessions each week.

During the first months, he constantly called me on the phone, screaming and wailing. When he returned to school, four months into his treatment, he often telephoned full of anguish before leaving home to go to the high school. Three years later the patient still phones now and then to convey his anxieties, but much less often. After four months I decided that Lorenzo was able to go back to school. This was a personal challenge. I acted in an opposite manner to his father. His father told him repeatedly that he would never be cured and that his problem was genetic. As Lorenzo's treatment proceeded over the years, I gradually discovered how, in his quest for physical feelings and bodily sensations, Lorenzo was ensnared in the lights, the colours, and the sounds of video games. I noticed that he performed repetitive movements with his body, could not focus his eyes, gyrated as he walked, ritually tapped his heels when he came into my office on tiptoes, or washed his hands at the beginning of sessions. In other words: we discovered in Lorenzo primitive experiences, obsessive mechanisms, and movements similar to autistic enclaves or encapsulations from early childhood, which I thought related to his mother's severe depression before his birth.

The importance of teamwork—
the multiple support system

The treatment was approached as the work of a team, not only that of a psychoanalyst. As I customarily do, I saw the patient with the psychiatrist and clinical psychologist. The psychiatrist is in charge of medication and family sessions. It is important for me to make my scientific–clinical position explicit: that it is necessary, when treating psychotic or severely regressed patients, to treat the family at the same time. We consider that the patient is a spokesperson for the family group, and it is important to detect directly, in family sessions (Correale, 1994; Ferro, 1996, p. 115; Pichon-Rivière, 1959), and to interpret paradoxical double-bind messages and contradictory orders and their psychogenic effects. The psychiatrist also handles emergencies if I am out of the city over the weekend. The psychologist intervened when the patient had to be seen at home, and during my summer holiday visited him at home and saw him in his office. This team had regular meetings and frequent communication. When I need to arrange for the hospitalization of a patient in a psychiatric clinic, I usually include in the team a psychologist or resident, who functions as a qualified assistant or as a representative of the team. He or she spends about two hours with the patient each afternoon and goes out with him when he can for a while. When the patient is better this person accompanies him to my office for sessions.

Our criterion for hospitalization of a patient is the need to contain his psychotic part 24 hours a day. At the same time, we also attempt to recover fragmented aspects of the patient through the reports that we receive from the staff and the medical residents of the clinic or hospital.

Violence and delusions

I shall now relate some instances of violence with delusions and a psychotic transference during the first year of treatment. Very often Lorenzo began sessions with obsessive rituals like bringing his feet together, tapping his heels, and entering the room with his right foot, jumping twice, washing his hands before entering, walking to and fro across my office for a few minutes, or pirouetting while he talks. From the first session these movements and gyrations reminded me of what one sees in autistic children, which made me think of encapsulated autistic aspects. Verbal violence was continuous at the beginning of sessions, especially because, according to him, the therapist might harm him. He also displayed verbal violence at home, and he sometimes said that he did not want to come to his session. His mother often helped to make him change his mind and brought him to the office; she escorted him to every session.

Through Lorenzo I began to get acquainted with the characters and features of the video games that consumed him. In fact, it was clinically vital that I learned what happened to the patient while he played, so I decided to go with him to a video-game arcade and get to know the characters he played with, and those he identified with me and with the psychiatrist on my team. The patient projected my attributes on to some of these characters. He wanted to play a game called "Street Killer", and another one called "Street Fighter", both of which are extremely violent: you have to kill the characters with a sword, cut their throats, or hit them very aggressively. When he played with me, Lorenzo won most of the time, and he experienced his triumph omnipotently. But after winning at the games, he came to his session terrified because he had won—as though he had killed me and cut my throat. The same theme was projected onto many external objects; he was afraid of revenge, of being hounded by a schoolmate or by someone in the street, and he was even afraid that I would turn into someone dangerous who would smash his head in and drive him crazy. Sometimes he saw me as dangerous during a session, at other times it was a part of me projected onto the outside world that could hurt him. He confused people on the television screen with real, external people, and this occurred in relation to me. This was a dramatic example of a symbolic equation. The terror he felt about what I could do to him after he beat me at the video games generated in Lorenzo delusional fantasies that were often extremely difficult to manage in the transference. In these cases, psychoanalytic technique required relating the transference delusional fears to the fact that he thought he had killed me when I was representing one of the characters in a video game. My countertransference is difficult to convey in just a few words, especially in view of the long hours when I was in receipt of his anger and tantrums whenever the game failed to respond to his wishes, aside from the difficulty I had in entering the unknown—to me—world of video games and its characters with mysterious names. It was an enormous exercise in containment and holding. I was also obliged to learn the characteristics and names of all the video characters. The important task was to bring what had formerly been projected into the inanimate object, the screen of the video game or the computer, into the transferential relation with the therapist, and to play it out. My most important task was to drive him away from the screen and to connect him with the real, living human being that I am. It was often possible to see Lorenzo's thoughts becoming concrete: there is then no difference between the symbol and the symbolized. The word "demolish" reflects his fear of what I would do to him during our session and exactly what he did to the character in the video game: he demolishes his head with a sword or a karate blow.

Clinical vignette, first year of treatment

One day we played a particularly vicious video game, where the characters fight with laser beams. One week later, the patient began to be afraid of persecution. He thought that his schoolmates would hurt him and he went into frank delusion, afraid that they would attack him with a laser ray. He refused to go out into the street unless he could wear a protective suit against laser beams. His mother tried to calm him down and made him an outfit of aluminium foil. Lorenzo said he felt protected against the laser beams. This delusion amplified and developed to the point where for a few days Lorenzo did not go to school at all. The psychiatrist increased and modified the antipsychotic medication. We considered hospitalization, but we decided to wait for a week because I was interested in seeing the transferential origin that has triggered the delusion (this is the way I try to reason as a psychoanalyst). He came to sessions every day and he even had two sessions on one day, including at the weekend. Lorenzo came dressed in his protective outfit and said he wanted to play again the game we had played last time. I accepted with reluctance, but also with a good deal of curiosity. After the second session that day, he had taken off the aluminium suit, and we played the laser beam video. Lorenzo won the first time, and I won the second game; when we were about to start a third round, he told me: "Dr Rosenfeld, when you win, you can be transformed and become other characters, so even if I kill you now, you are still alive and have turned into another character." I am transformed into someone projected in multiple and varied characters, and even if he kills me, I am still dangerous: I go on living through the other characters in the video game. I am a mutating object that becomes other objects, and they still pursue him with laser beams. This is a symbolic equation and a disorder of perception and of differentiation of external from internal reality. It is only at that point, once I had become aware of this feature of the video game, that I could decipher and work psychoanalytically on the origin of his delusion of being attacked with laser beams. I had metamorphosed and fragmented into his multiple schoolmates, and from there I was attacking him with laser beams. This description that I was resuscitated and was becoming many other characters was the key, the code-breaker, the Rosetta stone, which allowed me access to the delusion in which the different and multiple characters of real life bad become fragmented aspects of Rosenfeld, Lorenzo's analyst. We departed from the screen and entered real life. On this basis I interpreted that when I won the game, my character became a mutant, and he was every other character in the video game. But since the patient confused real life with fantasy, Rosenfeld became a character that is fragmented and may become any one of his schoolmates who harasses him.

The patient thought that I pursued him not only through the characters on the screen, but also through hundreds of people in the real world. His need for the aluminium outfit was a piece of psychotic concretization that, when apparent in the transference, illustrates how the patient displaced onto the stage of the real outside world his feelings and his experiences with his psychoanalyst. After interpreting in the transference the origin of the delusion, and after intense work, I was able to resolve what appeared to be a clinical psychosis with delusional episodes. I found the work of Boyer (1983, 1990a, 1990b, 1999) very useful as a guide for the management of my countertransference. After overcoming this episode, the patient went back to school.

One month later, Lorenzo wanted to try a three-dimensional (3-D) virtual-reality video game. The psychiatrist and I went with him, and we decided to play a game that represented an aeroplane battle. While playing, the patient suffered a panic attack when he saw the objects hurling towards him, overwhelmed as he was by the 3-D effect. I believe that at that point he felt more acutely than ever before his fear of the vengeful persecution that could attack his mind. In a frenzy of panic he ran out of the place and refused to play 3-D games again. This event was crucial because with that game, the patient discovered that a two-dimensional plane is not the same as a space with depth and a third dimension. This coincided with his discovery that Rosenfeld's live image is not the same as the image of the characters and objects on a flat television screen. I think his encapsulated autistic aspects experienced a kind of evolution from a two-dimensional to a three-dimensional perception of space.

This experience with the third dimension in the new video game indicated a structural change in Lorenzo's mind: it was no longer a flat screen. We were beginning to leave the two-dimensional plane and to get into the real person. I remember that after this game we went to meet with the psychiatrist. We tried to calm Lorenzo's panic in a nearby coffee shop where we had tea, and only after that did we ask him to explain to us in greater detail what he had felt when the aeroplanes were rushing towards him in the third dimension.

During one of his subsequent sessions the patient expressed his fear of failing two of the courses at school, and I interpreted that he believed that there was an internal object within his own self that attacked him, abused him, or told him that if he failed a course or a test, it was because he was ill. Then I tried to carry this into the transference and told him that he often experienced the same with me. I asked him to read to me the essay he had written for his French class: It was the story, which he had created on his own, of a tourist who goes to Paris, and it was very well written. I think he needed me to return to him his valuable, healthy aspects, which he evacuated and deposited in me. I was aware of this mechanism, so I interpreted first the mechanism of projection, and only then did I convey to him my astonishment at the essay, which had made me think that he might have copied it.

For a period of time Lorenzo continued to be addicted to video games and to their violence. His involvement with some of the characters in the video game looked like a *"folie-à-deux"*, as described by Nicolò Corighiano and Borgia (1995). Once, while watching a musical on television with his parents and siblings, a scene of violence appeared, and the patient got up, screamed "we must stop this fight", bounced on the television set, and broke the screen with his head. This is perhaps the most significant and dramatic example of how he wanted to stop the battles that went on inside his mind among his internal objects and, at the same time, literally stop the part that was projected onto the television screen. I do not think I could have found a better example of a symbolic equation, where the mind is equated to the inanimate object, in this case, the television set. Segal (1994) has made useful contributions regarding the interplay of fantasy and reality through her distinction between symbol and symbolic equation (in which fantasy and reality are combined). Segal postulates that early processes of symbolic development and their pathological variables are analysable if one understands the patient–analyst relationship, as it offers the chance to explore and analyse the influence of fantasy and reality on the patient's perception of and behaviour towards the analyst. These ideas offered by Segal are extremely important for clinical work and for technique, because sometimes the analyst must decode and de-script who he himself is as a psychoanalyst: an individual, a fantasy, or a symbolic equation. Segal's ideas have allowed me to review my study and understanding of countertransference.

Nintendo versus Sega — collaboration and transition

Nintendo versus Sega

As part of the treatment we used to go to a video-game arcade where I could analyse and study the characters in his favourite games. I used the hour of play as if it had been the analysis of a child, but with modern-day toys—the video games. I came to know the characters, and I penetrated into his inner world. Lorenzo was given back his small video game, which had been confiscated on his previous therapist's recommendation, and a new issue came up: Sega games and Nintendo games are not compatible. The patient spoke about the problems he had when he tried to connect the games to the device he had at home. I interpreted about the problems he had to "connect", to connect with me, and the difficulty there was in finding one system through which we could have a dialogue, with two different minds, just like Sega and Nintendo.

Collaboration and transition

During a session Lorenzo related that he had been playing with a video game, but this was the first time the patient had chosen a game with no beheadings, no karate blows, no sabres, and no sword slashes. He said he chose this game "because there is a monkey who has to jump over a river to save his life, and the monkey finds a giant frog, as large as the desk in his office. The frog tells the monkey to get on her back, and they jump to the other river-bank. Then another animal comes along, who gives the monkey a banana to eat." The patient said that he had gone to bed early but had thought about this game for hours. I interpreted that this was the first time that he played a game where there is collaboration and help instead of fights, blows, and murders. "In the game you selected, they get together to help someone", and I added, "what you saw in the game is like what happens with me in the session. I support you, like the frog; I help you jump and cross the river. I carry you on my back, and I give you mental food, which in your game is the banana."

In that session we had good communication—so much so that at one point he lay on the couch as if it were a large frog that supported him. This was the first time he had used the couch. Previously he had stood or walked around the office.

During the following sessions, Lorenzo again brought up the frog and comments on my interpretations and on how his therapist and the couch give him support. He seldom showed good humour, but one day he started joking, laughing and mimicking the monkey, saying, "I am a monkey and you are a frog".

Periodically, the father and mother would meet with the psychiatrist (Cancrini & Pelli, 1995; Martini, 1995). The patient said that these interviews reminded him of the game with the monkey and the frog. I explained that this was because we are the two people who helped him—the psychiatrist and I. "You have never seen two people getting together to help you. Mostly, you speak of arguments and quarrels." At that point the patient remembered: "On my birthday, my mother cooked Chinese food in a big pan, and just before cutting the cake my mother and father started insulting each other because she said he didn't help her clean up, or pay for my treatment, or make dinner for my birthday. They ended up throwing the pan at each other's heads." I interpreted: "You realize that any boy can go crazy with fights like this, especially if it's his birthday." I think that the real outer world has an impact and intensifies the disorder in Lorenzo's mind. Lorenzo survived his parents' fights by projecting them on to the video games' screen, thus dislodging from his mind things that happen with real objects: he emptied his head of the real events in his house. In my view, the level of violence my patient experienced at home was high and very disturbing for him—therefore I indicated to the parents that they needed to have regular interviews with the psychiatrist, which turned out to be useful because the family decided to stay in town for a few days (Izzo, 2000). This was the first time the patient went on an outing with his father, who took him to a film and for a stroll around the city.

Lorenzo is able to express hatred and anger

Lorenzo began to fear that he would be hospitalized again, and he remembered the first time this had happened, at Christmastime. "Those who sent me to the hospital must have been Jews or atheists, because they didn't care", he said. At around that time Lorenzo related things that his father had said that bewildered him (I must admit, I felt bewildered too): "My father says that if I ever get married, I'll have to go through what he is going through—he is about to separate from my mother." Lorenzo was jumping and running all over my office as he shouted "Why the heck did he have me, if now he is not interested in this marriage. I could kill him, I could kill him, I could kill him!" I interpreted that he does this in the video games: he projects the hate he feels for his father on to the characters on the screen. I underscored that this is the first time he was capable of shouting his hatred for his father, shouting that he wants to kill him. "Before, all this was secret, and it was evacuated from your mind into the television screen. It is very important that you hate and have fantasies about killing, and this doesn't mean that you are really killing him." Lorenzo continued to scream and run around the office, so I repeated the words, to make sure he heard them.

Collaboration

Several months later, just before I had to go out of town for ten days, Lorenzo appeared to be serene at the beginning of his session and then said: "Mother broke a transformer, and I don't know if it can be fixed; I don't know if the technician can make the right connections. . . . I don't know if I will be able to catch up on the classes I missed at school, perhaps they will make me pass a test on the environment and health. . . . I thought you would be upset because I was a little late today." I commented that perhaps he is scared of replacements—a psychologist and a psychiatrist—who would be taking my place during my absence. Lorenzo asked himself if human connections can be replaced and be any good, and I interpreted: "You think your communication with me will break, and you don't know whether what you called today a "broken transformer" can be fixed." After remaining silent, he said he had rented some films that he planned to watch with his grandmother. I reminded him that there was a time when he only rented violent video games, full of monsters, in which there were no human beings.

Drawings, letters and dreams —
the beginning of symbolization

Phase of drawings

During this phase, Lorenzo asked me for a paper pad during our session and began to draw beautiful and willowy women. The men, on the other hand, were sketched in black, very schematically, and this led me to think that he was drawing something about his identity problems and his body image (partly masculine and partly feminine). It was curious to see how, over a few days, his functioning fluctuated between the psychotic and the neurotic parts of his personality. Lorenzo lived far from the city, so we sometimes concentrated four sessions close to the weekend.

The week before I was due to go away, Lorenzo fantasized that he had an orifice between his anus and his testicles. A fantasy about the therapist's absence appeared as a hole in his body, or a void in his object relations, and on a different level it could represent an operation he had on his testicles when he was 11, and perhaps also the void left by his grandfather's death. Absence, emptiness, death, loss of masculinity are all mixed together or equated in the fantasy of the hole. Also, it may have represented a confused sexual identity, partly male and partly female (possibly because his mother had so often turned him into a part of her body and her mind).

Volkan (1996, p. 106, 1997) and Quinodoz (1989) state that in transsexual patients who have undergone surgery, it is most often the mother who, via her fantasy, determines the gender identity of her son. Volkan says that the perception the mother inculcates in her son is the core of the "self infantile core" from which the future development of the self will evolve. "His future gender identity confusion could be seen in the mother's fantasies about him, which she deposited into the child's evolving self-representation, where it remained partly psychotic."

Phase of letters

The patient continued with panic and screaming crises, especially before going to school. While in this state, he often called me on the telephone. His terror and his violence increased towards the end of the school year: he bashed in the doors of his house, afraid he would fail, and he believed that his teachers and schoolmates were all his enemies. Over these months, the transference was characterized by his violence against me, with claims and accusations: "Why doesn't he cure me? You want to hypnotize me!" This violence against me provoked intense countertransference feelings in me. But the technical handling of the countertransference was always useful. The violence is now with the human person and not with a non-human screen. Other changes were taking place that also deserved to be taken into account: instead of playing at killing through his video games characters, he began to write long letters that he then brought to the office.

The red-ink letter

The patient brought a large, unruled sheet of green board, on which he had written in red ink the following list: "People I must kill: schoolmates, who think I'm an idiot and make fun of me; Caroline, because of the eternal love disappointment; teachers who want me to fail; the teacher who gave me a low grade; kill the school for everything that's in it and the teachers who think I'm stupid. Kill couples and lovers because they show me what I will never have. Kill Rosenfeld for not being with me when I need him most and for abandoning me at the end of each session, and for setting a time limit to each session instead of being with me when I need him. I also want to kill him for taking money from my mother for each session I come to. . . . The Brazilian soccer team for beating Argentina. . . . My father, for making me lose all the illusions in my life and for talking to me coldly and sharply and telling me he will have me hospitalized and come and visit me once every six months."

He read to me: "This Doctor Rosenfeld is a son of a bitch. All he does is debase my father in front of me and debase me in front of my father, he really wants to demolish me, and he pesters me about my masturbating and jerking off while I look at women on TV". When he finished reading, he tore up the page.

The patient was able to convey a message verbally, to read and be heard. This was the beginning of symbolization, and it was a great change from previous years, when he spent his nights killing characters through violent video games. We saw the emergence of oedipal levels, mixed with pregenital levels, but now the patient expressed them during the session in a limited space but no longer within the flat, two-dimensional screen of his video games.

Dreams

During the third year of treatment, Lorenzo began to remember his dreams and to bring them to our sessions. This phase was also characterized by greater eroticization, with sexual fantasies and more masturbation. At the beginning, the images in his dreams or in his imagination resembled those in his comics, where the women are drawn as exuberant, erotic, and sensual creatures. I agree with Green (1977, 1992, 1996, 1997) that the sexual instinct is a vital drive for this sexual exacerbation, and it is worth noting that this happens at a time when pregenital problems and primitive anxieties can be verbalized and interpreted. At times, the tremendous sexual arousal the patient felt was experienced as an instinct that was driving him mad. The inability to contain primitive anxieties and powerful arousal reflects the same problem, perhaps because they are both based in the self's mental space, which is sometimes not appropriate to contain instincts and anxieties (Freud, 1914c, 1914g). Affection and closeness triggered both his fear of not being a male and his fear of homosexuality.

The dream with "L"

During the next session, he said that once again his father had told him that "there are things that cannot be changed." He added that his father and his schoolmates think he is "weird" and somewhat crazy. I interpreted that perhaps he was confusing real people with the imaginary characters in his head that call him "weird". He continued to say that his sister screamed "crazy" at him, and that he hit her. I decided to give him a second session on that day because I was afraid he might turn violent against his sisters. This is when we discovered that violence was his defence against sexual arousal. Lorenzo felt contained by me on this day, and at the next session he related a dream: "I see myself as a woman and I look for a name like mine, with an 'L', like Lorenzo, and it is 'Lenora'. I don't know whether I have a penis or not", he adds. I interpreted his fear of losing his sexual identity as a male; he feared that if he received affection or was taken care of by his therapist (who is a man) he will be homosexual, or become a woman. I added that he thinks that this is the only way he can be accepted, loved by me. Lorenzo believed that to be loved by his father, he has to be a woman, like his sisters, because they were his father's favourites. Lorenzo responded to the interpretation with a sexual comment: "My schoolmate Carol arouses me." And he went on to tell me that he was also aroused when he saw a couple who were students in his school kissing and necking on a motorcycle (Resnik, 1994). At the end of the session he said that at his grandmother's there isn't the fighting that goes on at his parents' house; he would like to go to his grandmother's more frequently, so he could come more often to the sessions.

I think we can see here how he was afraid that he will not be accepted as a male by a male therapist. Moreover, primitive lack of differentiation with his mother's female body emerged. He was scared of being close to his doctor, of discovering that he could feel affection for him, and this leads to dreams such as the above. This is a transferential recurrence of his history with his father.

Negative therapeutic reactions and insights

Negative therapeutic reactions

Negative therapeutic reactions (NTRs), as Freud (1923b, pp. 49–50, 1933a, pp. 109–110) describes them, appear after progress has been made during treatment, especially in neurotic patients. I have described (Rosenfeld, 1992b) certain varieties of NTRs, among them a silent variety in severely disturbed or psychotic patients. In my experience with psychotic patients, I have noted that with the onset of perception of insight—simply with its onset—psychotic patients often violently attack the therapist, and I have developed a hypothesis that may explain this mechanism. The patient's perceptual apparatus, capable of insight, is emptied, evacuated, projected outside the patient, into the therapist. When the patient begins to have a first outline of an insight, an outline of a perception of who he is, he wants to attack his perception of himself. The next step consists in attacking his own perceptual apparatus, which has been evacuated and projected into the therapist, and he therefore attacks the body and mind of the therapist. When I say "attacks" I am referring to real experiences in treatments of psychotic patients. This theory differs from Searles' theory on violence in schizophrenic patients (Searles, 1986).

Lorenzo, our patient, after his moments of insight, of getting closer to the depressive position, begins to perceive who he was when he was psychotic, and who he is now. The so-called NTRs cannot always be explained by a theory of envy, which is extremely useful in other pathologies, as Klein has taught us (1975a, 1975b).

Some dreams related to insight

When Lorenzo came to the next session, he was in a hurry, but he was not scared. He remembered once again that his parents had had a fight at the dinner table and ended up throwing pots at each other. Then he said he had a dream: "I was with an adult, I must have been around 12 years old. The adult could have been an uncle or a grandfather. It was night, and we were going through a place with all kinds of gangs and criminals. A train arrived, which came from where my grandfather lives. My uncle and I had to fight against all of them." (When he said "them" he used the feminine pronoun, "ellas", in Spanish.)

In my countertransference I thought that "them" [*ellas*] could be the gangs as a feminine slip of the tongue, but it could also be a change of sex as in the video-game characters. At that time I thought that Lorenzo tried to survive his parents' real fights and screams by trying to project them and empty his mind of them, either in a video game or in a dream.

The patient continued his narrative: "*Then I was with my uncle, and I killed the woman, the big one, and I threw her on the rail track: the blow as she landed on the rails killed her. Then I suggested killing the young one. Later an ugly woman came along, like a witch or a thin, bony, ugly nursemaid. She was with a young girl of my age who was just as evil as she was.*" I asked him to explain why there were so many women, and exactly who was with whom, and he explained: "*By the look on their faces, I think they all wanted me to lose, they wanted to beat me, they defended themselves well, but there was a stalemate. I could do nothing to them, and they could do nothing to me. Then I realized I liked the young one.*" A little overwhelmed by the confusion of characters, I asked him which young one he was talking about, and he answered: "*I see her with long blonde hair, partly straight but with some curls, white-skinned; and then I thought that this girl was not worth while, but I still forced her to be with me that night. I wrapped my arm around her waist, and we went walking like we were a couple. Then the adult in the dream changed into my grandfather and told me 'Now, we are all doing all right.' My grandfather followed us and took care of us.*"

Analyst [*A*]: Was he protecting you from some danger?

Patient [*P*]: I was just a 12-year-old kid; I wasn't ashamed if my grandpa took care of me.

A: Perhaps I was the grandfather?

P: No, no. The grandfather was my grandfather. I miss him since he died. It would be wonderful to have a girlfriend like that and a grandfather. [Lorenzo's voice has changed dramatically as he says these words; he had never shown such emotion during his years of treatment.]

A: Tell me about your grandfather.

P: I think I was 11. Oh yes, he loved me very much, and I loved him too.

He then said that in his dream *there was a restaurant where he went with his girlfriend, it was quite a simple and plain place, but they served good food.* In the countertransference I felt moved and remembered vividly an important scene from my childhood with my own dear grandfather. In my countertransference I was able to deduce that Lorenzo had felt moved when he talked about his grandfather whom he loved so dearly, and now he had found in his treatment a place where he felt good, a simple place, but with good and abundant food. *"In the end, we didn't go into the restaurant, grandfather took us someplace else because he had work to do"*, he says.

A: This is the first dream where you recover your grandfather, who loved you so much. In your dream, he protects you from your fears, and you recover him, this character who was so important when you were a child, at a time when you feel protected by me from your nightmares and your inner monsters that pursue you within yourself.

The session ended in silence, which was unlike him, but I did feel that Lorenzo was in the process of recovering his internal objects.

Phase of insight and infantile dependence

In another session, Lorenzo brought a letter, and read it to me:

"OK, doctor, I understand that during sessions I must answer for myself, and not through somebody else's mind. . . . (a) I feel many kinds of hatreds, but I wonder why all my hatreds must be directed at you. (b) Video games represent my mind. (c) The rituals I perform are aimed at cleansing my hatreds. (d) I am afraid that you will do something to me in retaliation for my hatred of you."

The next point in his letter is extremely important, and I quote it verbatim: "The development of my mind depends on the video game, but only in part. I have the absolute right to attack you if you behave like an ass-hole." We must remember that once he tried to illustrate how he wanted to attack me, which he called defending himself, and while he was pacing in my office he gripped my head and my neck from behind to show me what he would do to me. I admit I was scared. At that moment I remembered a schizophrenic patient who had once punched me in the face because, as he said, I looked like his father because of my glasses and moustache. But once I took hold of myself, it allowed me to decode his act and to understand that he does to me what he is continually afraid I will do to his mind. "There is a video game I can never beat; when will I stop being driven to play it, unable to quit once I've started it? Will the video game in my brain never be erased?" These words that the patient had thought, spoken, and written, are a sign that he has understood the interpretations that indicate that the characters fighting and killing each other in the video games, that fascinated him so much, were already within his mind since he was a little boy, his parents fought, slaughtering each other in a sadistic coitus, with him in-between, in a terrifying mental video game. In the same letter, some fragments reflect his infantile aspects, in need of help, more clearly than ever before, when he wrote: "I know a boy that, if you are any good, really needs you, because he leads a miserable life, he can't find peace within himself." He went on to list other items, related to his masculine identity, which he brought to his sessions under different guises: "I think I will remain short. . . . I don't ejaculate any more. . . . Is the physical male in me dead?"

I admit that after the session I felt surprised and moved when I reflected that this had been written by the same young boy who had been hospitalized in a psychiatric institution when I was first asked to treat him.

Theoretical conclusions

In my opinion an accurate perception of countertransference is primarily the result of a good psychoanalytic treatment of the therapist himself and is associated with responsible supervision of his work. If we take black-and-white photographs we shall end up with black-and-white pictures, and we might even say that colour does not exist. The same happens if we work without the full richness provided by the proper use of countertransference.

The setting or frame

The setting is a dialectic creation that takes place over a period of time. It is created by patient and therapist together. The setting consists in what is fixed or formal—the hours, the place or space, the fees—and in what is mobile, which is the dynamic aspect, the process that occurs within the setting. This is essentially a human relationship. We can say that this interpersonal or intrapersonal relationship is empathic and is an attempt to get to know about the unconscious, the inner world, its internal objects, and the primitive transference that unfolds. In particular, it takes into account the countertransference in order to decode primitive levels of communication, which, in infancy, had no words available for their expression. Countertransference will be the most important tool for research in psychosis. The order, time of day, and place are important, as are messages that convey stability and order in the object relationship, rather than the chaos and disorder that are experienced as mental disorganization in the therapist's mind. In my regular work with patients hospitalized in hospitals or private psychiatric clinics, I always saw the patient at the same fixed hours. But at other moments in the process, especially in acute psychoses, the dynamic part of the process is more important, and in this case, the frame or setting is the creation of holding and of mental space in the psychoanalytic field (A. Anzieu, 1986; Bonaminio & Slotkin, 2002; Painceira Plot, 1997). Then it is the analyst's interpretation and attitude as a person that is fundamental for creating the holding. Within the mental space of holding we include the team, which always shares the work. Here I refer to the psychiatrist and the psychologist on the team, and I also include the hospital residents and assistants who have contact with the patient while he or she is hospitalized. In the case of Lorenzo I went to great lengths to protect the setting, despite the patient's difficulties and the daunting task facing the team. The team must be a unit that the patient experiences as adequate and holding. What is important is to be able to think psychoanalytically about the transference and the patient's inner world, as well as about the countertransference. No one can prevent me from thinking like a psychoanalyst, even when I am walking through the hospital with a patient, or going to a shopping mall and playing video games. Here, what is important is to create a mental space in common that is appropriate for holding and for psychoanalytic work. Even in a classical setting, which includes a couch, the psychoanalyst's existence can sometimes be denied. In my patient, Lorenzo, we see that not everything could be based on verbal or symbolic elements. It is the psychoanalyst who must decode and differentiate these distortions or different systems of communication.

The setting or frame is more than something passive, as Goldberg (1990) points out.

> The environmental provision of holding revealed to us by Winnicott involves much more than a passive state of empathy: indeed, the holding environment must sometimes be actively sought and created within the therapist, a process that may involve the therapist in a great deal of internal activity and struggle . . . [and] . . . not necessarily any external activity at all, but rather a certain internal activity or experimentation with internal mental states.

Lorenzo had several simultaneous defence systems that were used interchangeably and that were modified throughout the course of the treatment. Some of these are:

• powerful projective identification;
• symbolic equations;
• confusion, especially between the human and the inanimate;
• behaviour based on autistic manoeuvres or mechanisms.

Projective identification

The video-addicted patient emptied his mind in the imaginary space represented by the screen and projected onto it the characters of his inner world; he was like a glove that was turned inside out and emptied its content onto the screen. The characters in the video games—imaginary on the screen, but with some correspondence with persons from the patient's childhood—became real for him and pursued him with unforgiving vengefulness. The patient wielded an omnipotent power over these characters through powerful obsessive mechanisms, but he feared they would treat him as he treated the characters in the games.

Symbolic equation

The real outer world is also projected on the video game's screen. To explain this type of functioning, I use the theoretical model described by Segal (1994), which I find useful to explain the differences between a symbol and a symbolic equation. Segal insists on what I believe is crucial for our work with severely disturbed patients: the first symbolization processes, as well as the alterations or pathological distortions to which the symbol is submitted, can be analysed and understood because they surface in the patient–analyst relationship. This is where we analysts have the unique opportunity to analyse the influence of fantasy on reality and how it supports the patient's perceptions. Our most important task is to understand how the patient distorts his perception of the analyst. "In a concrete symbolism, the symbol is equated with what is symbolized. Concrete symbolism leads to misperception and false beliefs" (Segal, 1994).

Transference and interpretations

By emptying his mind through projective identification, this patient elicits states of confusion. I postulate that Lorenzo could not relinquish his video games because he needed to evacuate into the outer world—a non-human world—the violence, hatred, murder, and brutal sex that occupied his fantasies. Thus, until he does not succeed in killing the characters that pursue him and that he hates, he cannot abandon the video game or the screen. With regard to transference and technique, we use the concept of psychotic transference, also called delusion or regressive or primitive transference, to describe a type of transference that has extremely intense, primitive, and undifferentiated emotional characteristics based on part-objects (Rosenfeld, 1992b, 2001b).

Autistic sensations

Quite often, patients induce autistic sensations in their own body in order to create protective manoeuvres. Through bodily sensations or feelings they create what Tustin has called "a world of sensations that envelops them and in which they live" (Tustin, 1990b). This is a primitive survival system and a way of achieving an equally primitive concept of identity—a way to avoid disappearing. Autistic children usually touch objects in the office, or rub up against them. They may, for example, lick the windows or the furniture, or rub the curtains or the analyst's clothes with their arms and hands. They search for bodily sensations in order to create a protective shield. I found some drug-addicted patients who, as children, had some autistic features and who survived by creating their own world of sensations through drugs. In adolescents and adults the search for this type of feelings is pursued through increasingly stronger drugs in order to try to obtain powerful bodily sensations, which reflects how autistic children obtain these sensorial experiences through the body using bodily movements (Rosenfeld, 1990a, 2000). Autistic children use autistic manoeuvres to surround themselves with a world of sensory stimuli in order to protect themselves from all that is terrifying on the outside. This is a world of sensations created by their own body, and these are experienced in a concrete way. The main purpose in using parts of the body in this way is to shut out threats of bodily attacks and, ultimately, annihilation. For them, any separation or absence is a tearing apart, and any absence is experienced as a hole. For example, with this patient, when I interrupted the treatment because I had to be away, only then was he able to symbolize it in a fantasy. He expressed it by dreaming that he had a hole, a hollow, between his anus and his testicles. He expressed this separation and loss as a loss of a part of his body. Tustin (1990b) says: "Autistic patients are fearful, despite having this protective shell."

We have described some behaviours of our patient, Lorenzo, that we also observe in the treatment of autistic children. One example is his coming into my office on tiptoe: to be precise, on the tips of his big toes. Another activity was his whirling around and around, which is typical of the repetitive movement of autistic children (Reid, 1997). Another was his repeated seeking of sensory stimuli by twisting his fingers and hands and rubbing his hands together vigorously. I think that the autistic manoeuvre most closely linked to his addiction to the video games and the computer was his autistic-like attempt to procure sensory stimuli through the bright lights and colours on the video screens, the loud noises of his games and the vibrations he felt in his body. This is another way to procure, as Tustin defines them, "bodily sensations". Autistic children, absorbed by and closed in by this sensory world, cannot use projection and therefore are unable to make contact with the outside by means of projective identification (Bion, 1984). Learning is held up and, of course, symbolization is arrested.

The contribution of Ogden (1990, 1994) on the autistic-contiguous position is particularly important, theoretically and clinically. In this position, primitive sensory experiences provide the self with a sense of cohesion, an envelope for the skin. For Ogden, this is the starting point for the formation of a rudimentary structure of subjectivity and an incipient experience of an integrated self. This is still a non-symbolic area, a non-separation of self and object.

Regarding the effect of television, video games, and computers on the child's mind during the first stage of childhood, I should like to comment on some interesting issues described by Amati-Mehler (1987, p. 273; 1992, 1998), regarding the influence of television and video games on children's mental processes. Amati-Mehler begins by saying that "parents and teachers have become increasingly interested as well as alarmed *vis-à-vis* the invasion of games such a video games." Certainly, the unsettling issue of the "technological child", symbolized at a symposium by a cartoon representing a child with a cap (computer) on his head, proposes an area of study that has been largely unexplored. A more recent symposium about the same subject was entitled "The 'On–off' Child", in reference to the uninhibited use of all types of buttons and keys. We know that the development and functioning of the psyche result from the variable and unique interaction between the exquisitely individual innate intellectual equipment that every child is born with, and the world surrounding him or her. The mind is constructed by virtue of experiences and perceptions that we have within the scope of human relationships and the surrounding environment. Therefore, we cannot avoid thinking that changes in the psychic organization of children do occur. The lack of boundaries or differentiation between true horror and fiction are introjected with natural and increasing nonchalance. This leads to a massive invasion of the perceptive field and influences the time and mode of reaction to events that would, in order to be mentalized and elaborated, require adequate internal space and time. Subsequently Amati-Mehler (1987) says:

> We are particularly interested in establishing the boundaries within which certain objects, such as televisions or computers—when used at a very early age or inappropriately—may interfere with the mode in which the inner self establishes the subjective capability of valuing and generally understanding the events and information coming from either the inner or the outer worlds.

Amati-Mehler adds (assigning value to the introjective aspects of outward invasion):

> I will particularly dwell on the interaction with the computer and television. This doesn't mean that video games or other electronic games, to which I will refer later, are not important, but I believe that the television and computers are the instruments that have most influence on the adjustment of mental mechanisms and mainly on the development of the symbolic function.
>
> This is one of the main reasons for the alarm expressed years ago when the computer was triumphantly promoted—the earlier the better—with the rationale that it stimulated the development of logical processes in children. But how can we use logic when an adequate sense of reality has not yet developed? Or when fiction cannot be distinguished from reality? A sequence of facts may be very logical and true, but its adequacy to a certain situation requires more complex judgement and the appreciation of other contextual circumstances.

Amati-Mehler continues:

> Play is one of the more important elements in children's lives, because it is the natural arena for experimenting the difference between reality and fiction, between animated and inanimate objects, construction and destruction, finding and losing, pleasure and displeasure, interest and boredom, between the interaction with oneself and that with others.

And about the influence of television on children younger than age 6 she says:

> The excessive leniency of television decreases children's ability to properly focus on a problem during sufficient time. This is a very relevant point, since attention, a fundamental requisite for learning, may already be compromised before entering school. The capability of forming mental representations is also affected, and these are the building bricks for later categorizations and more complex mental operations. Television, in contrast with reading or play, precludes experimentation, exploring and a whole series of other mechanisms.
>
> But while our fantasies spring spontaneously from within, the images that dwell in our head while we (passively) watch television come from outside.

Final comments and summary

In this chapter we have presented the clinical material of a youngster addicted to video games and computer games. We presented clinical material, including dreams. We offered hypotheses about the mechanisms employed by this patient and believe that such hypotheses may be useful for understanding other patients with similar psychopathology. We described the mechanisms of projective identification, symbolic equation, confusional defences or mechanisms and autistic mechanisms. In these final conclusions and summary I should like to expand on the concept of autistic mechanisms, especially on the encapsulation of autistic aspects, which may occur in a patient who at the same time functions in a reasonably adapted way to reality with the other part of his neurotic self (S. Klein, 1980; Tustin, 1986). Carrying out an in-depth study of the mechanisms used by this patient, we should find different mechanisms, as I mentioned earlier. But I want to emphasize the autistic encapsulated areas because part of the material seems to point to the mechanisms of autistic encapsulation. In the encapsulation model there is a shielding or early identifications that are later found to be fairly well preserved in this patient. As an explanatory model I would suggest that there is a dialectic interplay between all the systems: one aimed at encapsulating—which does not mean integration but preservation—and thus shielding identifications, and another that, despite everything, loses valuable identifications as a consequence of powerful projective identification. The inner drama develops between these mechanisms. Technically it is advisable to bear all these mechanisms in mind. We need to pay attention to projective identification mechanisms in order to avoid a mental emptying due to massive projection. This may lead to either mental emptying, or severe confusional states, or even to the loss or dismembering of early identifications. It also plays an important role in disorders employing symbolic equations. Encapsulation is a way of shutting out and protecting oneself from the external world, against the unknown—the non-ego. These are children whose internal wounds are always open and painful. One of the aims is to preserve the premature integration of personality, which has occurred far too hastily.

Conclusion

On the basis of experience it may be concluded that in many neurotic children the processes of secondary encapsulated autism have become isolated in a "pocket" of functioning, so that the developmental process seems to continue normally. This is my hypothesis transferred to adult patients. (This hypothesis, in which autistic encapsulation is also useful to preserve early identifications, was originally described by the author in "Identification and the Nazi phenomenon"—Rosenfeld, 1986.)

Two years after discontinuing treatment with me Lorenzo came to see me, following the advice of his current psychoanalyst, who was going on holiday and suggested the need for containment. Lorenzo came to the office, and I saw a slimmer young man, dressed quite elegantly and with properly combed hair (which had never been the case in the past). He said that he was currently sharing an apartment with his sister in downtown Buenos Aires, and that both of them were studying. This would not have been possible had they stayed at their parents' house, which is very distant from the large schools, colleges, and universities. Lorenzo later related that he sat for the English course's exam and passed the "first certificate". Now he was about to sit another English test, for a higher level. But he had been very violent and anxious due to this and had quarrelled with his older sister. Later, when he remembered the discussions at his parents' house, he denied the occurrence of arguments where they failed and even threw food over each other's heads during his birthday party. I believe that forgetfulness or denial sometimes occurs in severely disturbed patients, when they deposit in their therapist extremely ill or crazy periods of their lives and then refuse to tolerate remembering and re-suffering these periods. We were also able to talk and remember good moments while he was in treatment with me, especially when he finished high school and had won three awards: for best qualifications in economics–mathematics, best in French, and a prize for best overall results in his class.

CHAPTER FIVE

Listening to and interpreting a psychotic patient

I hope to demonstrate, through a detailed clinical description, the usefulness of psychoanalytic technique for the treatment of psychotic or severely regressed patients, and also to communicate my own experience in detecting subtle transference clues.

I discuss only a very limited period in the treatment of a patient: the first interviews and the first months of treatment. I describe moments of psychotic transference and then the psychoanalytic work during the psychotic episode. Thus I hope to stimulate theoretical discussion on the basis of clinical data and in this way suggest a number of themes to be discussed, in particular the relationship between models or theories and their influence on the interpretative technique.

I would first like to enlarge on the concept of psychosis and the psychotic part of the personality. Freud's (1940e) description of the splitting of the ego in the psychoses into a normal part and another that detaches the ego from reality is of fundamental importance for the understanding of the psychoses.

In the course of treatment the analyst avails himself of the patient's neurotic part, with its minimal capacity for verbalization, in order to establish a transference relationship. In other words, if on the basis of some of Freud's writings we may infer that in every psychotic there is a neurotic part, this part could be the basis for the establishment of a transference relationship in accordance with Freud's (1912b) own definition. Abraham (1908, 1911b, 1916) had begun to suggest, perceive, and state that there is transference in schizophrenia. As Freud (1940a) points out, "Even in a state so far removed from the reality of the external world as one of hallucinatory confusion . . . that at one time in some corner of their mind . . . there was a normal person hidden" (pp. 201–202). He adds, "Two psychical attitudes have been formed instead of a single one—one, the normal one, which takes account of reality, and another which under the influence of the instincts detaches the ego from reality. The two exist alongside each other" (1940a, p. 202). I insist, then, that a healthy part is necessary in order to work with a psychotic patient. As Shakespeare puts it:

> No thing can be made out of nothing.
>
> Shakespeare, *King Lear* (Act I, Scene 4)

Herbert Rosenfeld (1979) has defined the term "psychotic transference":

> psychotic patients project their feelings because they are too frightened to cope with them or to think them themselves. The analyst, however, like the parents in more normal development, has the potential both to face the feelings and to think about them, and it is this capacity which he gradually offers the patient to develop for himself [p. 488]

Kernberg (1979, 1992) also discusses short, transient psychotic episodes in borderline patients. In the more recent book he has developed the theoretical and clinical concepts of sadism, aggression, and violence. I agree with Kernberg's technical suggestion, namely, not to interpret projective identification at the moments of psychotic transference. Herbert Rosenfeld (1987) says something similar in his book, *Impasse and Interpretation*.

"Charles"

The patient, whom I shall call Charles, was referred to me for consultation six months after he had had a psychotic episode. The picture was first perceived by his family when the patient returned from his holiday, and it became more acute and exuberant while he was spending a couple of days at a weekend cottage. By then he and his girlfriend had decided to put an end to their relationship. At present I have good reason to believe that there had been a previous episode approximately a year earlier, of which his family seemed to have been unaware and which, according to the description, was of a confusional nature.

The psychotic episode that led to my being consulted had, I was told, an exuberant and delusional onset with disorganized speech. The patient began to call himself by the names of some of the great current tennis players and, holding a tennis racquet in his hand, at one moment said he was Borg, or Connors, or Vilas. Then he assumed their identity. According to his family, he spoke in an incoherent and unintelligible way.

The patient, 21 years old, lived with his parents and a sister. His relatives told me that the patient's psychotic episode had taken them by surprise: "It was a complete surprise to us, because he was a very quiet, orderly, peaceful boy. It was a shock, a scandal, to see him talking and running, or speaking in a delusional way at the weekend cottage where there were other friends too." They mentioned, almost in passing, that the patient found it difficult to study and spent endless hours trying to get organized to prepare for his exams.

We agreed upon a contract according to which treatment would be started on a five-hour-a-week basis. In addition, I suggested that family interviews with a well-known psychoanalyst be started later on. Medication was left in the hands of my team of collaborators, and the patient was to end his previous treatment with a wild psychotherapist.

Interview and first dream

Charles impressed me as unexpressive and uncommunicative, nor did his gestures convey affective states. He never looked me in the face. He was undemonstrative and seemed to be armoured and/or blocked. His father accompanied him to his first interview. At the time of the consultation, Charles had finished high school and was trying to enter a school of fine arts, as he is a painter and musician.

In his first interview the patient seemed frightened. During several months of psychoanalytic treatment (one of the members of the family usually accompanied him to my consulting-room), Charles used an obsessive language that included the repetition of phrases, concepts, and grammatical structures of an idiosyncratic type, which were difficult or impossible to understand. He wanted to show that his logic and his thinking really worked; I was able to show him that he used the logistics of thinking as a defence against the fear of a new psychotic disorganization.

During the first months this happened quite often and always generated strong countertransference feelings in me as his therapist. (The question of countertransference in these moments of obsessive doubt—or of psychotic disorganization, despair, or suicidal threats—is perhaps the central axis on which the future of research on regressed and psychotic patients will turn.) Sometimes he brought written descriptions of feelings he had experienced during a psychotic episode, feelings that he found incomprehensible.

Charles's father had been orphaned at 9, and his maternal grandfather, who had lived with them, had died painfully of cancer. The grandfather, of whom Charles was very fond, had slept in the room next to his and spent many months there in agony before his death.

Sometimes the patient got mixed up about the time of his sessions. One day he looked at his pocket-diary and said something that surprised me: "My mother writes things down in my diary and has a look at it every morning, and she has been doing this for many years. She writes everything down in my pocket-diary and fixes my schedule every morning."

After the fifth month Charles brought his first dream, from which he woke quite shaken. He entered the consulting-room surprised at having had a dream.

Charles dreamed that *he was crossing a car-park; his father was behind him, and his mother was behind his father. They went into a big building through the front door. At that moment he did not know where he was going. They walked along a corridor and took the lift to the top floor: the patient, his parents, the lift operator, and the grandfather standing by Charles. As the lift was going up, the patient underwent a transformation: he was no longer made of flesh and bone but was like a doll made of transparent glass. When they reached the top floor, Charles was worried about his fragility. When they left the lift, the grandfather had disappeared, but a nurse led them to a ward and said the grandfather was there. At that moment Charles was no longer made of glass and felt he was going to be very sad. When he got to his grandfather's bed, his mother was behind him, and he thought his sister was coming along the corridor.*

I asked him for clarification and more details about the dream. The patient cooperated and I interpreted, "The fact that you can dream is proof that you have more confidence in the treatment, for now you have somebody to tell your dream to." In addition, I told him, it was the first time he had brought a dream where he was trying to elaborate the death of someone he had loved dearly in his childhood. The dream also showed an important part of the patient's personality. Actually, Charles (as represented in the dream) was showing that he was a fragile person who, faced with such a traumatic event as the death of his grandfather, had become aware of his fragility.

I said that he was showing a part of himself in the dream—a fragile person, made of glass, who could tolerate, without fragmenting or breaking, being near his ill grandparent's bed. While he was in the lift with his grandfather standing beside him, his body, his mind, and his self were fragile yet not fragmented and seemed to be contained by the characters in the lift—those of his childhood—as if they were some kind of skin or container.

The other part of the dream—when he entered the hospital ward and saw his grandfather in bed—implied bringing to the consulting-room all his pain at his grandfather's illness. I then said that the most important aspect of the dream was that he was going to visit his grandfather and say goodbye to him for the first time in his life. The patient replied, "I never attached any importance to my grandfather's death, and I always thought I hadn't cared at all. I never thought I had felt anything."

Later on I told him that perhaps he had never been able to say goodbye to his grandfather because no one had helped him to cope with his sorrow and pain. We mentioned the fact that his mother had suffered a severe depression and that his father became quite depressed and isolated after the grandfather's death. Then I told him, "Here you seem to have found a place from which you can start to work through this painful childhood mourning." I added that the dream seemed to reflect his belief that he was a fragile being made of crystal, who could become fragmented any moment.

In later sessions Charles returned to this dream, and thus I could realize and interpret to him that the parking place also meant he had found in his treatment—his father always drove him to my consulting-room—a place where he could park his mind; he could get into a building and make a long journey in his inner world, which was represented by the lift space where he made an analytic journey accompanied by all his inner objects (Ogden, 1986).

Some time afterward I was able to get a full and more detailed picture of his mother. The patient described her as a domineering, demanding woman who could not tolerate untidiness and was intrusive but also affectionate as well as basically depressive. At one time he described his father as a man who made a very sad face if he was contradicted and, above all, when another child was in the house, someone who had to be taken care of.

Two dreams about identity and transference

On a Monday that same month Charles brought a very important dream, which condensed the transference and his life history, particularly as regards the loss of personal identity. He entered the room dishevelled. He had not shaved and wore an expression of astonishment. He said he had had a nightmare from which he woke up screaming with anxiety. This was the dream:

"You were in front of me, but you were some kind of demon, and with different features. Your hair was stiff, long, and standing out of your forehead . . . your eyes were strange. Then we spoke about something that frightened me. And here is the most terrifying part: my face began to change, to transform, it was gradually changing and started being another face. My face was changing, my cheeks, my mouth, my nose, very slowly—the feeling was so vivid, this feeling of becoming transformed, that I woke up screaming and sweating and I woke up my whole family. They all ran into my room and stayed with me." Then he added something quite significant: "But that person didn't do anything to me; I realized he hadn't done anything to me."

After asking him about some details of the dream, I interpreted that the dream condensed in a plastic way everything that was taking place in his relationship with me. He felt that receiving an interpretation designed to make him think meant I was going to change his identity, represented in the dream by his face; he believed I could model his face, as if I were a monster. "Besides, it accounts for the transference crisis you are going through and the psychotic episode last year, when you thought people brought things by means of the dream, your fear of my wanting to change your identity."

I emphasized his final remark, for I saw it as a sign of hope. The end, which he added on waking, was really quite hopeful. After all, in the dream he expressed his terror of receiving something from me, but he also said "[he] didn't do anything to me."

The dream was analysed in the course of several sessions, partly because it was a key dream showing his history and his identity crisis and partly, too, because after several days the patient was still under the impact of the nightmare. I pointed out that bringing the dream was a way of showing greater confidence in me; more precisely, it was proof of his confidence in me as an analyst capable of containing him with his nightmares and fears.

A week later Charles narrated a new dream. *He had written a piece of music and taken it to his music teacher. He felt happy at having composed it, but his teacher made so many corrections that the composition was transformed into something quite different. In the end, only the corrections made by the music teacher were left. He was unhappy, for his own musical composition had disappeared.* I asked him for clarification and more details of each of the different parts of the dream.

I interpreted the dream to be a continuation of the previous one about my transforming or changing his face. Here I was the teacher to whom he brought his thoughts and personal ideas. But he was afraid I was actually changing his ideas, probably mistaking an interpretation, which I gave him to stimulate his thinking, for corrections that would modify or do away with his way of thinking or, more important, modify his identity. This was the most urgent or important aspect of what was taking place in his transference relationship with me. He brought something that formed part of his own thinking or personal identity and thought that I corrected it or modified it, or that I ultimately turned him into a piece of me. He feared that when he left my consulting-room he would not have his own thinking but the corrections—the personality and identity of

Rosenfeld, his music teacher. The patient's associations confirmed the adequacy of this interpretive line.

For many weeks Charles used a monotonous, repetitive, obsessive language, devoid of emotion and abounding in empty, hollow words. In my notes at that time I wrote that, apart from conveying boredom and monotony, it included new elements: complaints and reproaches. This went on for several weeks, until one day in the sixth month of treatment he brought a dream that seems to announce the return of a split or psychotic part. This is how the patient told it:

> I saw flying saucers coming closer from afar, from space. Extraterrestrial beings like those in the movie E. T. came down. I felt terrified when I saw the flying saucers coming closer from outer space and even more terrified when the extraterrestrial beings began to come near.

After asking him for clarification and associations, I interpreted the flying saucers and extraterrestrial beings to be an unknown part of himself that had been previously dissociated, projected far from him, into another galaxy or space far removed from his mind. I suggested it was a disturbed or crazy part that he could not recognize as his own.

The dream shows the mental functioning of the patient's most regressed or disturbed part. This dream about extraterrestrial beings reappeared in treatment, but with a significant difference: as the extraterrestrial beings came closer, they were no longer terrifying and not so hostile. But this corresponded to the second version of the dream, not the first. The patient's mental dynamics seem to be as follows: Charles made massive splittings and projected those contents outside (Klein, 1930; Segal, 1988). The dream led to my feeling worried about the possible renewed invasion of the patient's mental apparatus by the psychotic part.

Clinical considerations about these dreams

In the dream of the flying saucers, I chose to interpret the dynamics of the patient's inner world (the return of the parts of the self that had been projected). In the two other dreams I chose, instead, the transference dynamics. We might say that the fact that the patient can bring dreams to the session may be conceptualized as his first attempt at differentiating between inner world and outer world.

As regards the first dream (in which Charles is with his grandfather), we may assume that the patient thus brought his libidinal bond with his grandfather; perhaps he was looking for an affectionate, infantile bond.

We might try to compare the dream of the transformation of the face and the dream of the musical composition. In the former the patient expressed modification through his body; in the latter there was a more symbolic intermediary element. There, the musical score involves primitive verbal language (Avenburg, personal communication, 1992). The patient seemed to distance himself from his body, that is, he shifted to another level of representation. The first dream corresponded instead to a narcissistic or hypochondriacal level (Ahumada, 1990; López, 1985). In the dream of the body made of glass (when he visited his grandfather) there was a more obvious bodily fantasy, which may be a hypochondriacal fantasy.

Embracing the father

This stage was followed by many weeks during which Charles made detailed, obsessive remarks. On several occasions he brought copybooks in which he had written down his ideas—obsessive ruminations about a question, an idea, or a problem. On other occasions he read what he had written in the course of the psychotic episode. The patient came regularly to his sessions, often accompanied by one or another member of his family, but sometimes alone.

I interpreted his obsessive narrations as logical defences against disorganization.

One day, after a session in which he had managed to communicate well with me, Charles introduced some changes into his obsessive language or system. He told me he had felt weak while walking along the street and so had held on to his father's shoulder. "That frightened me a lot", he said. "After I had embraced Dad, I felt paralysed. My left foot became paralysed." I interpreted, "You wanted to hold on to your Dad's shoulder, as a child would. The boy inside you wished to embrace Dad." I added, "Perhaps you were so frightened because you thought that was something a boy would not do that you paralysed a part of you that you regard as a female part."

Later on in that session I interpreted: "It's as if inside you a boy had said, 'I want to be helped by Dad, that's all.' But you got frightened and so you paralysed the female part that frightens you every time you come close to Dad or to a man. I, Rosenfeld, am a man, and perhaps what happened to you has to do with the fear of your coming close to me."

It seemed to be clear that intense homosexual fantasies were expressed through bodily sensations. Another theoretical subject for discussion has to do with the analytic technique to interpret the emergence of sexual and hysterical levels that may coincide with pregenital levels in many patients. Yet another subject for theoretical discussion is the analyst's choice of the patient's developmental level he will interpret at that moment.

The rest of the session was devoted to showing Charles that his expression of affection towards his father was also a way of communicating with me, that he wanted to embrace me, to show me his affection, but this frightened him. I said that perhaps even thinking of me and remembering me with fondness outside the session might be experienced as frightening.

Psychotic episode

During the week in which the patient became disorganized, his communication with me was characterized by greater emotion and affection. A few days before we had seen that he could embrace his father, an unusual show of affection that had shaken him.

One day the patient wondered out loud, "I asked my family therapist to kill me, then take my neck strongly." I told him again that what he actually wanted was to have someone kill the crazy part he had inside that was controlling him, but that he should take into account that he was asking a psychoanalyst to do it, both the previous night and at that moment. "Besides, what you want to kill is a part that believes it is a woman if it gets close to me, like when it got close to Dad and embraced him." Then I added, "But

I will try to cure you with words. There's no need to kill the crazy and female parts."

In the last minutes of the session the patient recovered a new infantile memory. "Do you know something, Doctor? When I was a child, they made me wear a tuxedo when the school kids had their birthday parties, and sometimes I wore white gloves to go to the party so I wouldn't get dirty." Then he added, "I feel as if I were far from here, I feel stiff." I said to him, "It's as if every time you tell me something, you get frightened and end up drawing away, feeling that you're far away. It's as if you were repeating with me your own history with your Dad."

The crisis

In the following session, the patient was connected to me. He seemed to be far more relaxed, his body less rigid, and he told me he had had sexual intercourse with his girlfriend. Then he said that something strange had happened to him, bodily sensations he had never had before, and he had been frightened, "as if they were frightening sensations or coming from outside". He added, "It happened while I was having an orgasm during intercourse." (I want to clarify that up to that moment the patient had never mentioned sexual feelings or intercourse.) "The bodily sensations you have now", I told him, "are similar to the dream with the flying saucers and the extraterrestrial beings."

The following day Charles's parents phoned me to say the patient had become disorganized and was very "excited." Charles arrived at my consulting-room that morning terrified and rigid and said, "I'm delusional, I'm psychotic." "I am being telepathically controlled." "I have funny sensations and I'm crazy." "Out there in the street there are men who are half men and half women. . . . I'm delusional, I'm being telepathically controlled from outside and I feel funny things all over my body, they are making me feel funny things. . . .

I told him to calm down, that over the previous days and in the last few sessions he had had good, affective communication with me, as perhaps he had never had before. "Perhaps that frightened you", I said. "You have a fantasy about me, a kind of delusion of what's happening to you with me here, and then you project that onto the street and you see what happens to you here in the others. What is happening is something that originates exclusively in your own emotions towards me and what you feel here with me. You've never had such intense affects because you've never allowed that to happen . . . or else you were a boy forced to disguise himself in a tuxedo, rigid all over and having to repress his affects. You think that when you show affection here that implies loss of mental control or some kind of madness. In addition, you imagine, you suppose, that you will turn into a woman if you are affectionate."

In the same session the patient moved the chair and placed his legs—he had his shoes on—on the top of my desk, almost in front of my face. Then he put his feet down, walked around the consulting-room, quite angry, and took some earthenware dishes on which flowerpots stood and broke them violently against the floor.

Later on, having broken the saucers, the patient said, "You are controlling me." And I interpreted, "You believe that this happens just when you remember or think about my interpretations after a session." I emphasized, "You believe that to receive my words is the same as to receive orders. That's why you feel that I am telepathically controlling you from a distance. You think I am directing you telepathically, and perhaps this is because there was a real story with your mother: she directed everything you did and you ended up thinking I would do the same with you." The patient answered, "If I receive an interpretation, then I become the interpretation."

In the evening the patient's parents and the psychiatrist and psychoanalyst in charge of the family therapy got in touch with me and told me about what had happened that day in the course of the family therapy session. Charles became violent: he grabbed his neck and then tried to seize the psychiatrist by the neck. It was the first time he had attacked the psychiatrist physically. Faced with this violent reaction, the psychiatrist gave him an injection to tranquillize him, to which the patient did not object.

I was also told that in the course of that session the patient kept talking about "penises, phalluses, having sexual intercourse with his parents", and insistently repeated that he was "psychotic". In the conversation I had with his mother, she remarked that Charles saw "penises and men everywhere", as if he were having hallucinations. However, he appeared to be calm at that moment, thanks to the tranquillizer.

> In his session with me early the following morning, Charles stated again that he was being influenced and that he was convinced that he was being telepathically directed and that outside, "in the street, men are half men and half women."

> My interventions continued along the interpretative line adopted in the previous sessions. Then he spoke again about "penises and phalluses" and read to me from a book dealing with those subjects. He gave verbal expression to suicidal ideas, which led me to decide upon his immediate hospitalization.

When the session was over, I explained to his parents in his presence that the repeated emergence of a suicidal idea led me to decide to hospitalize Charles.

Hospitalization

In the clinic I spent several hours with the patient to contain his anxiety and disorganization, but I also interpreted his fantasies as an analyst.

> While we were walking to his room, Charles started expressing a delusional fantasy. He repeated again and again, "All this is a lie. You are not doctors and those people down there in the dining-room are neither doctors nor patients."

> When we got to his room, I sat down and Charles sat on the bed as if he were trying it. When he seemed to be feeling more relaxed, he opened the wardrobe to put his clothes there: that reassured me because it meant that he had accepted staying at the clinic and his hospitalization. Suddenly something unexpected happened, something that shook me and the staff deeply.

> When the patient opened the wardrobe to put his clothes there, he took the hangers out and shouted: "You have lied to me. . . . I know that all the people down there are actors. This is the unquestionable evidence: this is the Ritz Hotel."

Deeply shaken, I jumped up. At the same time the doctor at the door came in because he had heard the shouting. The patient was beside himself but triumphant, for he had corroborated his delusional ideas and the omnipotence characteristic of psychosis. He took the hangers out and showed them to me, one by one. As a matter of fact, the hangers really did belong to the Ritz Hotel: the words "Ritz Hotel—Buenos Aires" were written on all of them.

It is hard for me to describe what took place between the moment when the patient saw the hangers and shouted his belief that he had seen his delusion of omnipotence confirmed by external evidence and the moment when the doctor came in and explained to Charles that a foreign patient had been in that room, someone who before his hospitalization had stayed at the Ritz Hotel and must have brought those hangers with him. The doctor repeated this explanation for approximately half an hour while Charles listened attentively. Later on, when he had calmed down a bit, we went through all the rooms in the clinic to show him the hangers in all the wardrobes. Fortunately, the name of the clinic was written on all of them.

Nevertheless, the search for corroboration continued, and at one point Charles said that the woman he had seen in the dining-room was not a patient and asked us to show us the rooms where the women were staying. The head nurse asked the female patients' permission to show him the rooms and then told Charles he could see them. The patient calmed down somewhat.

I told him he needed to know that the female area—that is, his own female parts—was far away, not mixed with his own male part. I insisted he needed to corroborate that he would sleep with his male part: that is, in the men's area.

This was the shocking episode in which the patient thought he had found external evidence corroborating his psychotic omnipotence. We went back to his room, and I stayed there to accompany him in accepting and elaborating his hospitalization. When I left, after a mutual "See you tomorrow", Charles asked me not to close the door between his room and the room of one of the clinic doctors.

* * *

On one of the parents' visits to the hospital where the patient was, I was finishing the psychoanalytic session we had on fixed days and timetables, while his mother and father were sitting at the waiting-room.

I approached to greet them and heard the mother says to the patient: "You look as if you are cured, you are cured, you do not need to be here, you are already cured, your face looks cured." This was repeated several times.

To my great surprise, the patient answered: "Mother, I'm very ill, and I'm here because I want to get well." I only remarked: "Try not to confuse a patient who discovers what is ill in himself and wants to get well."

A couple of weeks after this incident the patient was no longer hospitalized, and he was to coming to individual sessions to my consulting-room. The patient had two sessions in silence but then, in a soft, broken voice, he said:

"My mother forbade me to tell you ... [long silence] ... but my mother drives me to a wild doctor that gives magic potions and performs magic with her hands and Tarot cards." He went on to say: "my mother prohibited. ... " ... "but she said the wild doctor would cure me better than you. ... "

Luckily I could keep in silence my countertransference emotional reactions (which I tried to write down after the session), and, calming down, I told the patient I wanted to have an interview with him together with his parents to speak about this.

We decided to have the interview together with the family psychoanalyst. I asked the mother whether what Charles had told me was true: "that you drove him to a wild doctor saying she is better than me". Her only reaction was to shout at the young man, "Why did you tell him!"

In front of Charles, I told both the mother and the father: (1) "You cannot stand the idea of stopping to manage Charles' head, as if he were a puppet and you the only one to manage his mind." (2) "You make him believe I am stupid and inept and the only one that is useful is the mother." (3) "It's the same thing you do with Charles and his father: you make him believe his father is stupid, an idiot, as you make him believe I'm stupid, an idiot, and don't not know how to cure." (4) "That's how you drive Charles crazy." (5) "You are jealous your son has become independent of you, and you want to go on treating him as a part of your body and of your mind."

At the next individual session I asked the patient what had he thought and whether he had understood what I had said. He answered that at first he had been frightened by the violent reaction of his father when I showed he was also treated as a fool. He added: "I could not sleep the whole night, but I understood much more about how my family works."

The later evolution of the patient was good, in the sense that he continued with his sessions at the consulting-room. But the mother was over-jealous when he applied for a scholarship in a foreign country to distance himself from his family.

Theoretical and technical remarks

My purpose in this chapter has been to show how I interpret and how I use theoretical models in psychoanalytic practice—specifically, in the technique with a psychotic patient—and to describe my intense countertransference feelings in connection with him. In this particular case one important technical requisite had to be taken into account: the need to avoid being intrusive or invasive, like the patient's mother.

With a patient who has had a delusional episode (my patient thought I was telepathically directing him), interpretations should not be rigidly stated but suggested in the interrogative, because he can take interpretative statements to be orders he has to carry out—for instance: "Do you think these flying saucers coming from outside could be a part of you? What do you think? Could it be something like that?"

Another technical aspect to be taken into account is that the analyst has to be cautious and must avoid the early use of words the patient can distort and interpretations about the oedipal and sexual levels.

I suggest avoiding words that the patient may take as definitions of identity, accusations, or seductions. The use of the word "homosexual" may be risky when prematurely made. At the beginning the therapist should say that the patient feels "weak or not very strong if he trusts the therapist", "he feels fragile" or "feminine" and so "less manly". Only after many months do I use the word "homosexual", and only if the patient brings the obvious kind of material in a dream, a fantasy, or a delusion. The same applies to aggressive or murderous fantasies directed at the therapist or at the internal objects, paternal or maternal.

It is true that these elements—homosexuality and aggression—are there from the beginning of treatment, but I suggest that we must be very careful when interpreting them. I waited a long time before I made a direct interpretation of this patient's aggression, and I did so only on the basis of a dream in which the patient crashed and damaged his mother's car. Incidentally, at that point I learned that the car was in his mother's name. In the dream the patient was accompanied by a man.

It is important to note that throughout my analytic work with this patient I tried to bring together the fragmented, dispersed, and projected aspects of the self—an extremely difficult task indeed.

The analyst makes a great effort to integrate his countertransference feelings with his thoughts and his theoretical background. As Schafer (personal communication, 1993) points out, we can very seldom leave behind all the theories in which we have been trained; we have our own internal map, and we use it in the course of the analysis. I could add that we accept and use theories on the basis of our affects and our own life histories, and our infantile histories are probably as important as what we have learned from books and teachers. I accept theories and use them as an internal map, but I accept them on the basis of my affective and emotional background. Perhaps I have not learned from theories more than from my grandmother in order to construct a model and be able to listen to, understand, and think about a human being who is talking of his life and his feelings. I think my personal history determines the way in which I make use of my internal theoretical map.

I have tried to show how we can apply some of the theories we employ in the psychoanalytic treatment of patients whose transference shows regressed characteristics, also described as psychotic or delusional.

I believe theories do not change patients. They are valuable to explain psychopathology more or less richly or broadly. What theories do change is the explanation, but not the patient's actual pathology or his clinical picture.

I do believe that a valuable aspect of this chapter is the detailed clinical account and the way in which it shows the practical and technical use of theoretical models. Searles (1979) says that theories are useful or not depending on the moment the patient is going through. Green (1986), an important author in the field of psychoanalytic theory, is another clinician who has dealt with this question.

A true master in the investigation of severely disturbed or psychotic patients, Boyer (1982a) says something very interesting about impasse situations and countertransference:

> The type of psychoanalytic impasse described above is due to a combination of factors which result in a specific kind of interaction between the patient's psychopathology and the analyst's ego ideal and self-representation. In each of the cited instances, the impasse was transient because the analysts were able to resolve the countertransference reactions which had created the impasses. The impasse arose in each instance because the analyst sought to remove his own discomfort by expecting the patient to change the manifestations of this psychopathology.
>
> The question can be raised whether it is inevitable that the analyst feel disturbed. Because of particular character adaptations, it may be necessary for the patient to seek to provoke certain reactions in the analyst as the transference relationship develops. But should the patient be allowed to succeed? If one were familiar with such situations and could anticipate them, perhaps it would be possible to simply analyze them without feeling personal upheaval. [p. 83]

In his contribution to *Master Clinicians*, Boyer (1990a) deals with the developments of psychoanalytic technique in connection with countertransference. His view coincides with mine when he stresses the importance of using countertransference in the psychoanalytic treatment of severely regressed patients. I would like to stress once more that, in my view, the future of the investigation of psychotic or severely disturbed patients depends on two factors: first, the therapist's personal ability to contain the intense affects and emotions aroused by this type of patient, and, second, the detection and decoding of the messages the patient sends us via verbal means, nonverbal means, and communications systems of which we know very little as yet. These patients force us to experience intense emotions that they cannot feel or express in words. Our task as therapists is to decode these emotions, in the course of supervision analysis or personal analysis, in order to be able to adequately discriminate the personal aspects from what is projected or communicated by the patients through different means.

I believe this hypothesis changes the theory of insight and mental space. In the treatment of psychotic patients insight sometimes takes place first in the therapist's mind and not in the patient's, because the patient's mental space may be projected onto the therapist's mind. This is part of a broader theory with which I try to account for the violence of schizophrenic patients. Sometimes these patients attack the therapist, hitting him or her violently and mercilessly because their perceptual apparatuses have been projected into the therapist's mind. What they attack, or actually try to murder, therefore, is their own perceptual apparatus placed in another space, in someone else's head, when they detect painful experiences they cannot tolerate.

The following quotation from Freud (1910d) helps us to reflect nowadays, especially as regards the treatment of severely disturbed patients: "We have noticed that no psychoanalyst goes further than his own complexes and internal resistances permit. . . . " (p. 145).

In this chapter countertransference is used in the sense of certain feelings, certain affects, that the therapist experiences when confronting facts specific to the transference field and to his or her emotional relationship with the patient. It is therefore a signal—just a signal—that needs to be decoded, reflected upon, and finally evaluated by the therapist to be better understood, and not projected. The therapist must try to translate into words the feelings evoked by the patient through preverbal language, or through the phonology or music of his or her voice. Above all, he or she must differentiate these feelings from personal neurotic problems.

Countertransference is a phenomenon that can shed light on certain elements of clinical psychoanalysis if it is kept in mind during all investigations. In my opinion it is an indispensable tool, especially for very perturbed or psychotic patients.

> Occasionally it may fail to express itself overtly as a fact or a phenomenon, and stems from an a priori methodological definition of our objectives. If we take black-and-white pictures, we might say that colour does not exist; but, of course, colour pictures also exist. The same happens with the greater richness provided by the proper use of countertransference. [Rosenfeld, 1992b, p. 83]

CHAPTER SIX

Autistic encapsulation

T he theories of autistic encapsulation in one part of the mind, which also "preserves" parts of the infantile world and the individual's identity and relationships, as we shall see in the clinical material, were proposed by me at the Hamburg Congress in 1985.

The hypothesis differs from Frances Tustin's. My proposal is that these mechanisms, used as defences in autistic children, can be used again in parts of the mind by adult patients. Unlike Tustin, I show that they are useful for "preserving". In this chapter, I also discuss the importance of autistic mechanisms or defences in patients who are drug addicts.

Another part of this chapter shows the importance of autistic mechanisms or defences in patients who receive organ transplants. These patients provoke sensory stimuli in the body—"bodily sensations"—as defensive ways of filling the emptiness that they feel in a part of their body whose original organ has been extracted.

Additionally, I would like to present to the reader a new problem: We are currently receiving cases in psychoanalytic practice of people who have undergone vital organ transplants and who have consequently developed a hypochondria—and, at times, a psychosis and psychosomatic illnesses—based on a specific psychodynamic mechanism. These patients with psychosomatic disturbances generally present with autistic mechanisms. Like autistic children, they are enveloped in a world of bodily and tactile sensations. Their psychosomatic symptoms give this type of patient a "sense of being" that is similar to the bodily sensations autistic children attempt to achieve by pressing a part of their body against a "hard" object. This use of bodily sensations—the disappearance or annihilation of a primitive identity—makes these patients difficult to cure. Even in patients who seem to make use of more "healthy" or neurotic mechanisms, it can be very useful to look for autistic pockets. It is also interesting to observe how these very primitive autistic pockets are hidden by apparently sexual or neurotic behaviour (Tustin, 1986, 1990b).

As Tustin points out (1988), autistic patients are fearful, despite having this "protective shell", because they feel there is a hole in it. She also states that even parts of their bodies can be used by these children as "autistic objects" that create a cluster of sensations that provide them with the illusion of being impenetrable, all-powerful, safe, and protected. I think today that the "holes" in the body that adult patients experience might be filled with psychosomatic disturbances. Just as the autistic children described by Tustin cover over the "holes" through the use of autistic mechanisms, psychosomatic symptoms with bodily sensations might be used to provoke a "sense of being", a very primitive experience of identity.

Organ transplant and autistic bodily sensations

I have revised my ideas on this case. I believe that, with the revolutionary surgical breakthroughs of recent years, patients do in reality lose very vital parts of their own bodies. To cover up this loss, the patient creates a "protective shell", just as autistic children do, to cover up the "black hole" left after the event of the loss. As a consequence, patients with transplants often present hypochondriacal symptoms. My thought today, after treating and supervising a number of cases of organ transplant patients, is that these patients repeat the same evolution and mechanisms as described by Francis Tustin in her studies of cases of infantile autism. Autistic children suffer a terrible depression after their birth, because they have the sensation that they have lost a vital part of their bodies and that vital part which has been lost is represented as a "black hole". The "black hole" is so terrifying that it needs to be covered with a "protective shell".

When an adult undergoes a vital organ transplant, he consequently needs to cover the loss, and he does so by developing a hypochondria, the hypochondria being a sort of mental protective covering that will keep the mind occupied with rumination and repetition on what has happened to the bodily part that has been separated. If this covering of the hole is not successful, then these patients will become psychotic and delusional. My conclusion is that these transplant patients seem to repeat the same defensive manoeuvres and mechanisms as autistic children who move from autism to psychosis.

In my book *The Psychotic: Aspects of the Personality* (Rosenfeld 1992b) I presented the case of a heart-transplant patient about which I now have new thoughts. I would like to establish clearly two aspects that are evident in the following clinical case: the transference psychosis and delusions—expressed in the transference–countertransference interplay—and the role of the father in the evolution of this patient. These two elements, within the framework of the sessions, allowed the therapist to detect the rejection of the transplanted organ.

In the clinical material we can see how the patient sometimes became his own father: he imitated the latter's voice, his accent, and his mannerisms. At other times he became his own son, who had died at the age of 19. He believed that he was resurrecting his son as he carried inside himself the transplanted heart of a young man of the same age. At one point during the treatment he played the father taking care of his son, and it was then that he best took care of the heart of the young man he fantasized to be his own son, and for whom he was caring.

"Hamlet"

The patient, whom we shall call "Hamlet", was 51 years of age and had sought psychoanalytic treatment after being told that he had to undergo cardiac surgery, with an indication for a heart transplant. He was in a state of extreme anxiety and despair, and in this condition he began treatment. He appeared to be an intelligent, tuned-in, thinking person, with sensitive feelings. He had divorced and remarried, and he had a 10-year-old daughter. One of Hamlet's sons had died a few years earlier, at the age of 19; before that, Hamlet's father had died as well. His mother had died when he was 2 years old. She had been very ill for a year after the birth of his younger brother.

Hamlet was prepared for cardiac surgery; he was waiting for the moment when a donor heart was obtained for transplant. The donor turned out to be a young athlete who had died in a car accident. After surgery, once he was authorized to leave the special care unit, Hamlet resumed analysis.

In one of the sessions, the patient greeted the analyst in his hospital room, shouting: "Out, you intruder! I want no intruders, you're invading me!" During this episode the patient was in a state of delusion, in which the analyst was one of the intruders who invaded him. Let it be clear that this delusion did not appear on the day following the transplant, nor immediately upon his leaving the intensive care unit, but, rather, when he was about to be discharged from the hospital. The analyst had been seeing Hamlet every day, and when Hamlet was near his recovery and discharge, he suddenly and surprisingly received the therapist in this state of delusion, which enhanced the impact on the therapist. (The therapist made a note after the session to the effect that he believed that this delusion might indicate a rejection of the therapist in the transference and that he feared that it might presage or indicate Hamlet's rejection of the graft.)

I believe that the patient was projecting into the external space—into the hospital room or the consulting-room—and into the transference the unfolding of his inner world something that in a persecutory or delusional way was felt to have got into his body. The room seemed to represent his body, in which the alien heart or the analyst were intruders (Searles, 1960). It is in this space that we suppose he rejected the therapist. Could it be possible that he is also rejecting the introjection of the primitive protecting figures of his childhood, possibly his mother-the-breast, and his father? Is it the spectre, the ghost, who comes in as an intruder, the ghost of his mother or that of his son? Is it Hamlet's ghost that is reappearing?

In addition, we believe that he was reacting to this very special situation in the same way that he experienced his childhood bonds or introjections. The following day, a routine heart biopsy showed signs of rejection, and the cardiologist asked the therapist to prepare the patient psychologically to receive the news of the rejection, which implied that his discharge would be delayed. (We are not saying here that psychoanalysis can always detect transplant rejections. We are only presenting an experience interpreted as a hypothesis that the patient was rejecting part of himself, of his new identity, or something coming from outside, which was very dangerous and was invading him.)

The following session began as follows: The patient said that in the hospital, with the doctors and the nurses, he felt that he was being taken care of, since they came rushing as soon as he called. Using the same words as the analyst, he added that the prospect of going home made him feel helpless, unprotected, and in danger. The therapist interpreted that the prospect of going home also meant that he was well and getting better, that he would rejoin his family environment, and, above all, that he would be reunited with his small daughter, whom he missed very much.

In another part of the session, the therapist interpreted that the small daughter represented the infantile part of the patient, which had been left unprotected. The patient went on to say that "the intruder was inside him and that he had to perform mental immobilization exercises and send messages from his mind to his sick heart in order to attain harmony between his mind and his heart." (The similarities with some phases of the Schreber case are remarkable.) The therapist told the patient that the intruding heart was the healthy heart.

After a period of recovery, the patient was discharged. From October onward he was able to go out, walk, and attend the consulting-room. The insomnia that had afflicted him became less serious. Sometimes he came: (1) with the more adult part of his self; (2) as a trembling—2-year-old—child, as he had come during the beginning of his treatment; (3) as another part of the patient with his omnipotent self; (4) with his adolescent part; (5) confused with his adolescent son, whom he brought back to life and resurrected inside himself, as he carried inside him the heart of a young man whom he believed to be his son, or the heart of his son; (6) looking like his father, when he imitated his voice, his accent, and his verbal mannerisms; or (7) as the mother, in the transferential dynamics, projected into the therapist, who thus assumed the role of the mother (or of the grandmother, who had lovingly taken care of him as a child).

It was at this time that the material about the patient's feminine aspects, which he mistook for homosexuality, became clearer: This was a total or narcissistic early identification with his mother, which became more intense two years later, when she died. We could see that for him, searching for and being with his mother was in fact like becoming and being the mother–feminine–woman. In moments of regression, this was the way in which he could find his mother, though at the expense of feeling tied up and confused with a woman. His defence before this had consisted in: (1) promiscuous sexual escapades—particularly some years earlier—to prove to himself that he had a penis and that he was a man for many women; and (2) appearing as a child with an omnipotent self—trying to prove that he needed nothing from anyone—the breast, the mother, the therapist. All this was mixed up with an intense homosexual panic.

Autistic bodily sensations in drug addicts

I will propose a new hypothesis, based on autistic mechanisms in drug-addicted patients.

The patients Type "C" needs to provoke bodily sensations with a drug.

In my book *The Psychotic: Aspects of the Personality* (Rosenfeld, 1992b), I proposed a classification of different types of drug addicts that may be useful for the evaluation of the clinical and prognostic status of these patients as well as the therapeutic approach. (See the section on "Categories of Drug Abuse" in Chapter 3.)

"Mr A"

One of my patients, Mr A, had a mother who had suffered from a severe post-partum depressive state. She had then suffered from another depressive state after the death of her father, the grandfather of my patient, when Mr A was 5 years old.

During the first interview with him and one member of his family, it came to my patient's attention and to mine that the grandfather had committed suicide. During the treatment, in one session, Mr A. showed me a photograph album. The photographs exhibited the mental state of the mother very clearly. In one we could see the mother lying on the floor in a depressive state, looking at nothing, while a 3-year-old Mr A tried with one hand to reach his father, who is standing behind her.

In another case, discussed in a clinical seminar, a 5-year-old girl, diagnosed as autistic, provoked bodily sensations by pressing her tongue around her lips. As she repeated this constantly, her lips became very sore, and it was difficult for her to eat. She had to be put in an intensive care unit. She also refused to eat because she preferred her own bodily sensations, with which she felt protected from dangers in the outside world.

In general, patients in Category C are children with autistic features who survive by creating their own sensation-dominated world. However, the adaptation of these patients is very fragile. Faced with any kind of external or internal catastrophe, they try to repeat their early autistic functioning by means of drug consumption or other corporeal activities that provoke bodily sensations.

In the case of Mr A, his mother had died when he was 12 years old. One year later, he began to experiment with drugs, apparently in an effort to deny this unbearably painful situation but also to find, in the drugs, his bodily sensations and to live inside them, as in his early childhood. I see this kind of patient not just as a drug addict, but as a *survivor*.

Even with good treatment and some hospitalization, one cannot always be successful with these patients. They are prisoners of a pragmatic paradox: They use drugs to obtain very primitive autistic sensations which seem necessary for them to survive and be protected, as in a "shell". They fear that if they cannot obtain these sensations through drugs, they will lose all sense of identity and will disappear. However, if they continue with their level of drug consumption, they become more intoxicated each day, and finally they may die. This is the real pragmatic paradox: Whatever they may decide, whether to abandon drug use of to continue with it, will always be wrong for them.

Autistic encapsulation to preserve childhood and identity

I would like to introduce the use of the concept of autistic encapsulation in the treatment of survivors of the Nazi persecution. These are patients who used autistic mechanisms as a way of preserving childhood memories and identity. I will present a summary of one case to show how Tustin's theory applies.

"Mario"

The patient, Mario, who was over 40 years old, looked younger than his years. He was tall, dark-haired, and athletic-looking, in spite of which his fear, anxiety, and withdrawal were obvious. In the first interview, he spoke about his problem: A stomach pain had returned. His physician had diagnosed gastric ulcer and advised him to start psychoanalytic treatment, which Mario did. He was a typical representative of the Jewish–Spanish Sephardic community of the Bulgarian city in which they were born. Roustchouk, on the Lower Danube, was a wonderful city for a child. People of very different origins lived there together and spoke seven or eight different languages. When asked about his father, Mario said he was a gentle, affectionate man whom everybody loved and who frequently used to play with him. He also remembered that his father used to make fun of him when he could not pronounce certain words correctly.

His first memories concerning fear dated back to his eighth year of life, at which time the Germans had bombed Roustchouk. Mario recalled blood, mutilated bodies, death and terror. The Nazis were looking for his father, but Mario and he left the city disguised as Moslems. They reached the Dalmatian coast, but Mario's father was arrested there. Luckily, he fell into the hands of the Italian army and was set free. The Italians and Italy had since then become an admired symbol. Mario and his father ran away to Trieste, where the "men in black" tied them with chains and took them to the city of Turin, where they were released and then lodged. After that, Mario lived alone in an orphanage. Those months were like long years for him (Rosenfeld, 1997, 2005).

Some time after that, he arrived in Buenos Aires, where a relative secured a job for him in a small factory. In the meantime he had learned that his grandparents and two of his mother's brothers had been killed in Bulgaria. He was over 30 years old when he had his first sexual relationship.

During his first three years of analysis, the patient preserved his apparent formal adjustment, his pseudo-identity, and his narrative–

obsessive linguistic style describing real facts and speaking about his commitment to his job.

While I supervised this case, Mario's therapist and I attempted various hypotheses on technical approaches in order to get in touch with the encapsulated or supposedly dissociated areas. One of these approaches was to suggest that, since one of the following sessions coincided with the most important Jewish religious festivity—Atonement Day, or Yom Kippur—the therapist might make it clear that if the patient did not want to come to his session, he did not have to—that is, his therapist would respect his being a Jew and that he did not have to hide again.

Three sessions later, something completely new happened: The material brought by the patient showed how important his Jewish identity was for him. This had not become manifest before; it seemed to have been encapsulated and kept apart, preserved by the patient, as well as he could, within his self. In this session, he remembered the time when he used to ride on his grandfather's shoulders and was filled by the peculiar smell of his grandfather's hair. He went as far as to say: "I seem to smell it in the session." Then he told the therapist he had watched "Holocaust" on television and described an episode in which the father of the family in the film met a brother, and they both walked together along the railway tracks.

At that moment, the patient stopped. His mind seemed to go blank, he remained silent, he skipped the next scene, and he started speaking about another part of the film. The therapist, who had seen "Holocaust", pointed out his mistake to him, saying that he had stopped, remained silent, and then gone on talking after skipping a whole scene in which the father walked with a man called Moses. The patient's tone of voice suffered an abrupt change and, deeply impressed, he said: "Doctor, you're right. I've just remembered my name is *Moses*." The patient had lived in Argentina for more than 30 years, and in that time that name had never reached his consciousness, nor had he ever spoken about it or mentioned it at home. He was 14 when he arrived, and it was as if, ever since then, part of his identity had remained encapsulated; now, after the long hibernation, it had emerged again, well preserved, in the course of a session. Deeply moved and trying to overcome his own surprise, his therapist asked: "But then, your name isn't Mario but Moses?" "Doctor, I have just remembered, they used to call me Misha, as a diminutive of Moshe."

In another session, the patient reported that he had attended an important event in the Jewish tradition: the celebration, known as Bar Mitzvah, of his partner's 13-year-old son. Obviously moved, the patient said he had found himself crying at the Synagogue. He added that he had felt frightened and that, as in his dreams, he was suddenly filled with emotions and memories: Roustchouk, voices calling him Misha, an image of himself on his grandfather's shoulders, the strong smell of his grandfather's hair.

Then he told the therapist: "I will never recover that name, because the registrar's office where my true name is written down was destroyed, burned down by a bomb." The patient remained over-whelmed by deep emotions for the rest of the session. Childhood feelings and memories connected with his father, prior to the Nazi persecution, also began to emerge. This made it possible to deal with the mourning over his father's death from another perspective, for instance the memory of some mischief. When he was a child, Mario had pulled away the chair as his father was about to sit down, so that he would fall.

The 1982 war between Argentina and Great Britain over the Falkland Islands aroused feelings of exacerbated terror in Mario–Moshe. Although in the course of the session he said, "This is too much for a child", it was our belief that he now had new and better resources to face this war as well as the kidnapping and abduction of people in the streets of Buenos Aires during the military regime, which always reminded him of the day his father was taken away and sent to jail.

Very early childhood memories cropped up suddenly and in a dis-orderly way. The patient himself realized that there was a "hole", a gap, in his earliest childhood. One day he asked his mother what had happened in his early years in the town of Roustchouk. The mother told him facts and anecdotes, among them one in which a neighbour gave him a present. The patient, in a deeply regressed state during the session, unwittingly spoke in Italian. In this way

he expressed, in a very concrete manner, the linguistic regression
he allowed himself. And, as the poet says:

He has now reached the end of his journey, he takes
Off his veils and
Clarifies the twenty years of silence elapsed under his
Own shadow. He could not
Have revealed so much if he had not remained
Silent for so long. . . .

Elias Canetti, Territoire de l'homme

Psychosomatic problem
based on autistic bodily sensations

"Clarisse"

To illustrate, I will here present a short vignette: the case of a patient
I will call Clarisse. This patient tried to maintain a tenuous "sense of
being" and a primitive sense of identity by provoking bodily sensations. I believe that this was the only way she was able to feel that she
existed.

Clarisse was 24 years old when she was sent to me by a colleague
for psychoanalytic treatment. She arrived in my office looking so
untidy that she gave the impression that she was psychotic. She told
me she was under psychiatric treatment and that she was receiving
medication since a transient psychosis, which had begun when she was
undergoing treatment at a weight loss clinic.

Her father came with her to the first interview, and he told to me
that Clarisse had a delusion in which she felt that men were following
her. In the clinic, she had felt that one of the male nurses was pursuing
her. Both Clarisse and her father also mentioned that she frequently
wet her bed at night.

Clarisse was black and, when she started treatment, she explained
to me that her biological mother was black and from another country.
Clarisse had been adopted by a white family. Her adoptive parents
were divorced when she was 14, so now she lived with her father in
Buenos Aires. When she was 11, something very important had happened to her. She had moved from a quite distant province to Buenos
Aires, leaving behind her beloved adoptive maternal grandmother.

During our work together, Clarisse often repeated comments that other therapists had told her during previous treatments, as if these were slogans. For example, on one occasion she told me that she masturbated with urine. I was never sure whether she was saying this because it was something she actually did or rather because it was something other people had said it to her.

The patient started to recover memories that I had asked her to bring to the sessions. She remembered how, during her first year of life, she was absolutely immobile, rigid, and silent. She told me that she had weighed 5 pounds at birth and that her adoptive mother was so afraid of hurting such a "tiny thing" that she would never touch her with her bare hands, but only with cotton wool. She never dared to pick up Clarisse. Members of her family remembered Clarisse as lying absolutely rigid and immobile in her cot. She was always silent, with her little arms crossed in front of her chest. It seemed to me that Clarisse had formed a rigid shell in order to protect herself. I interpreted in the session the times when I felt that she was doing the same thing with me in the transference, and I pointed out to her how she always arrived at the sessions absolutely enveloped in a large shawl that she would never take off.

In another session she spoke about the person she loved most in her life: her adoptive grandmother, from whom she was separated at the age of 11 when her family moved to Buenos Aires. At the time of this session, the grandmother was still alive. The grandmother was very affectionate—she had contained Clarisse when she was a child and had held her very close to her in her arms. She always caressed Clarisse. She had been the one to help her get dressed, to help her with her school homework, and to take her for walks. Clarisse repeatedly said: "I love her deeply." I discovered in this session that the patient had felt absolutely empty and that she had suffered a terrible affective catastrophe and loss when she moved to the city, losing daily contact with her adoptive grandmother. As we recovered these events during the session, Clarisse said, "I feel a hole in my soul."

Two months later, Clarisse brought a dream at the beginning of the session. The dream was of *a white geography teacher at Clarisse's primary school*. Clarisse had been the only black child in her school in Buenos Aires. She remembered that this teacher was the only one in whom she could confide, especially with respect to her feelings of loneliness. In her dream, *the teacher had black skin, just as Clarisse does, and not white skin like her adoptive family or her beloved grandmother.* Based on her associations, I told her that in the dream she seemed to transform her grandmother—who was alive at the time, although old and ill—into a young woman with whom she could talk easily, just as she had been able to do before she was 11—the age at which she had moved to Buenos Aires (Kliman, 1998; Rosenfeld, 1992a, 2001b).

I asked Clarisse to remember that in the dream she is a young girl at primary school, before she moved to the city. However, I also interpreted that the teacher could also be her biological mother, represented by the black skin, which was the same colour as Clarisse's own. I added that perhaps the dream appeared today for two reasons: one, because the grandmother was more ill than before, and second, because she felt that she had found—in the therapist—a person to whom she could confide her feelings and emotions.

Since moving to Buenos Aires, the patient had started to provoke sensations within her own body as a way of feeling that she was full rather than empty. She achieved this by compulsive eating and by retaining great quantities of urine in her bladder. After a couple of months I began to understand that her bed-wetting was not of the typical variety—that is, due to loss of control of her bladder—but that she would withhold urine for as long as she could stand it in order to have the sensation of being completely full. Only when she was full and about to burst would she run to the toilet. Often, she would wet her bed in her scramble to get to the bathroom.

In that same session she told me that, during her psychotic episode, she had put on 50 pounds. I interpreted that it was very important for her to feel that she was full up and not empty by retaining urine until she was full to bursting and by eating compulsively in order to feel full. I did not take these actions at a sexual/masturbatory level, but at their most primitive level: to be empty or not empty, full up or not, therefore to exist and to have a "sense of being" or to be annihilated. The patient quickly replied that she also retained faeces and then asked me if this might be for the same reason. I replied that I thought it was and that she had probably been doing this since she was a little girl in order to feel that she was complete.

In the following session Clarisse began to recount more of her experience of the loss of her grandmother. She cried inconsolably throughout the session. She said, in her own words, that she now understood that this loss was the reason why she ate so much and held her urine. I added: "If you don't obtain this sensation in your body, you suppose that you will lose your sense of being, and you will cease to exist."

At the same time, I thought something that I did not mention to the patient: that the bulimia was a way of searching for sensorial experiences. As I write these lines, I am thinking that these bodily sensations are similar to those that autistic children have in early childhood, and that this patient was doing the same, although she was an adult. Although an autistic child will actually insert something hard or metallic into the mouth, ear, or anus, this patient was able to create the same sensations as an adult by retaining faeces or urine or by eating. This was, in my view, her way of provoking sensorial feelings inside her body. On the more primitive level, this patient was trying to survive terrible and painful losses by obtaining a primary sense of identity.

As for Clarisse's psychotic delusion that men were persecuting her, I believe that this was also related to her attempts at survival. In her delusion, she is the centre of the world, the centre of attention of all the men around her. For her, it was better to be the centre of persecution than to feel she had been abandoned to solitude—as a little girl by her biological mother, then by the adoptive mother who would not touch her, and later by her adoptive grandmother.

Clarisse was trying to obtain a very powerful sensation and a sense of omnipotence. Tustin suggested that this state of omnipotence differs from that usually referred to by psychoanalysts. In this case, the patient used part of her own body as an autistic object, which provided the sensation of hardness. An autistic child in the same situation feels invulnerable, impenetrable, armoured, and safe. The "holes" are filled by a cluster of sub-sensations—the autistic shape—and these are comforting and tranquilizing. This is what I believe happened to Clarisse: she used her own body and bodily substances as autistic objects to create sensation shapes, to feel that she was utterly impenetrable and invulnerable and that nothing could destroy her.

When we treat these adult patients, they gradually develop more of a sense of their own existence, and their terrors are mitigated. Using this concept, we can begin to understand many psychosomatic disturbances in a very different way.

Psychotic body image

> Learn this, Thomas,
> And thou shalt prove a shelter to thy friends,
> A hoop of gold to bind thy brothers in
> That the united vessel of their blood. . . .
>
> Shakespeare, *King Henry IV, Part II* (Act IV, Scene 4)

This chapter is a theoretical conceptualization of the body image, based on psychoanalytic psychotherapy with psychotic patients going through acute crises as well as some psychosomatic disturbances. I will try to define and describe, from a clinical point of view, a new concept of psychotic body image and neurotic body image.

When Freud (1914c) speaks of the body, he refers to the projection of the ego onto the body's surface and describes the organization of the libido in the body. He also deals with the development of the erogenous zones, the way in which they are represented, and their importance in the formation of the body ego. The development of sexual libido takes place in major concentration zones that are in contact with the external world—hence the paramount importance attached to orifices and their relationship with the external world; the relationship of each of them with the outer world prevails in the different developmental stages.

Anzieu (1974, Anzieu et al., 1987) points out that Freud did not confine the so-called oral phase to experiences related solely to the buccal–pharyngeal zone and the pleasure of sucking. He stresses the importance of the subsequent pleasure derived from feeling full inside. Anzieu also adds that just as the mouth provides the first experience of a differentiating contact and of an incorporation, feeling full inside, though usually neglected in the literature, would provide the infant with a more pervasive and lasting experience: the perception of a central mass, fullness, a centre of gravity. Anzieu uses the term *moi-peau* [ego-skin] to describe an image used by the child's thinking during the early developmental phases to represent himself as self, on the basis of his experience of the body's surface. This corresponds to the period in which the "psychic ego" becomes differentiated from the "body ego" from an operational point of view but remains fused with it on a figurative level.

Bick (1968, 1986) has presented a wealth of clinical material to describe the development and growth of a mental perception of a skin and its relationship with introjection and projective identification.

I have discussed previously thoughts about the body image and its relationship to the patient's conceptualization of the skin (Rosenfeld, 1975). In that presentation I described how a patient who suffered from a skin disorder acted out in his relationship with me the period of his infancy in which the skin disturbances had their origin. Additionally, in his sessions he repeated one of the aspects of the fairy tale *Peau d'Âne* ["The Skin of the Donkey"]. This patient felt he had lost his skin, comparing his experience to that of a crab that has lost its shell, and he was afraid of becoming an amoeba or a slug without any external envelope or endoskeleton. When I discussed this case with Esther Bick, we were able to detect the mechanisms the patient employed to enable him to believe he could penetrate into the object in order to live parasitically inside someone else's skin (Rosenfeld, 1984, 1985a, 1986, 1988; see the section on skin disturbances in the transcript of Julian below).

I would like to draw a distinction between these cases and those I shall now discuss: patients in whom the conceptualization of a skin has been lost. Rather than attempting to explain the disturbances in the notion of a skin, I will try to describe a certain type of body image where that notion does not exist. Another new concept is the notion of liquids as the nucleus of the psychotic body image and their possible transformation into solid or semi-solid substances as an indication of a change in connection with the body image—that is, a more integrated ego nucleus, which shows a different type of structuralization of the self and the body image. This may be seen, for instance, in the material of a patient, Agnes, when she dreams for the first time of *something semi-solid, chewing gum, in her mouth* (see below).

By *psychotic body image* I mean the most primitive notion of the body image to be observed in certain patients whose work begins while they are already regressed or who regress during their treatment. In my view, the extreme notion of what can be conceived of as psychotic body image is the thought that the body contains only liquid, one or another derivative of blood, and that it is coated by an arterial or venous wall or walls. These vascular sheaths take over the functions that are normally fulfilled psychologically by the actual skin, the muscles, and the skeleton. There is only a vague notion of a wall that contains blood or vital liquids.

In turn, this membrane containing the blood may be perceived—as can be seen mainly in crises associated with acute psychosis—to have broken or to have been otherwise damaged and to result in a loss of bodily contents, leaving the body empty, without either internal or external containment and/or support. Sometimes the experience of becoming empty is expressed linguistically through a sudden and incessant verbal flow: the patient cannot stop talking.

The notion of a psychotic body image is not limited to clinical cases that are phenomenologically psychotic: it may be present in personalities that are neurotically adjusted to reality. I would even say that the psychotic body image prevails in personalities that may be very well adjusted to reality—some psychosomatic cases, for example (see the section on skin disturbances in the transcript of Julian below). This psychotic conception of the body breaks through and invades what up to that moment was a different kind of mental functioning, and this may be expressed either through words or nonverbally through body language, in the psychosomatic disturbances. Additionally, the regression to the concept of the psychotic body image occurs at times during periods of personal crisis, as I have observed in patients following cardiovascular surgery (Rosenfeld, 1992b).

We can speak of a *neurotic body image*—closer to the notion of normality—when there is an unconscious mental representation of the skin that covers with warmth and contains the body image. The most normal psychological notion of skin is that representing the parents who hold with warmth and contain the child's body (Bick, 1968, 1986; Tustin, 1986).

Transcript 1

"Agnes"

"I am mad in the blood."
[Words of a female patient, Agnes, in the course of a session]

This material pertains to "Agnes", a patient in whose functioning the psychotic body image prevails—a fact that is expressed through a body language in a psychosomatic illness. The patient, a 26-year-old woman, said she became aware of her illness after she and her boyfriend had broken off their relationship. She wanted to be treated because "I am depressed, I want to die." She said that her illness consisted of necrosed sores in various mucosal areas and the skin and that, according to the many doctors who had sought to diagnose and treat her, their origin was unknown. The physicians considered her case to be hopeless in view of the severity of her illness: When she underwent any emotional crisis, the vascular inflammation and necrosis of the mucosae of the mouth, larynx, and lips were, indeed, severe. On one such occasion, she was unable to speak or eat for six months and had to be fed intravenously. One acute crisis resulted in a coma that lasted for three days. The patient added, "There is no longer a prognosis for my illness", and, "At this moment I don't have so many necrotic sores on my legs."

I briefly summarize a startling phenomenon. Each time Agnes was left, her transference reaction could be understood as giving evidence of the psychotic body image. When she felt that she had been abandoned, her ulcerations actually became more severe and her bleeding and oozing increased. When she began to improve, she had a physical defensive response, a vasoconstriction of the arterioles that reduced both the dermal and the mucosal necrosis.

This case is typical of the way in which the use and functioning of the psychotic body image becomes rigid. The re-emergence in times of crisis of the old psychotic body image becomes chronic, and this takes place in cases of infantile or psychotic autism, where what was once primary autism becomes pathological later on (Tustin, 1972, 1981, 1986).

Three years of treatment led to an understanding of the nature of the patient's transference and enabled us to study more thoroughly— almost microscopically—the origin of her bleeding sores and necrosis, which were correlated with specific stages in the analytic transference. Agnes could say that she felt something *before* the appearance of her sores. This was the first step, a small one indeed. She began to perceive affects instead of expressing them concretely through her body. On the basis of the psychotic body image, menstruation meant for this patient that her body self was going to be completely emptied of blood. That same year she had to undergo plastic surgery in order to reshape her mouth and lips, distorted by the severe skin and mucosal necrosis. Here we can study in greater detail material associated with the relationship between the nipple and the mouth—that is, her transference relationship with her female therapist.

Due to the lack of psychological boundaries between her body and the therapist's breast that she imagined sucking, every separation or loss meant to her that: (1) The nipple takes or tears away from her fragments of her own skin; the nipple decorticates her, depriving her of her body's outer boundaries. (2) There is a fantasized murderous attack on the objects that abandon her: in this period it became possible to understand the deeper reasons that triggered the organic disturbance in connection with the loss of her boyfriend. (3) The lost object takes away with it pieces of the membrane, and she bleeds through her pores. (4) The confusion of subject–object–lips–nipple leads to the attack on the object in a space within her non-differentiated body; therefore, to attack the nipple implies an attack against her own lips. The lack of boundaries (fusion) (Mahler, 1968; Searles, 1979) is the reason why, by attacking the object that abandons her, she becomes identified with parts of her own body's surface. This explains how she can attack and destroy her own body's casing: she is left with venous or arterial walls containing blood as her only conception of a body image. In this case, *the arterial and venous walls take over the function that should be fulfilled by the normal skin.*

In connection with the transference experiences, it was possible to detect, on the basis of childhood material, that her mother had become pregnant again when the patient was not yet 12 months old—in other words, she had been prematurely abandoned by her mother in connection with her affect needs and during the period of structuralization of the body image (Abraham, 1945; Pichon Rivière, 1964; Schilder, 1935; Scott, 1948). Before the holidays there was a new intensification of the feeling of becoming empty of blood, manifested mainly in bodily terms—sores and necrosis—during the therapist's absence.

I would like to stress that I deal here with the *psychological* experience of the notion of a protective skin that covers and protects the body. The same applies to the psychological notion that Agnes's body is a kind of large artery or vein about to be perforated, but in no way do I refer to the organic concrete body, or to its anatomy, such as can be studied in anatomy or histology.

In my view, the type of hypochondria centred on and expressed through the psychotic body image is different from all others, not only because it concerns the blood or the psychotic body image, but also because in my experience it implies the danger of "accidents" or suicidal attempts. I refer to more active methods than those implied by Pierre Marty, Michel de M'Uzan, and Christian David (1963, p. 355; see Oliner, 1988). Everything concerning the psychotic body image corresponds to a more primitive and psychotic level. Here, as in the case of other patients, the fantasy of suffering from leukaemia is an example of a hypochondriac disturbance centred on the psychotic body image. It may indicate anything from becoming empty of blood to a severe persecutory delusion in connection with monsters or organisms that eat away the blood or an attempt at achieving hypochondriac control. These delusions sometimes bring about suicidal attempts, such as cutting one's veins to expel and get rid of persecutory objects that have already invaded the psychotic body image. There may emerge transient hypochondriac fantasies concerning blood in every neurotic personality, and always when there is a re-emergence of the body image based on the psychotic body image.

I will attempt to illustrate this point by presenting dream material obtained from Agnes. It should be noticed that in the case of severely disturbed patients nocturnal dreams may appear only after a long period of treatment.

The first dream, six years after the beginning of treatment, concerns *some chewing gum the patient has and keeps in her mouth*. This is the first time there is a representation of something she keeps. Besides, it is semi-solid—different from the fluid that oozes out through all her pores—and, additionally, it is centred in a circumscribed erogenous zone: the mouth.

There was a period in which she could symbolize her fantasies through her dreams, while the disturbances of the body image were expressed on the linguistic level in a very peculiar way; for instance, the orifices appeared not in her skin but in her speech, which began to lose the normal linguistic structure, that is, the "social skin." At a linguistic level, speech disorganization might express destructuration of the body image (Liberman, 1970–72). The loss of the body's surface or skin was now expressed as the loss of the structuring envelopment of speech, but without reaching the point of psychotic disintegration at a linguistic level. During this period that patient dreamed of *"a little woollen dress, knitted with holes and given as a present to a little girl"*: fragments of skin–dress that covered her incompletely. The fact that the dream material shows that the loss or emptiness is not related to liquid or blood and that more solid materials that are easier to retain—for instance, solid faeces—began to appear, is a very important clue that marks the beginning—though only the beginning—of her functioning on the basis of the neurotic body image and shows that the psychotic body image was not so dominant. In the content of this dream the body is also emptied of its contents, but this time they are not only liquids or blood, but also faeces that are hard and seen as a penis (Freud & Hawelka, 1974). Besides being more solid, they are contained or introduced inside an orifice in her own body (vagina), which contains it.

In connection with the psychotic body image, this was expressed at a different developmental level.

The patient says in the course of a session: ". . . Oh! I remembered a dream. . . . I was in the waiting-room, laughing to myself, when I remembered. Is the session over?" (She laughs.) "I took out a . . . I don't know what to call it . . . puff . . . ouch . . . uff . . ." (She makes noises.) "I kept quiet to see the expression on your face." The therapist points out that she, unlike the patient, is *not* alarmed or frightened. Then the patient seems to believe the therapist and continues: "Well, shit carne out, a very long. . . . My God! It wasn't sticky, it was not disintegrated . . . to put it into my vagina . . . what a masturbation fantasy!"

Six years after starting treatment, the patient brought a dream including material related to the loss of blood associated with menstruation, in which she showed that a towel was not stained with menstrual blood. But menstruation was not expressed as before—that is, when she believed it implied bleeding through all the pores (we are reminded here of her every month). It could now be seen that she denied the bloodstain on the towel, and this implied a denial of the loss of blood, which was closer to containment than to becoming empty. It was the equivalent of what the patient had expressed before through sores: now it had a symbolic manifestation in the fact that blood did not come out and did not stain. The important thing now was that she could dream of this and symbolize it. Before, she had expressed through the psychotic body image her empty feeling and the sores through her skin injuries. When an inner space may be created (Bick, 1968), and also a mental space between the patient and the therapist (Anzieu, 1974; Anzieu et al., 1987; Winnicott, 1957), another stage has begun. In a patient with such a severe illness, this stage brings with it the hope that the struggle or the battle will cease to be expressed through the body and will reach mental transference levels.

We hope, as Shakespeare says, that

> . . . if God doth give successful end to this debate that
> bleedeth at our doors, we will our youth lead on to higher
> fields. . . .
>
> Shakespeare, *King Henry IV, Part II* (Act IV, Scene 4)

I have been able to observe in various clinical disturbances that the idea of the protective membrane or skin sometimes disappears, especially when there is object loss or destructuration. These patients retain the idea that their bodies remain continuous with that of their mothers: when she leaves, the child feels she takes parts of its body with her. Such patients are left without a skin every time there is a separation or a relationship is lost. Thus, in periods of crisis, of mourning, and due to object loss, they react as follows: the blood vessels function as a self-containment membrane in the patient's response to feeling empty. Bick has suggested the concept of a second skin as a substitute for the psychological notion of an external skin; this second skin is sometimes achieved through muscular hyperactivity. In neurotics there may be hypochondriac ideas related to the psychotic body image, as of suffering from leukaemia or haemophilia. Clinically, under these circumstances a psychotic body image prevails. Every hypochondriac disturbance expressed through the psychotic body image should alert us to the possibility of a suicidal attempt or some accident of a suicidal nature. The likelihood of suicidal risk should also be taken into account in cases of drug addiction in which a psychotic body image prevails—for instance, intravenous self-administration of drugs or when the patient has hypochondriac fantasies concerning the possibility of a blood infection. As an example, a patient may inject himself intravenously with antibiotics on the basis of such a hypochondriac fantasy (Santamaría, 1978).

The notion of becoming empty of blood has its origin in the earliest infantile relationships and in experiences based on body object relationships; every psychic activity is based on a biological function. For instance, the notion of projective identification does not arise in a child as an abstract theoretical conception; rather, it stems from body experiences and object relationships: for instance, putting out the tongue in search for the nipple without being able to find it. According to Tustin (1986), the baby then feels that he falls into a vacuum, and this becomes a model of becoming empty through projective identification. The hand of a baby who tries to get hold of the breast and cannot find it is a similar model. The hand and the attempt to grasp the breast allow me to express my own "model" related to the psychotic body image. When a child tries to grasp the breast with his hand and cannot find it, he may, in a second step, try to contain himself by pressing his fingers hard against the palm of his hand, even to the point of hurting himself with his nails. But if this self-containment system fails and there is no other, the idea is present that the arteries and veins begin to function like the palm of the hand in order to achieve self-containment: They close up or contract in the person's desperate effort to achieve self-containment, but at the level of the psychotic body image. The idea of a skin is displaced to a notion of vascular walls. The normal concept that the baby or regressed patient can derive from its primary relationship with the breast is that of a mouth with a nipple that has a warm skin, accompanied by a familiar smell and voice, as described by Bick (1968). But when a relationship is based on the psychotic body image, the relationship with the breast seems to become established without the notion of a nipple covered with skin. A liquid merges with another liquid: milk, saliva, blood—a cocktail of liquids. This is particularly true when a child loses its mother or is separated from her; having been abandoned by the maternal object is experienced by the infant not as losing the nipple from inside its mouth but as if it were being skinned and as if the mother takes with her the external surface or skin of its body covering when she leaves. Due to the infant's experiencing his skin as continuous with the mother's and the equation of skin with vascular wall, the psychotic body image arises.

It is my belief that this notion of psychological self-containment provided by a wall or by arteries or veins may be at the root of certain psychosomatic disturbances.

The notion of liquids that spill often emerges in schizophrenic patients when they express their feeling of emptiness at the level of the psychotic body image. I have observed that, after many years of treatment, and if the patient improves, instead of the loss of liquids or blood, he sometimes begins to express fantasies of becoming empty of more solid substances—for instance, through dreams in which the car "loses" oil—and later of even more solid substances, like faeces. I believe it is only here that the ideas of holding the object at the anal retentive level begin to manifest themselves. As an example, after six years of treatment a schizophrenic patient no longer dreams before the holidays that he becomes empty of liquids or blood; instead, he dreams of losing solid faeces, and this is accompanied by a period of anal masturbation. On the other hand, in the psychotic body image the notions about becoming empty correspond to a more narcissistic level, and the patient is emptied not through an erogenous zone but through his pores.

I think it is only after this stage that anal masturbation, as described by Meltzer (1966), can be analysed. I suspect that when the psychotic body image prevails, the function of the rectum, of the anus, and of anal masturbation lacks the structuralization it has when it is based on the neurotic body image. (This formulation is important in that it im-plies the need for technical approaches to anal masturbation, involving sensitive timing and different levels of interpretation. This is different from Meltzer's theory.)

Avenburg (1975) made us aware of the great similarity between what I am describing here and the concept of libido stagnation formulated by Freud, who spoke as if what became stagnated was a liquid. It is, then, a process of fluidization, of loss of quality, of dedifferentiation, similar to what happens when one liquid becomes mixed with another in the psychotic body image, in which self-discrimination is lost. According to Avenburg, the German word *Stauung* used by Freud refers specifically to stopping the flow of a liquid.

On the basis of my experience with regressed patients, I am currently more convinced of the possible relation between hypertension and the conception of the psychotic body image. Through dreams and fantasies brought systematically into the analytic material, a patient revealed that he conceived of himself as possessing neither skin nor muscles but, instead, imagined that his sensations of movement were produced solely by contractions and other movements of arteries. The following two examples come from patients under supervision.

The first patient develops hypochondria and imagines she has hypertension; she takes her blood pressure five or six times daily in an effort to corroborate her fantasy. What is of special interest is that she conceives of her body as a bag of fluids or blood, which empties out. The imaginary hypertension defends her against the feeling of emptiness, and the hypertension is conceived to result from being full of blood.

The hypertension of a second patient has developed into a psychosomatic illness. The onset of her high blood pressure had coincided with her acting out by abandoning her psychoanalysis a month before the summer holidays; she required medical treatment. When she resumed treatment, her hypertension disappeared, and did not reappear. This patient also functions with a psychotic body image. Not being in a position to contribute a physiological or other medical explanation for this observation, I resort to citing the words of an eminent hypertension researcher, even though they are not original with her. "Hypertension is a riddle wrapped in a mystery inside an enigma" (Page & Durstan, 1962, p. 433).

Models, philosophy of science, and methodology

The concepts described constitute, from the methodological point of view, an explanatory model. Many of the hypotheses we formulate result from what in the field of methodology is known as *inductive generalization*. But if I make a hypothesis or model as an explanatory model, albeit empirically based, there is no reason why it should be of a very low level of abstraction; on the contrary, it may attain a high explanatory level, even as a model. Atomic theory, for example, was formulated not on the basis of direct observation but of an explanatory model (Meadows, 1969).

Every model is a pattern of symbols, rules, and proposals that are regarded, partly or wholly, as consistent with the set of existing postulates. Thus, every model postulates its correspondence with reality, the possibility of establishing its usefulness in the structure of reality. It should be noted that the construction of a model is an inner logical creation and, as such, sometimes a function of the cultural model. As was the case with Niels Bohr, the model is invented. In psychoanalytic practice one may sometimes find examples like those I present, and that is why the psychotic body scheme is a useful explanatory model for a variety of clinical cases. This model helps me to incorporate into a single idea developmental genetic and transferential concepts that apply to schizophrenic and psychosomatic patients and others when regressed. When we invent a model, we find it useful first for one particular patient but then for other patients as well. If I add to it, provided it is consistent, a developmental–genetic theory of infantile bonds that may be empirically demonstrated in the transference with the therapist, I may say it is already a hypothesis of a high level of abstraction, and I may even develop a sound theory—if it passes the philosopher Karl Popper's test (Popper, 1965; see also chapter 8, this volume).

The psychotic body scheme is a nonobservable entity, but when we invent the model, it becomes powerful from the explanatory point of view. This does not mean that the model represents the ultimate truth, but only that it is a useful model for the time being.

Perhaps the origin of this scientific model may be best described through clinical observations: (1) Two of my schizophrenic patients showed their fingernails or their hands to me and stated they were losing blood—all their blood. (2) Post-surgery cardiac patients very often have delusions in the course of which they say, for instance, that nothing is left in them except veins and arteries. (3) Another psychotic patient kept talking about his low blood pressure but eventually said to me, "I don't want to have a corn removed because if I do, they will realize I am hollow and with no blood inside." For this, I had to create a new and different explanatory model: When this psychotic patient speaks of his "low blood pressure", he really means that he is bleeding or that there is no blood left in his body. Then the observation was completed with the psychosomatic patients, and the model acquired paramount importance (see the case of Agnes).

In other words, the model began to evolve and to show its usefulness for various psychopathological cases and then became a more comprehensive model. If I then add a hypothesis about its genetic–historical origin, its evolution, and how it is shown in the transference, it becomes a fairly comprehensive and acceptable theory, if corroborated by clinical observations.

The model began to be used for all these "psychopathological cases, and I found it useful from an explanatory point of view. When applied, for instance, to a severe psychosomatic case (Agnes), it modified not only the theory but also the interpretive approach and, thus, the chances for survival in a seriously ill psychosomatic patient. The clinical evolution and the predictions that emerged may be quite novel.

"Pierre"

Pierre, another patient, had a delusional episode after the removal of a (benign) brain tumour and, in the course of a session said: "I'm afraid of having leukaemia. . . . I have begun to despair . . . to worry."

At that point I asked him: "Why did you think of leukaemia?"

And the patient answered immediately: "Because of the destruction of the red cells by the tumour. As if I were afraid of becoming empty . . . emptied of blood . . . as if I were soft all over.

Then I asked him: "Soft?"

He replied: "Yes, everything soft . . . like a sack full of blood. I'm afraid of having a haemorrhage, and that everything . . . will come out. . . .

The accuracy with which this patient expresses his fantasies concerning his body image is remarkable. The conception of the body as a sack full of vital fluids or blood—primitive psychotic body scheme—is clearly formulated here on a verbal level. The patient can express it in words, whereas Agnes acts it out through body behaviours and haemorrhages through the skin, because she cannot symbolize it verbally.

I also found this model quite useful for other psychosomatic pictures, such as ulcerative colitis—that is, patients with diarrhoea and loss of blood through the bowels. We have postulated that this illness may be explained on the basis of the primitive psychotic body scheme model and invite validation. In several patients with ulcerative colitis I have observed that the fantasy was more closely related to bleeding than to the anal level. These patients let a part of their bowels express the most regressive and primitive levels of their self, and it is on this level that they express their emotions, persecutions, sorrows, and aggressions.

Blood is lost through some kind of skin—in this case, the bowels (Agnes loses it through the oral mucosa and the skin of her hands and feet). The patient with ulcerative colitis bleeds or loses vital fluids, but through another type of skin. The two are similar as regards the infantile models of object relationship. Therefore, I would like to insist once again that the conceptions of vital fluid and blood constitute a *different* "observational model" that provides another approach to patients with ulcerative colitis, who used to be understood only in connection with the anal stage.

These patients conceive of their body image in a different way, and this is a new model for further research.

Another example is H, a 30-year-old woman, who, before the summer holidays, dreamed that *she had lost her scalp, part of the right side of the skull, and also the brain, and saw, in the dream, only an artery on the right side—a large brain artery. This artery, containing blood, had lost part of the wall on the upper right side. She was afraid of having a haemorrhage through this open side of the artery.* It was her way of expressing her feelings in connection with my desertion. But exactly a year later—that is, again before the holidays—she had the same dream, but with one fundamental difference: that *the artery was whole and no longer open.*

Not all patients are capable of expressing such regressive and deep transference feelings through body images. It may be that this theory is valid only for those patients who can express it in this way. I do believe that this model or hypothesis will help many analysts to be more on the alert and will provide them with a methodological framework better suited for an accurate understanding of these clinical observations.

Methodologically, many loose and unconnected clinical observations may be put together by means of a hypothesis designed to explain a larger number of observational facts in psychoanalytic practice.

The primitive body scheme model, for instance, also helped me to create new hypotheses concerning a type of hypochondriasis that has different origin and dynamics (Rosenfeld, 1985a).

Transcript 2

In order to show how a psychotic patient may express himself at the level of the body image, I present two brief clinical illustrations. These patients express, through visual or corporal images, the most primitive notions of their self, which we call *corporal scheme* or *body image*. The first of these is case material pertaining to "John", a 19-year-old patient of a supervisee, and the second are fragments of clinical material pertaining to "Pierre", a patient treated by me. We will be able to observe the way in which I intervene and interpret the transference in a postoperative psychosis rooted mainly in fantasies about the psychotic primitive corporal scheme.

"John"

John started treatment in July when, after a journey, he was hospitalized in an acute psychotic crisis. He said, early in the first interview, "Every time I meet a girl, I surrender, I fall in love, and I bleed in her." He also said repeatedly, "I want to kill myself; there is no love in return, I bleed in her." He fixed his eyes on the therapist's eyes and told her something that he would repeat several times in the course of his treatment, "Your eyes give me life." (It is usual during this type of acute episode for the patient to rivet his eyes to those of the therapist, as a baby looks into his mother's eyes during nursing.)

In the first session John verbalized another fantasy of the emptying that occurs in the presence of the psychotic body image: "I came into the world to bleed myself because of my love for all human beings. I am paying for my guilt over my sins." Later on he added, "I masturbate, and people see it on my face." This material—that is, that people in the outside world see something specific on his face—seems to be an attempt at restitution through a self-reference delusion. He related a dream: "*I was going to school. I came across Miriam* but, Doctor, even if I wanted to I couldn't love her more. Are you going to watch Monzón's fight today?" (We may see here that dreams and material from waking life are mixed in the description, which points to a dream-like mental state.)

Apparently this is taken up again in the following session: "Suffering prevents me from loving." The understanding of this concept is essential for our comprehension of the suffering of a psychotic patient. Next he described another fantasy of the emptying existent in the primitive or psychotic body image, talking about cows that kill the butcher who is about to slaughter them. At that moment we understood this material as a retaliatory fantasy in which a breast–cow becomes revengeful.

Another possible meaning is that the attempt to bleed his mother's breast very soon turns into his own bleeding, showing the prevalence of the psychotic body image. Such material reappeared a week later, after he had been afraid that he would faint if he went to a party. It is interesting to distinguish between the different diagnoses: the fear to "feel sick or have low blood pressure" in a case of hysteria or anxiety hysteria, where the body may express sickness directly and, at a schizophrenic level, when a patient speaks of feeling sick or of having low blood pressure, he is likely to have felt bled empty in the previous sessions. The same may hold true in distinguishing the material of patients who speak of "having a low blood pressure" or of "feeling empty or weak inside". It is important to make a differential diagnosis between a depressive patient who expresses his sadness by saying his blood pressure is low and a schizophrenic patient who, in the course of his treatment with me, spoke about having low blood pressure, which we could understand to represent a fantasy of his having been emptied. Some months later he said that his body was hollow; that is, he then experienced the psychotic body image. Another time, when he had to have a wart removed, he felt panicky because, "If that wart or corn was removed, they would know that I am hollow inside." That is, although phenomenologically the words are the same as those a depressive neurotic might use, this psychotic patient expressed to me through them his experience of emptying out the inside of his body and the presence or prevalence of the psychotic body image.

But let us return to John, our patient:

In December, he had another fragmentation episode, this time expressed through projective identification as his being in many pieces, in the form of thousands of cards that he distributed.

But how did he return in March, after the summer holidays? He no longer spoke of the cards he had distributed. Instead, he regressed, saying he was "empty and hollow": he was functioning at the level of the psychotic body image. Such material persisted until July.

In March the following year there was another fantasy related to the emptying of the psychotic body image: The patient said his mother "takes away from me and leaves me empty." A week afterward he organized a delusion and produced material including a satyr–penis or persecutory satyr.

In June of the same year he dreamed again about the regressed body image: he had nothing left except his skeleton, and no other support. Here the fantasy of being emptied of liquids and blood seemed to be a kind of retribution for the possibility of retaining the skeleton. In my experience the skeleton by itself in dreams or drawings—no matter how ill the patient may be—has always proved, in the long run, to indicate an identification with the father or the paternal role. Some patients hold that the penis provides the breast with firmness. It may also be the father who is capable of taking care of the nursing mother. I thought that John's compulsive masturbation was an attempt to prove, among other things, that since at least some liquid came out from inside his body, he was not completely empty, thus reducing the intolerable feeling of utter emptiness and hollowness that implied madness. This schizophrenic patient felt that sexual intercourse amounted to bleeding; an acute psychotic crisis was for him a way of expressing his becoming empty in coitus, while a delusion was an attempt at restitution vis-á-vis what he experienced as the bleeding of the body–self. During the following summer holiday he was unable to retain an image of the therapist. Following the loss of her intrapsychic representation as an object, in March he experienced fusion with her as fluid in a vascular sheath. He brought a restitutive delusional fantasy: He felt capable of finding God, with whom he identified and whom he hallucinated.

In May the patient described his fantasy of bleeding during coitus. (To imagine that one bleeds during coitus is at the root of many cases of sexual impotence that are difficult to cure and derive from the psychotic body image. Before having intercourse he shot several cats, watching them bleed to death. Later on he expressed object losses at the level of the psychotic body image: "I am afraid of being emptied of you and of losing you.

A year later, in June, he expressed clearly for the first time that becoming hollow was being emptied of something *good*: that is, a prior introjection of the benevolent therapist had taken place. Expressing his gratitude to his therapist, he said that in his loss of her "One is emptied of what is good." In another psychotic area, of course, the belief persisted that he was God and that the devil was in others.

The fantasies near the end of that year concerning parting from his therapist before the holidays were expressed in terms of blood and of the psychotic body image through a fantasy of anastomosis and fusion with the therapist (Searles, 1961). In December he said: "If my blood spills, after me the others which will exist will spill too."

In March the following year, after the end of the holidays, he developed a delusion, intensified by the fact that his sessions were reduced from five to four times weekly. He tried to compensate for the object loss and feeling of emptiness by hallucinating the body of a girl. We understood this to mean that the search for the missing breast was carried out by means of an identification with the breast and that he tried to come close to the therapist on the basis of this feminine identification.

Three months later the patient tried to re-establish his relationship with the therapist through an organizing delusion, something better than the complete loss of the object. He then chose a singer, Sandro, with whom he identified through a fantasized homosexual relationship. Here I would like to point out something important: This is the first emergence of an aesthetic hysterical level concerning blood or the psychotic body image. Ordinarily, the object loss experienced due to the loss of a single session meant to the patient the end of the world and was expressed at the level of the psychotic body image as the loss of blood. This time he expressed his becoming empty of blood at an aesthetic level, as happens with certain patients who have reached the hysterical level. He spoke about condoms that were as red as blood and about others that were blue. The emergence of red and blue expresses the emptying of blood or of the psychotic body image in some patients with their attempts to express it at an aesthetic–hysterical level. Garzoli (1979) reported that a female patient dreamed that "while on the stretcher she had a transparent vision of herself, in which thick blue veins and red arteries could be clearly seen." An example of this may be found in Bob Fosse's film, *All that Jazz,* when the final ballet expresses the death anxiety of the main character, who dances with his veins and arteries drawn in blue and red all over his body.

Once John became empty of the liquids of the psychotic body image, he tried to compensate by developing a strict obsessive order in connection with timetables and the like. The obsessive level was new and provided very important clues that must be taken into account to understand how this patient then behaved in December. For the first time his pre-separation fantasies did not include bleeding.

In July he could express at the verbal level the fantasies of emptying of his psychotic body image: "Before I became empty, I could throw you out by masturbating. Now I can't." On earlier occasions of psychotic crisis the loss of semen, liquids, or blood had been equated in his thinking and had caused total emptying. Additionally, the patient now expressed on an apparently genital sexual level how he tried to expel his persecutory objects. This is quite interesting from a clinical point of view: if he had remained fixed at the level of blood, the diagnosis could be different. For example, patients who have delusional persecutory objects—the mother, for instance—fixed at the level of their psychotic body image may attempt to cut their veins in order to get rid of the thousand persecutory objects that have got into their blood.

I want to make clear that when I speak of persecutory objects in very disturbed patients, I mean that they are genuine delusions, sometimes not fully expressed at the verbal level. For instance, some patients take high doses of diuretics in order to expel, through their urine, persecutory objects that have become fixed in the body's liquids. To extend an earlier remark, I have come to the conclusion that every expulsion of persecutory objects through the body's liquids—like blood, urine, and so on—should make us more alert to the patient's suicidal potential. For example, in the case of drug addicts who take amphetamines, it

is interesting to observe that if the fantasy accompanying the introjection of the drug is believed to help them expel parts of the body such
as urine or faeces that prevent them from thinking, special attention
should be paid to a possible hidden, suicidal fantasy or, which is the
same, proneness to have a suicidal or drug-induced accident (Boyer,
1982a, 1983).

Returning to John, there came a time when he expressed his emptiness at all possible levels. I would like to add that becoming empty
of the liquids or blood of the psychotic body image can be expressed
verbally, but when it is expressed in the body without any kind of
verbal symbolization, we are faced with some of the psychosomatic
disturbances. It is a peculiar type of dissociation, described by Liberman (1970–72).

"Pierre"

I will now present some fragments of clinical material concerning
one of my patients, a prestigious veterinary surgeon in his province.

According to Pierre's relatives, he went through periods in which
he lost control of reality. One psychiatrist who had seen him thought
his increasing alcohol intake was an effort to be unaware of periods
of mental disorganization. He had been treated in supportive psychotherapy for two years and received medication.

Pierre's relatives brought him to his first appointment. He looked
older than his 43 years and appeared to be exhausted. He lived with
his mother and two brothers. His father had died five years previously,
from multiple myeloma.

During the first session the patient was oriented as to time and
place but was confused and felt persecuted. Previously he had sought
to escape from apparently delirious persecutory episodes by fleeing
from his home while carrying firearms and/or drinking great quantities of alcohol.

Noting that he had certain speech problems and nystagmus, I referred him to a neurologist, who found a tumour to have spread across
the optic chiasma; immediate neurosurgery was recommended. Pierre
was terrified and asked me to remain by his side every day that he
was confined to the hospital and especially requested that I hold his
hand when he was anesthetized. While firmly clasping my hand, he
said, "Dad, Dad. . . ."

The extension and complexity of the case prevent me from transcribing it in its entirety, so I will present only brief fragments corresponding to the immediate postoperative period. This material brings to light in a very clear way the most primitive images of the patient's corporal scheme, and at the same time shows my interpretations of the transference. I beg readers to interpret my brief account as an example of how a patient may express this model of the psychotic body image.

Pierre underwent an immediate postoperative psychotic episode: a delirium in which he was convinced that vital fluids were being extracted from his body, encephalic–spinal liquid, blood, semen, and urine. The third night after the operation he sought to verify that he had not been completely drained of liquids, and, for this purpose, he had sexual relations with his girlfriend in his hospital bed. His intention, according to his own words, was "to see if any liquid came out. . . ." This was when the hospital doctors woke me at 2 am. and I had to rush there in the middle of the night.

During the postoperative period, Pierre oscillated between confusional states and semi-clarity. At times he was convinced that he or I was his dead father.

I will now reproduce parts of the material corresponding to the first weeks after the operation. These fragments underscore fantasies regarding Pierre's bodily image or corporal scheme and show the way in which I intervened when he identified with his dead father and believed that I was persecuting him.

1. During a session the first week after the operation, the patient said:

Patient [P]: I want to urinate, it scares me, three times a day. I'm going to urinate.

Analyst [A]: You're afraid to go urinate. . . .

P: It scares me because . . . [he stutters] you know? I might get wet, right? . . . In reality I try not to urinate very much. I hold back.

A: What did you say? That you're afraid to urinate?

P [in muddled language and stuttering]: Yes, I'm afraid to urinate, I'm afraid to bleed . . . to have blood come out, you know? . . . That urinating blood might rush out, and I could bleed to death. . . .

> I am afraid that the tumour is lodged in the bladder, prostate gland, testicles. . . . I think I have bone marrow metastasis.

In this and following material it became increasingly clear that the patient was convinced of the following: (1) that the tumour had not been removed; (2) that he had malignant metastases; (3) that he was his father with bone-marrow cancer; (4) that I was deceiving him as his father had been deceived.

In a session later in the week, the following interchange occurred:

P: Well . . . uh . . . last night I defecated and also urinated, right?

A: And did the fear remain?

P: Well, the fear seems . . . uh. . . . What was the faecal material like?" . . . I told Mum . . . because she was with me, it seems like I was afraid to go to the bathroom alone, right?

A: And what did you think?

P: Well, I thought I would bleed, or something like that.

A: You thought lots of blood would come out?

P: Well, yes. . . . I think like an external haemorrhage. I made Mum look at what came out.

A: Ah . . . and did you believe your mother when she looked at the faeces, or did you have to look yourself?

P: No . . . I . . . uhh . . . yes, believed her, she said it is . . . [stutters] not very . . . hard, she said . . . it was a bit, we could say, mushy.

A: And did you believe it was blood, or did you have to look?

P: No . . . no . . . no . . . I believed her that it was not blood . . . let me see . . . but I also looked . . . I also looked.

A: Ah, you looked, just in case.

P: Yes, yes, yes . . . I also looked, yes.

2.   In the third week after the operation we can observe my intervention in the delirious transference. I must make clear that the delirious transference with me increased every time that spinal–encephalic liquid was extracted from him for examination. I became someone who hurt him or took his vital fluids—a vampire. (He had been placed on

anticonvulsive medication and was apprehensive, believing various people were seeking to harm him.)

During a session after he left the hospital, Pierre said:

P: Yes, I thought that the fact that you could not hurt me . . . that you did not tell me the truth and did not solve my problem, you know? . . . that is that I would not have . . . fear of going out on the street, to walk. . . . It seems that being confined here, it seems it would be better . . . being like this in a daze taking the pills that made me somewhat dizzy . . . and . . . like this in a daze, in a dream, you know? It seems that I wouldn't like to think . . . the reality of the operation, right? . . . It makes me shudder . . . it seems it would make me afraid of the treatments I would have to undergo, right? The puncture, the Epamin [anticonvulsive medication].

A: But perhaps it is also me that you fear . . . you may believe that everyone will hurt you . . . including me.

P: That, that, that they hurt me [stutters], that they could not make me overcome the tumour . . . that they did not love me, you know? That everyone is lying to me as to a child, right? And me living with mistrust and with . . . we could say on the verge of departure, you know? . . . without stepping soundly, it would seem, isn't it true? The earth could split at any moment . . . [silence] and I would be ashamed of crying, you know? That is why it's as if rage gripped me, it seems that I do that before crying in front of you . . . of . . . [stuttering] today . . . I was crying in front of my mother, right? This morning she made me have trust, you see? But I started crying because she was explaining to me the case of Pinky, a girl who had metastasis and a number of operations.

3. The following fragment, which occurred during the third week after the operation, depicts my interpretation of the transference related to the psychotic identification where the patient believes he is the father with bone marrow cancer.

During the session, while he talked about his meals, Pierre said:

P: It's as if this were . . . uh . . . the desire to gain weight, don't you think?

A: Are you afraid of losing weight?

P: It would appear so. Dad lost weight when he had the myeloma.

A: Do you realize this panic you have is because you think you are your father?

P: It seems as though I were Dad with all the same symptoms, right? That I might limp, that the medication was destroying me, as dialysis seemed to destroy him, right? And it seems I'm afraid I might have to undergo dialysis, right? It's as if I had the tumour . . . and the tumour had invaded all of me, that the operation was too late, you know? That you had lied in the diagnosis, when you read me . . . how do you call it?

A: The anatopathological?

P: The anatopathological, yes.

A: You speak as if you were convinced that you still have the disease—bone-marrow cancer—and they haven't solved anything. So now you stopped being Pierre and turned into Dad, you think you are Dad with the myeloma and make me take the place of Pierre who is deceiving you, and you think you are Dad. . . . Do you follow me? And you believe I deceive you like they deceived your father with the diagnosis . . . and you pretend or believe to be the deceived Dad. . . .

The patient's gradual acceptance over a period of several days of this interpretation relieved this particular psychotic regression. Interpretation was the regular means, throughout his treatment, of helping him reverse psychotic regressions. Although the use of regression as a defence was not emphasized in the given example, it was an almost regular element of effective interpretations.

I shall discuss how the fantasy of bleeding is expressed in the actual body through a severe illness where the patient really bleeds . . . she loses blood through the skin.

Transcript 3

I will now present a clinical case based on the envelope of the skin and not specifically based on the psychotic body image.

Psychosomatic skin disturbances
due to early abandonment

"Julian"

Julian[1] was a patient about 35 years of age. He had been asthmatic since his childhood, and he had also had eczema and desquamatory and eruptive disturbances all over his skin since then. He was a researcher in the field of entomology. In the year he had been in analysis with me, I was able to establish that he inoculated others with his depression. In the course of his life he had had a number of suicidal and melancholic friends, which characterized his way of relating to people. He seemed to choose his friends on a sadomasochistic basis, with projection of his own suicidal tendencies and a tendency to function as the parasite of a host (the other person). He sought friends with melancholic traits, people who needed people, with whom he established a *folie à deux* in which Julian inoculated the other with his melancholia. He identified himself with the object the others desired, through which he also became an ego ideal for his friends, whom he helped and advised.

In his sessions he subtly belittled the analysis. He objected to everything I told him and then tried "to cooperate" in order "to help me" so that I did not "feel bad". As I had achieved nothing up to that point, he was going to try to make up for that by doing me the favour of continuing to be my patient. In this way he transformed me into the needy and destructive one and helped me by projecting his own destroyed part onto me. It was a defence against envy through the projective identification of his own devaluated and dependent aspects. He became the nurturing breast and denied his need for help—a situation that seemed to be connected with his experience of early object relations. According to the patient, his mother had "got rid of him" in his first year of life and had had him breast-fed by a hired wet nurse in a remote place. The wet nurse spoke a different dialect. In this respect, a construction may be made: namely, the hypothesis that his mother must have had a post-partum psychosis. Likewise, the language spoken by his wet nurse might correspond to the mother's idiosyncratic language during that period, meant to be understood only by her.

The father seemed to be psychotic, with a rather brittle façade of social adjustment. He talked about everything and nothing and made remarks about facts known to him alone. He would begin a sentence, interrupt himself, and then continue with some other idea. According to the patient, his father sometimes even became incoherent and flooded his son with his own chaos. Thus, the father seemed to be an incoherent man, and the mother had to put up with him.

The patient endeavoured to turn me into a kind of automaton who gave the answers as he led me to through his material. These answers were no surprise for him but, rather, what he had expected. I seemed to be a hired wet nurse who appeared when he called me, not to satisfy him but to gratify myself, as I was the one in need. Actually, this was a situation of mutual slavery, in which he said what he believed I wanted to hear and tried to make me say what he expected. By inverting his real relation of dependency and making the wet nurse need *him*—a situation that included some elements of reality, since it was a *hired* wet nurse—he used a defence against his narcissistic injury and feeling of dependency. However, at the same time, he ultimately established a mechanical bond with the others.

> For the first time, Julian brought a dream on a Monday, after the weekend holiday. He came in, looked at the couch, and said, "This leather couch looks like a urinal, it's dirty, the leather looks creased on one side: it looks like a used sheet." He lay down and added, "My arms are bitten to pieces by mosquitoes, they bit me all over the arms, here and here" (he showed me his arms and shoulders up to the neck, including the lower part of his jaw). Then he said, "I got a letter from my brother, who is in Mother's house. Mother's house is always the same, he writes me. You know the kind, a big house in a far-away province. The windows are never opened, maybe once a year if there happens to be a visitor. All that makes it a closed place, with a smell of mould, filth, and confinement that is horrifying, frightening, and oppressive. And my brother tells me she served the same old biscuits. D'you know what they are like? She doesn't offer a biscuit less than a year old. She keeps them in closed tins and won't give them to you when you ask her; only when they are old, covered with mould, and can no longer be eaten, then she opens the tin and offers them to her visitors or children. The smell in that living-room, that huge living-room, is unbearable. My brother also tells me that he was at a wedding party, and they made the usual jokes. For example, the bride and the bridegroom were at the party, and when soup was served, some of the guests

defecated into the soup so the others would eat the shit. It's disgusting to mix shit with soup or food."

Immediately, he added: "I had a dream, a dream where *I fell into a deep well, I fell into a very deep well, maybe with mud at the bottom. I was shut up and didn't know how to get out. I tried to get out of that well with mud and earth, where there were a kind of nails*" (he shows the size), "*roughly 40 centimetres, half a metre (two feet) long. Some were securely nailed to the wall, others were loose, others were in bad shape, some were bent. I attempted to climb up the well through those nails surrounding me. As they were loose, I slipped or fell down or got pierced all over. I tried to climb up; I felt smothered, suffocated, I was covered with mud. After a great effort, when I was exhausted, pierced all over, slipping down, I succeeded in climbing up those nails covering the walls and getting to the top, near the surface. That wasn't the way out. Before that there were marble stairs and then the scene changed. The stairs were made of marble, polished stones, with a lovely artificial light, and now I could come out, climbing some beautiful stairs leading to a living-room, as if it were the way out of a living-room or a very beautiful hall.*"

He associated this with the memory of an occasion when he had been absolutely alone in a field, without his parents, looking for frogs or tadpoles to avoid experiencing feelings of loneliness. He tripped and fell into a puddle. He narrated this episode so as to make reference to "things I do when I'm alone". This situation was connected to a period in which his parents had left him in another house (note the connection between this period of his life and his early experience of being breast-fed by a hired wet nurse). He associated this fact with his high-school days. He had stayed in the school all day and with some fellow students had stolen bread from a bakery.

Julian's material was interpreted in the following manner. I had abandoned him on Friday, and he felt no analyst would support him, no one would hold him in this arms, he would fall into a deep well where there was nothing to hold on to, like a baby who feels his mother, instead of holding him to feed and cuddle him, drops him, suddenly lets him fall and, what is worse, leaves him alone without food. The fact that the scene occurred in darkness represents the period in which the baby is left alone, as he felt during the weekend. I pointed out that this is what he felt had happened since Friday and that is why he tried to get inside me, to steal the biscuits, the food, the thoughts I had, since I did not hold him and let him fall.

It is necessary to emphasize once again that this is the first dream the patient had brought on a Monday. Furthermore, the dream shows evidence of this having experienced emotions for the first time after a weekend.

The staircase of nails represents my arms transformed into something piercing him. He had violently, intrusively, got inside me in order to empty me of my contents (the biscuits he had stored) and retaliatively he felt surrounded by teeth. (In a personal communication, Esther Bick adds that the nails really symbolize his fingernails; these represent the first expression of an aggressive contact previous to the teeth. They can be turned against the self: for example, when one angrily makes a fist. We find in this an example of an attempt at illusory self-containment, in which the baby believes himself to be his own armour, before the real ministrations of an external object allow him projections. The nails represent the fingernails in their dual role—aggressive and self-containing—as they also help him to hold on, to support himself, to keep from falling, and to climb up instead.) In his fantasy Pierre had transformed me into the mother who kept the valuable analytic food in a box and only gave it to him much later (one year later, the following week), when it tasted rotten. His voracious attack included dental and excretory elements, which he used to try to disparage me.

But, as we have seen, the inside into which he had got turned against him, with nails that wounded him, which were the same teeth with which he had attacked me, a hypothesis corroborated by his reference to the appearance of the couch and to the faeces that had changed the valuable elements into something disgusting. His allusions to the mosquitoes–teeth turning against him are along the same lines. Thus, I had become an object that turned itself vindictively against him, with the same weapons he had used to attack me. The nails seem to be the equivalent of the teeth (for instance, there is a saying, "to hang by tooth and nail"), and in this sense the clinical material would seem to indicate a search for self-support when he experiences de lack of environmental containment. This search comprises—as that of the infant who, being alone, closes its fists and sticks its nails into his palms—both the illusion of self-support and independence from others and an attack equivalent to what was experienced by the baby on feeling abandoned. Moreover, in the following session another aspect was clarified with respect to the marble stairs at the top of the well. He relates it to the entrance of the building where my consulting-room is—that is, with entering a more luminous, solid world, on Monday, when he could feel there was something under his feet. (In an investigation I have been carrying out for the past ten years about certain psychosomatic disturbances of temporal–mandibular joint articulation, with pain and persistent contractions, I found three factors from the psychoanalytic point of view: (1) illusion of self-support *vis-à-vis* feelings of having been abandoned; (2) melancholic attack upon an object; and (3) closing oneself up against the fantasy of psychotic depletion–fear of a lack of container and a closure of orifices; fear of becoming empty.)

Throughout the weekend the patient remained a prisoner inside me, as in the well he had dreamed about. For this reason the couch remained the bottom of the well until Monday: a urinal with mud, piss, shit, and nails that persecuted and pierced him. For this reason, too, he alluded to his swollen skin and his feeling surrounded by a number of damaging objects. From the material about his mother's attitude with the biscuits, we can also infer the patient's experiences of having been retained inside her only to expel him, as if he were faeces. There is also the fantasy that his mother's breast gives putrid milk, and that was why he was condemned to have a hired wet nurse, which, in turn, was the equivalent of being fed by a breast with putrid contents.

The patient's answer to my interpretations was the following: "It's only with my wife that I'm not afraid to surrender myself, to get into her. On the contrary, I'm very much afraid with P and G [lovers]." After a brief silence, he said: "I'm thinking about something, I don't know why, but I suppose it has to do with this. I happened to think about crayfish and slugs, worms, jellyfish, because they strike me as weak animals that spread out, disperse. They have no consistency, especially the jellyfish, since it doesn't have a shell. I always thought the same way about the crayfish, that if its armour were removed, it would turn into that kind of animal: drivelling, diluted, spreading out."

I pointed out to him his need to get inside another skin, inside me, inside his wife, inside P or G, so as to feel surrounded and not spreading out. This is what he did in the dream, in order to feel in an enveloping analytic shell, although he devoured me inside, as we had seen a moment before. Herbert Rosenfeld (1965, 1987) remarks that there are patients who try to penetrate, not through the fantasy of chewing the nipple but through other means, such as piercing the other's skin.)

"When the crayfish's skin or shell falls off—I don't know how to say this—I believe it is something I was always afraid of about my-self, as if I were left without a skeleton, weak, inert, had nothing, was spread out. You know, the jellyfish was always my problem, I even wrote about it. I don't know if I suck, if I steal by making people talk, but I remembered something you told me once, that I make people answer, respond, I get responses from them, I take things out, it's like emptying them."

I interpreted that he wanted to get inside me, to live inside my skin, and that from Friday to Monday he had tried to by resorting to another shell, the well. He tried to be like a parasite. (Bick suggests that this patient seemed to function as an external parasite, that is, he attached himself to the other from the outside.) But then, having got inside me violently and greedily, with fantasies of biting, uri-nating and defecating, he ended up feeling that what surrounded him pierced his skin; the couch merged with his skin and he filed it with urine and faeces, as a revenge. The patient thought about the interpretation.

In addition, everything he had referred to with the name of "armour" corresponds to a special kind of defensive system the patient used and which I had succeeded in detecting after several weeks of hard work, which included the working-through of my own countertransference feelings, since I felt like a conditioned and manipulated automaton. Finally, when I understood that Julian's linguistic formulations here were a kind of diluted and implicit question that induced only one possible answer, I discovered that the armour corresponded to his defensive system.

With respect to the material connected with a shell, its connection with Bick's hypothesis of a second skin is evident, a hypothesis that in the context of this session is linked to other formulations that account for it: those referring to terror. Indeed, Julian seemed to have built the "protective" although restrictive armour as a defence against terror. His dependency from this second skin preserved him, in this way, from the massive loss of control over his own emotions.

The references to his difficulties to surrender seem to illustrate Winnicott's (1971) hypothesis that the pseudo-self must surrender to the ego. They also seem to illustrate Julian's fantasy about the lack of a mother who could contain his projections, together with the material about the smothering living-room. However, the fact of having brought a dream with these characteristics on a Monday is a sign of a greater capacity to surrender, of some hope that he would be able to overcome his impotence to establish bonds of useful dependency. The "happy" ending of the dream has to do with his overcoming his omnipotent projective identification (armour) and the ensuing tortures at the thought of the imminent session. In this sense, the dream creates a sort of bridge or link between the weekend's experiences and their communication in the session.

> After remaining silent for a while, Julian referred to M, a young woman with whom he had been impotent abroad. He had met her at a "very crazy" time. He thought that he had fooled her and that perhaps the same thing was happening now with another young woman, with whom he was afraid to be impotent again. I interpreted to him that he was afraid of having destroyed himself and remaining trapped, smothered—as when he suffered from asthma—vindictively by me. He was afraid that, instead of nourishment, good food, I may give him back excrement, and, at the same time, of being trapped inside me, as with M, the equivalent of being inside a mother who induced his asthma, closed windows, and surrounded him with stink, mould, and poisoned air. He was afraid I may give him inedible, useless interpretations–biscuits. This seems to correspond to a confused moment in which he did not discriminate between hate and affection, just as he was afraid to receive a violent reintrojection from me (H. Rosenfeld, 1987).

Moreover, this patient showed muscular hyperactivity in his everyday activities, which seemed to be a compensation for the lack of an adequate container (skin). In this muscular activity he lost energies through his body, as if he lacked something to contain them. With this activity he tried to find limits for his self, but this attempt was always unsuccessful, and his energies vanished. Thus muscular activity seemed to be related to the need for an immediate motor discharge of anxieties, rather than to a capacity to control his own muscles, which he could only have acquired through a better-organized notion of the skin. This view coincides with Bick's ideas about the creation of a "second skin" through exaggerated muscular activity.

With respect to this clinical material, I want to stress a particular kind of omnipotent projective identification, which is observed in certain patients who in their fantasy remain imprisoned inside the therapist's body, with their whole skin surrounded by piercing, harmful teeth, by excrements threatening to suffocate or burn, as a consequence of getting inside the object, which they attack through the different parts of the body. In their fantasy, these patients can use different orifices of their parent's organs to penetrate. In this material, a non-existent orifice is chosen omnipotently, as if the patient were convinced that it is possible to gain access to the other's inside through any zone of his body image.

The patient can also be considered as identifying himself with the object through a violent projective identification—that is, ending up inside the object, confused with it, and experiencing what happens to the other, as Donald Meltzer (1966) and Herbert Rosenfeld (1965, 1987) pointed out. Instead, I prefer to follow the theoretical and clinical description given by this patient, that is, the return of the penetration with teeth and nails from outside and his experiencing in the session the continuation of the dream. (Besides, I always consider it important to detect a dream's continuation in the course of a session.)

All this constitutes a set of hypotheses allowing us to understand some patients' skin disturbances in a different way.

With respect to Julian, the skin disturbances involved the whole body, which is connected to the fact that he was asthmatic. It should be remembered that asthmatics are people who experience object loss at the skin level in terms of cold. In Julian's case there is, furthermore, an aggression against the skin (in the dream)—that is, an attack on the part of the self-experiencing loneliness. Piercing also represents grief over the object loss. Some patients use the hand that scratches the skin as an equivalent of the retaliatory object that has been attacked and which turns against the ego, of which it had previously been a victim.

Julian resembled those cases showing a tendency to resort to a pseudo-self, as described by Winnicott (1971). These patients present an armour of false maturity that includes an underlying underdeveloped ego.

In the case of "Irene", a drug-addicted patient to whom I referred in a previous paper (Rosenfeld, 1976), the lack of a containing skin seemed to determine the need for taking drugs, which was designed to make her experience the cutaneous stimulus of heat, that is, of a container, the opposite of object lack. She got inside the inanimate object, the drug, so that it would envelop her.

Transcript 5

"Juana"

I will now consider another case: a woman who seemed to have less significant problems in relation to the skin. "Juana", 25 years old, resorted to an intense omnipotent projective identification in order to get inside the object. She very often lost herself inside the other, a situation that was manifested through prolonged silences in the course of the session, forms of catatonia, or else extreme bodily tension.

One day Juana brought the following dream: *"Several thieves break into a house, turn everything upside down and steal all the hens and clothes they find inside."* The previous clinical material had had to do with her wish to re-establish a bond with a mother who was not as stingy and hoarding as her own. In the following session she came in and said, "Oh, but this couch is a carving fork rather than a toilet." From her associations we understood that she saw sharp-pointed carving forks in the leather of the couch, in the cushions, and that there was nothing that could receive her defecation.

This implied that in the preceding session the patient had made a violent projective identification inside the therapist, expressed through the dream, in which she had stolen hens (food) and clothes (skin), which allowed her to feel surrounded by a skin that enveloped her. But, in attacking it with urine and faeces and with her teeth, she came to the following session feeling surrounded by the same aggressive elements that she had used to attack the therapist, which were now directed against herself. The couch appeared as the body inside which she was surrounded by the aggressive elements she had previously used against the therapist (teeth–mails that carve and faeces). In the dream, clothes were stolen, and there was a reference to hens, which, of course, have feathers. Juana's underlying fantasy was that, *vis-à-vis* the end of the analytic week, she had to steal the therapist's contents in order not to starve. This attack upon the analyst's inside is qualitatively different from Julian's and is connected to anxieties of castration in women (fantasies of a penis–baby that destroys her inside).

As for catatonia in the sessions, it seemed to be the expression of an attempt to control her emotions—above all, her resentment when she did not feel understood and had fantasies about an impatient and greedy attack, in order to get what the therapist kept from her. But this control affected only the voluntary muscles and, because of this, had to do with hysterical conversions. The counterpart was the possibility of dramatizing conflicts—unlike what happened with Julian, whose conflict involved one organ and had to do with psychosomatic illness, which was much more difficult to overcome. Juana's conflicts seemed more associated with maternity (hens) and, on the other hand, the clothes were not the equivalent of a shell, as may be observed in Julian's case, but something less rigid, in the nature of body preservation rather than the restriction of its development.

Correlations between the clinical material and Perrault's Peau d'Âne

In Charles Perrault's tale of the Ass's Skin, the princess puts on an ass's dirty, filthy skin, which amounts to an overestimation of the faeces. The girl does that on account of the object loss, loneliness on her mother's death. Thus, we find here a clear connection between both materials. The young girl and the patient regard the skin partly as generated by them and partly as if it were the surface of another body. On the other hand, the "treasure" of the patient's mother, the biscuits, have an anal connotation, and the same may be said of the soup at the wedding party. This is similar to the riches (golden coins) created by the ass through defecation.

Other correspondences can be found in this case study. In the tale and in the clinical material we observe a precocious pseudo-genitality as a defence against the working-through of losses. We also find another aspect usually associated with precocious pseudo-genitality: hyperkinesis as self-support and an attempt to re-establish one's own identity. Thus, hyperkinesis functions as a second skin containing one's self-feeling; but at the same time it implies a rudimentary attempt at regulating interpersonal distances, in the service of drawing near and drawing apart.

The patient repeated in the transference several aspects of the princess's story, including mourning and the use of a second skin, which she afterwards struggles to get rid of. To regard the couch as a urinal or creased leather indicates that the conflict and the dream continue in the session. Besides, aspects of a defensive pseudo-genitality against the feeling of loss become manifest.

Notes

1. This clinical case was published in Rosenfeld (1988), pp. 65–77.

Dialogue with Shakespeare
and Jean-Paul Sartre
about psychoanalysis
and scientific methodology

All the world's a stage,
And all the men and women merely players:
They have their exits and their entrances;
And one man in his time plays many parts. . . .

Shakespeare, *As You Like It* (Act II, Scene 7)

Freud's method

D avid Rosenfeld [DR]: Let us begin this seminar by trying to express the questions we have about "Analysis Terminable and
Interminable" (Freud, 1937a).

Gerardo: What was the personal and social background of Freud's
treatment of this subject?

Elsa: Freud put it that the main purpose was to think again about what
psychoanalysis achieved with patients.

Goyo: It is a taking stock of his life in 1937. With the Nazis already
in Germany, perhaps he was thinking that he, as a scientist, was
powerless to cure the diseases of cancer, Nazism, and war. So he

returned to the destructive instinct, the death drive, and to the possibility of an equilibrium between Eros and Thanatos.

Arturo: Freud tried to deal with the question in the field of research with which he was familiar—that of psychoanalysis. He was particularly concerned with situations where a complete cure was not achieved. He examined clinical cases familiar to him.

Elsa: He also wondered whether the duration of treatment could be reduced, whether a permanent cure was possible, and whether the patient could be inoculated against falling ill again.

Coco: Although he had so much to say about the possibility of reducing the time, what Freud in fact achieved was to prolong our training analyses from three weeks to six years!

Elsa: To me it is almost a testament of his life, work, and doubts.

Aída: . . . with the aim of locating the obstacles to the cure.

Goyo: Rather than trying to confirm his successes, Freud looked for the obstacles. His work is a model of how a researcher and epistemologist of science should explore an unknown area of which he is still largely ignorant. He demonstrates a specific approach to research in the philosophy of science. Epistemology is concerned with the validation, verification, or refutation of the theories and models we are creating in science. It studies how scientific theories, and scientific knowledge in general, are produced and investigates the criteria for acceptance or rejection of a theory.

DR: It was Karl Popper who introduced and championed the idea that the most important thing in science was not to try to verify but to falsify a theory. If it was wrong, it could be discarded, but if it was not wrong, it would show its strength by not allowing itself to be refuted (Popper, 1965). Refuting theories reduces the risk of error. One of the most valuable lessons Freud has taught us is how a scholar ought to confront new problems and difficulties.

Goyo: Another scientist might have called the value of psychoanalytic theory into question in view of the clinical failures. If cure or improvement in the patients is taken as the criterion, it may be felt that the theory is of no use if the patients are not cured. . . .

DR: Freud believed in his theory and did not abandon it, although, according to orthodox epistemological models, it might seem to have been refuted. Freud's view was that auxiliary or complementary *ad hoc* hypotheses could be added. These would draw attention to local areas of difficulty without causing the theory to collapse. In this paper (Freud, 1937a), one such hypothesis concerns earlier alterations of the ego that he had not taken into account. For Freud, a failure does not mean that a theory is completely wrong. The core of the theory may be correct and may remain intact. Freud would think there were additional factors that had not been sufficiently analysed or taken into account. Here the epistemologist in Freud would try to find auxiliary hypotheses, either to track down what was at fault or to preserve the core of his theory. Examining what new auxiliary hypotheses could be added was the tactic he adopted in order to find out where previous hypotheses had failed.

Goyo: When we talk about "obstacles", what we mean is that Freud was looking for unknown factors that might be responsible for the peculiarity of the clinical results.

Gerardo: He was more inclined to look for epistemological factors that would enable him to maintain the theory. In seeking auxiliary hypotheses to explain the failures, Freud tried to examine those factors closest to the clinical situation that were responsible for the failures. He had done this long before, in the case of Dora, where, after encountering difficulties, he discovered which factors led to breaking off the analysis or to acting out.

DR: Here again, he tried to round off his theory with appropriate additional hypotheses. We could say that Freud was attempting to complement his theory by introducing new models to explain the difficulties. If this tactic were successful, the theory would be enriched. I should like to stress that Freud was not discouraged by the difficulties he met and did not abandon his theory. His attitude was to re-examine the problem, and this led him to important discoveries.

Elsa: I believe that Freud showed partial discouragement when he wrote: "Every step forward is only half as big as it looks at first" (Freud, 1937a, p. 228).

DR: As the champion of analytic theory, he did not allow himself to be defeated. He preserved that theory and used it. Thus, in trying to uncover the obstacles responsible for the apparent failures of analysis, he rediscovered the existence of primitive and severe alterations of the ego, which he had not previously considered in their full magnitude.

Arturo: Had he referred to alterations of the ego before?

DR: He had spoken of the ego in the 1890s in "The Psychotherapy of Hysteria" (in *Studies on Hysteria*, Freud, 1895d), although he here connected it with an instinctual force. By the time of *The Ego and the Id* (1923b), it was presented as an organization having specific functions and properties. In "Neurosis and Psychosis" (1924b) he described an ego that restricted, modified, and deformed itself in order to adapt. He had become interested in this question when he considered the structure of the ego in "On Narcissism: An Introduction" (1914c).

Arturo: I would also mention the book on Leonardo (1910c), in which he referred to narcissistic object choice. The ego appeared there as a structure.

Bruno: We should also not forget Schreber.

Arturo: We should remember that previously Freud had been using a dynamic concept of strength, with repression opposed to the repressed. Now he places more emphasis on defences altering the actual structure of the ego.

Coco: Another problem Freud discussed was the role of the constitutional versus traumatic aspects. He wrote, "An aetiology of the traumatic sort offers by far the more favourable field for analysis. . . . Only in such cases can one speak of an analysis having been definitively ended" (1937a, p. 220).

Elsa: In another paragraph, Freud refers to innate modifications of the ego due to defence mechanisms that exacerbate the alterations of the ego.

Aída: But here he explains that the ego alterations are of mixed origin. "The aetiology of every neurotic disturbance is, after all, a mixed one. . . . As a rule there is a combination of both factors, the constitutional and the accidental" (1937a, p. 220).

Trauma

Coco: It seems to me that the word *trauma* as used by Freud here means something external.

Arturo: Freud's conception of trauma in Part V of this paper is not the same as in *Beyond the Pleasure Principle* (1920g), where the implication is that the excitation breaks through the stimulus barrier.

Bruno: I think that here he is talking not about traumatic neurosis in the external sense but about the internal release of a quantity of libido. From this point of view, trauma can be a normal quantity of libido that enters the mental apparatus and surprises the *weak ego*. When he refers here to the *traumatic factor,* he is referring to psychoneurosis.

Goyo: For me, *trauma* means a relation between the entry of a quantity of libido and the defences. It occurs whenever the sum of excitation overcomes the defensive barriers.

Arturo: I see it differently. I believe trauma is related here not to internal things but to external ones, as it was in the works on hysteria.

Bruno: This excitation may come from outside or inside. If it comes from outside, we are dealing with a traumatic neurosis. If it stems from internal sources, we are in the field of the psychoneuroses of traumatic aetiology.

Arturo: I should like to add that the concept of trauma as used in *Beyond the Pleasure Principle* (1920g) is seen as something that *does* give rise to alterations in the ego. But I would emphasize that in this paper Freud (1937a) gave added meaning to his concept of trauma of 40 years earlier, when he was talking about hysteria.

Coco: You say that this sum of excitation comes from outside only. . . .

Arturo: But I wonder whether the developments that took place in experience were paralleled in theory. In this seminar I stand for the person who doubts that theories evolve with the passage of time. Might it not be that a theory regresses instead of advancing in a straight line?

Gerardo: I, on the other hand, am the one in this group who thinks that the theories evolve and grow along a straight line of development.

DR: I think that there are some arguments about Freud in which people forget that they are talking about different thoughts, periods, and times.

Jean-Paul: All thought goes through different periods of growth and retreat—the process is dialectical.

Goyo: What an interesting methodological problem! I believe that this discussion concretely illustrates the ebb and flow in the history of a theory, and in general the methodology of the sciences. . . .

DR: The relation between the strengths of the trauma and of the ego is a dialectical one. The concept of interrelated structures and sub-structures and the dualistic dialectic of conflicts in Freud's work are fundamental.

Food for thought

Arturo: In "The Psychotherapy of Hysteria" (1895d), Freud took an-other look at his method of treatment and catharsis, and it was only 40 years later that he discovered that a change in the technical approach to interpretation was necessary. If only the id (and not the ego) is interpreted, we have interpreted only for ourselves not for the patient" (1937a, p. 238).

DR: As regards technique and the formulation of interpretations, what you say suggests to me that sometimes the fact that a message is given does not mean that it is received, listened to, classified, un-derstood, or decoded by the recipient. Present-day communications theory has thrown a great deal of light on the specific problems involved.

Aída: What you are saying is there in Freud's text: "We have increased his knowledge, but altered nothing else in him" (1937a, p. 233).

Jean-Paul: He already had something to say about this in the papers on technique. He was now adding a new structural understanding to it.

Goyo: This point is one of the "obstacles" to the cure, which we may identify as one of the themes of communication theory. To return to what you were saying, Freud's point is that the theories and techniques were not bad, but they were insufficiently complete for the patient to acquire knowledge. As the analyst's theoretical knowledge increases, so he is able to modify his technique and capability.

DR: Yes, but consider what a difficult job we have. After all, not only do we have to ensure that the patient acquires a certain knowledge, but we must also judge the patient's own theories about himself. The epistemology of the psychoanalyst is much more active than that of the physicist, who does not have this problem. Psychoanaly-sis raises a fascinating epistemological problem because, in addition to what happens in other sciences, where the scientist acts on the material and observes how it responds, the psychoanalyst performs a specific epistemological function. He causes the patient to know something and to evaluate the knowledge he has acquired.

Coco: This is complicated, because he is also involved as a person in this function.

Gerardo: This is one of the obstacles that Freud includes under the wider heading of "obstacles to the treatment".

Aída: In other words, it again becomes clear that obstacles are not a result of mistakes in psychoanalytic theory, but an indication of areas of research still to be carried out. These include the limitations of the therapist as a person.

Goyo: Freud was an epistemologist who modified the auxiliary hypotheses of psychoanalysis in order to preserve a theory. It was these auxiliary hypotheses that were not complete—for instance, once the childhood of the Wolf Man, his archaic narcissism, his paranoid regressions, and his aggression were reviewed and reconceptualized, a much wider and more severe psychopathology was uncovered.

DR: It was the same with Newton. There is no need to change Newton's theory because someone suddenly discovers a part of the sky that he did not investigate sufficiently, and in which there is a disturbing mass. This is not a flaw in the theory but a new piece of information to be included, one that will be taken into account in future calculations. If we relate this to clinical practice, the issues relate to prior alterations of the ego that had not yet been discovered and had as a consequence not been studied. To characterize this unknown factor, it is necessary to make new hypotheses. The appropriate epistemological tactic is one that will enable us to penetrate further into this unknown factor. One obstacle to this is the name we give to what is not yet known and has not yet been studied, and which changes the outcome of our predictions.

Coco: How many psychoanalysts and scientists have believed they already knew everything!

Elsa: Again and again there is the discovery of something new that can be appropriately incorporated into one's own theory.

Gerardo: We may even believe Freud's metapsychology may have been an enterprise of theoretical creation—that he created a metapsychology for each individual or particular type of patient. So we would have the conscious/unconscious dichotomy for hysterics; ego, superego, and id for melancholics, depressives, schizoid patients, and so forth.

Elsa: Sometimes not even the creators themselves can appreciate the full theoretical implications of their own discoveries.

DR: Something like that happened to Einstein. Revolutionary as he was, when Heisenberg and his followers argued, on the basis of the master's ideas, that the ultimate laws of the universe might be probabilistic and not deterministic, Einstein turned aside and pronounced the famous sentence "God does not play dice."

Coco: There is much that we still do not know.

William: "There are more things in heaven and earth. . . ." [*Hamlet*, Act I, Scene 5]

Aída: When Freud describes resistances to the uncovering of resistances, he is theorizing about something that was hitherto unknown.

Arturo: Not entirely. In *Inhibitions, Symptoms and Anxiety* (1926d) he describes one of the ego resistances.

Aída: The relevant quotation from "Analysis Terminable and Interminable" is: "we should not reckon on meeting with a resistance against the uncovering of resistances. But what happens is this. . . . The ego ceases to support our efforts at uncovering the id" (1937a, p. 239).

Bruno: This paper was used as a foundation for subsequent theories, such as Hartmann's (1964) idea of ego development, and the concepts of autonomy, changing states of ego organization, adaptation, perception and so on discussed by Hartmann and by Anna Freud in her book *The Ego and Mechanisms of Defence* (1936), quoted in Freud's paper.

DR: According to Blum (1987), other authors in the United States stress the importance of this work in stimulating their ideas on and interest in pathogenesis and theories of evolutionary development.

Aída: While others—for instance, Melanie Klein (1975b)—emphasize earlier aspects of childhood object relations.

Analysability

DR: What sort of patients was Freud referring to, and what sort of analysts was he thinking of?

Gerardo: The patients I see in my hospital practice—borderline, psychotics, and drug addicts—are, I believe, different from the ones Freud is referring to here.

Arturo: But let us remember that Freud taught us about serious pathologies in regard to such cases as those of Schreber, the Rat Man, and the Wolf Man.

DR: What concept of analysability does each of you have in mind?

Aída: What Freud says is that a patient might not be amenable to analysis owing to a structural alteration of the ego.

Goyo: In addition to the criteria of analysability given by Freud, we now have the ability, 50 years later, to make new and better diagnoses with the new theoretical knowledge we have. A psychosomatic clinical picture, a neurosis, a borderline case, and a temporary psychosis are not the same thing.

Aída: I am surprised Freud did not include here theoretical concepts such as psychosomatic illnesses and nonverbal languages.

Arturo: It seems to me that he did discuss psychosomatic illness to some extent in the work on President Wilson.

DR: Returning to the subject of the analysability—or otherwise—of a patient, I believe that today we know more about the concepts of intersystemic and intrasystemic conflict, weakness of the ego, negative therapeutic reactions—whether true or false—and primitive forms of transference, sometimes called delusional, psychotic, or highly regressive transferences.

Aída: As someone interested in child analysis, I should like to add that, by helping us to locate or to date conflicts within the ego in the patient's development, this paper was partly responsible for allowing child analyses to begin at an earlier age. This changed our ideas about analysability and prognosis.

Gerardo: It had the same effect on the psychoses.

Aída: I should like to ask a question about the part of the paper where Freud says, "In states of acute crisis analysis is to all intents and purposes unusable" (1937a, p. 232).

Coco: Is he referring to acute internal states—for example, an ego absorbed in mourning—or to acute external situations, or to acute psychotic crises?

Arturo: There is a reference in "The Psychotherapy of Hysteria" (1895d) to the clinical pictures of acute hysteria. Freud had the feeling that everything he said was diluted for patients in the midst of these acute symptoms. However, he seems to wonder whether treatment in acute states prevents the appearance of subsequent symptoms.

Gerardo: On the subject of acute psychosis, if I may answer you, I would say that we are now able to confront and investigate episodes of acute psychosis with more theoretical and technical knowledge than we had 50 years ago. The work of Herbert Rosenfeld (1987) and Harold Searles (1979) clearly illustrates the usefulness of strictly psychoanalytic interpretations in dealing with psychotic patients. Might this not indicate a change in the concept of analysability since 1937?

DR: Since this paper makes us think about the concept of analysability, I should like to refer to the developments of communications theory by Bateson (Bateson & Jackson, 1964), Watzlawick (Watzlawick, Beavin, & Jackson, 1967), and Liberman (1970–72). It was Liberman who applied this to psychoanalysis, maintaining that the concept of analysability should not be considered from the point of view of the diagnosis of a single person but depended on the possibility of establishing good communication between the members of the analytic couple. Some analysis, owing to their personal characteristics and theoretical knowledge, may not perform well with some patients.

Aída: Do you think this paper encouraged the analysis of psychotic or very disturbed children?

DR: I would say yes, it did so by encouraging the analysis of earlier disturbances and of alterations of the ego. My interest is aroused by Freud's statement that these resistances are *"separated off* [italics added] within the ego" (1937a, p. 239). In the German edition the word here translated as "separated off" is *gesondert*. Freud does not use, instead, the word *Spaltung,* which is closer to dissociation or splitting. I want to stress this point because it touches on a field of research that particularly fascinates me—that of parts that remain *encapsulated but separated off within the ego.* This relates to the area of autism and infantile psychosis and especially to encapsulated autistic nuclei that, according to some recent conceptions, survive in adult patients. These separated nuclei may reappear in a different way from aspects that have been dissociated or split off. This is a mechanism that may define new forms of diagnosis in clinical practice.

Feelings, affects, passions, and illnesses

Aída: The negative therapeutic reaction as an *obstacle* that appears before any progress in the treatment is a clear phenomenon about which there can be no argument.

DR: Provided that you can detect *when* there is progress—that, at any rate, you have your own personal definition. The analyst does not always notice negative therapeutic reactions, because very often they take silent, hidden forms. We are not dealing with concrete, static facts like those in physics. In other words, any concept is relative and depends on the definition given to it by the analyst in the clinical field. The same thing happens with the concept of acting out. This is not a concrete fact, a "thing-in-itself". It is only a definition that I give in the psychoanalytic field to an *action* performed by the patient. If I then define it, I add it to the theoretical baggage I carry with me. Learn to think that everything is relative. . . .

Aída: But the negative therapeutic reaction is an obstacle. . . .

DR: No, *I insist on the relativity of the concept*. For example, the negative therapeutic reaction may be a step forward in cases of obsessional character pathology, in silent schizoid states, and in patients who discover that arguing is not the same thing as killing. In the psychoses, apparent negative therapeutic reactions may be attempts to preserve a little piece of the self reconstructed in the treatment. The patient is afraid he may be robbed of this. In a reanalysis, it may be a violent reaction against the previous therapist. This last type of negative therapeutic reaction can, if diagnosed early, be overcome.

Aída: We can expand from the problems of Ferenczi with his ex-analyst Freud to the problems of *termination of analyses* and *training analyses*.

Bruno: Yes. A key point is that what the analyst received in his own analysis must continue to operate within him. Freud says, "But we reckon on the stimuli that he has received in his own analysis not ceasing when it ends and on the processes of remodelling the ego continuing spontaneously" (1937a, p. 249).

DR: An analysis may be *terminable* for the therapist but *interminable* in the mind of the patient.

Gerardo: Changes in the personal or scientific life of a psychoanalyst usually cause him to think again about the values he received from his own past analysis. Even the good aspects of this treatment may be called into question.

Coco: During the Argentinean military dictatorship around 1977, patients and therapists sometimes had opposing, dissimilar, or contrary political opinions.

Elsa: Something like that happened to psychoanalysts in 1937 in the Berlin Society, with the Nazis in power.

Goyo: I find this beautiful sentence remarkable, "And finally we must not forget that the analytic relationship is based on a love of truth— that is, on a recognition of reality—and that it precludes any kind of sham or deceit" (1937a, p. 248).

DR: Being honest as a therapist means teaching people not to falsify reality.

William: "This above all: to thine own self be true and it must follow, as the night the day, thou canst not then be false to any man. . . ." [*Hamlet,* Act I, Scene 3]

Coco: On behalf of the neurotics—sorry, of the psychoanalysts, as we are all a bit neurotic—I should like to draw attention to this sentence: "Our aim will not be to rub off every peculiarity of human character for the sake of a schematic 'normality,' nor yet to demand that the person who has been 'thoroughly analysed' shall feel no passions and develop no internal conflicts" (1937a, p. 250).

William: "Have we not eyes? Have we not hands, organs, dimensions, senses, affections, passions? Fed with the same food, subject to the same diseases, healed by the same means, warmed and cooled by the same winter and summer? If you prick us, do we not bleed? If you tickle us, do we not laugh?" [*Merchant of Venice,* Act III, Scene 1]?

DR: As Lagache (1961) wrote, the notion of conflict is inherent in psychic structure. We need to know simply that we are human beings but with a very special quality. When Freud speaks of the capacity for introspection and self-observation, I think this is one of the most important things for us, as well as having the capacity to learn to learn.

Goyo: After all, if the analyst does not have an epistemophilic function, if he has no curiosity and imagination and is incapable of learning to learn, his capacity for psychoanalytic research will be greatly reduced.

Elsa: What will be the future of research?

DR: We are talking about the therapist. I believe that psychoanalysts must be prepared to acquire new knowledge and *greater tolerance of the impact* of severely disturbed patients in long treatments. The future of analysis at the clinical level calls for a greater capacity to study the very primitive types of transferences called psychotic, delusional, or highly regressed, which give rise to very strange and intense *countertransference* effects in therapists. These are seen particularly with regressed, borderline, highly disturbed, psychotic, and drug-addicted patients.

Bruno: How does this differ from the neurotic transference?

DR: The psychotic transference is quantitatively much more intense than other types of transference. Qualitatively it has more delusional characteristics than in the neuroses. *Psychotic transference* is the patient's total and absolute conviction about a delusional belief which he has concerning his therapist and—more important—acts out in consequence. "Acting out in consequence" is important in cases where this psychotic transference is not manifested openly but is hidden or silent and detectable only from its effects.

Coco: How many things we have to learn. . . .

DR: The most important thing is human sensitivity and common sense. Unfortunately, it seems to me that these cannot be learned in psychoanalytic seminars.

Bruno: Freud makes us think of the *countertransference*.

DR: Because *empathy*—being able to feel with the patient—is one thing, while analytic technique, in which it is important *not to* make confessions, is another. We have to use our feelings simply as a signal for understanding, followed by decoding them and putting them into words with the appropriate timing. That is how we explain some aspects of the term *countertransference*.

Gerardo: The analyst also must have undergone technical training and must not use patients for the projection of his own problems, as Freud clearly states in his paper. He says, "It seems that a number of analysts learn to make use of defensive mechanisms which allow them to divert the implications and demands of analysis from themselves (probably by directing them on to other people). . . ." (1937a, p. 249).

William: "By the fool multitude, that choose by show, not learning more than the fond eye doth teach, which pries not the interior, but, like the martlet, builds in the weather on the outward wall. . . ." [*The Merchant of Venice*, II:9]

Before and after

Coco: At the time Freud was working on the case of the Wolf Man, was he looking for a traumatic origin for the disturbance?

DR: Yes, but something else as well. He was also looking for the symptom as a transaction that he could go on investigating, step by step, in the patient's childhood. He described the Wolf Man's infantile sexual wishes, his primal scene and castration fantasies. "Instincts and their Vicissitudes" (1915c) was based partly on what Freud learned from the Wolf Man.

Goyo: Here again we see how a theory of high general level is the result of observations with a specific patient or group of patients

Coco: How was Freud to conceptualize this in 1937?

Arturo: In *Inhibitions, Symptoms and Anxiety* (1926d) he took another look at the neurosis of the Wolf Man from the point of his theory of anxiety, his new theory of conflict, and a new theory of defence. He shifted to a new psychopathological conception in 1937.

Bruno: So in 1937 Freud had more to say about the ego in the case of the Wolf Man. The attempt to coordinate the demands of id, superego, and external world, and the failure of the ego to accomplish this coordination, caused him to locate this failure at an earlier developmental stage. He shifted from symptom analysis to the study of pathology more connected with the ego.

Aída: He was now thinking in terms of the life and death instincts. This interplay between Eros and Thanatos is one of the factors determining prognosis.

DR: We have just seen how Freud modified the description of the conflict from the structural point of view and from that of instinctual
conflict. He did not speak of a conflict between narcissistic libido
and object libido, but of a conflict between Eros and Thanatos. He
did not say that the passivity of the Wolf Man gave rise to his maso-
chistic attitudes, but spoke of primary masochism.

Arturo: The masochism of the Wolf Man seems in 1937 to be within the
bedrock, that is, connected with the intensity of the drives and the
innate structure of the ego. It is an apparent "obstacle" to cure.

Goyo: In this way he explains how the idea one has of a patient and
his prognosis may change as the frame of reference and the theories
gradually change and as new knowledge is acquired.

Jean-Paul: How would you now study the Wolf Man, Dr R?

DR: I would prefer to look at the transference relationship between the
patient and the therapist and to study Freud's countertransference
reactions (if I could find them) in his notes. I have already done
this with the material of the Rat Man in a paper on the handling of
resistances (Rosenfeld, 1989). An example of my approach might be
the speculation that the Wolf Man's fantasy of having an operation
on his nose was due to his confusing himself with Freud and wanting to have an operation on his face just as at the time surgery was
being performed on Freud's mouth tumour.

William: Reality could be worse than any dream.

Termination

Elsa: Freud's concept of a natural end to an analysis makes one think.
Did it have just one meaning, or a large number of different ones?

Jean-Paul: Each school or geographical area may have a different way
of conceiving of it and theorizing about it, or may adopt different
criteria relating to the development of an analysis. It is rather difficult to distinguish clearly between the idea of a phase of termination or concepts about it and the notion of a natural end. I think
they are two aspects of one and the same problem.

DR: Yes, for some schools, the aim may be to attain genitality. For
others, it is to work through what the Kleinians call the depressive position. Others take it to be the resolution of symbiosis and
nondifferentiation. Some have the criterion of a self-sufficient ego

structure with appropriate defences, while others refer to the possibility of expression in words. Then there are those for whom the
termination will be detectable in the analytic transference, with
the linguistic possibility of measuring the greater flow of information and the increased linguistic transmission of affects in human
communication. Others look for indications of changes in phonology and the music of the voice in analytic terminations. All this is
extremely interesting. And we all know about working through,
dreaming, insight, and so on.

Gerardo: Some of us have severely disturbed patients in psychoanalytic
treatment. We have learned *to treat patients for a much longer time.*
So the criteria for *termination* are also connected with the severity
of the psychopathology.

DR: Not all patients can separate and introject. For some, separation
may be equalled with a catastrophe, with the end of the world, with
being flogged, with no longer having a skin and being exposed in
their rawness. But this is discovered after many years, with subtle
linguistic clues that may appear once or twice a year in analysis, or
in psychosomatic language. We can theorize about it in many ways.
But treatments extending over many years are necessary. There is
much that we still do not know.

The pendulum

Arturo: It seems to me that when Freud speaks of alterations of the ego,
he includes technical points he has suggested before: "It sometimes
turns out that the ego has paid too high a price for the services they
render it" (1937a, p. 237).

Elsa: In the Dora analysis Freud says that we concern ourselves first
with the unconscious and then with the ego, while on other occasions we deal with resistance. He gradually re-conceptualizes the
entire model, which is nothing more nor less than the psychoanalysis he is creating, developing dialectically.

Bruno: It is clear that defences appear that do not oppose the ego or
the repressed but, rather, alter the structure of the ego itself. This
point seems fundamental to me.

Coco: I do not understand this business of the pendulum (1937a, p.
238).

Aída: I believe he is saying that, in one and the same treatment, and with one and the same patient, you proceed from resistance to the repressed, from the repressed to resistance, or, if you like, to the defence mechanisms, which appear on the surface. There is an ebb and flow.

Goyo: Originally the protagonists were the id and infantile sexuality. However, in 1937 we have an interplay between the ego and the id. Hence the pendulum. And what about the superego?

Arturo: It seems to me that it is the same as Freud described in *The Ego and the Id* (1923b). I do not think it has been greatly changed. The superego sinks more into the id.

Bruno: May I say that "impoverished" does not mean "altered". In 1937 Freud speaks of *alterations*. I think he is indicating something else, namely the type of alterations be described in "Neurosis and Psychosis" (1924b) and in "Splitting of the Ego in the Process of Defence" (1940e). I am quite certain that by 1937 he was thinking more about the actual structure of the ego.

Arturo: I still think that this is explained—indeed, explained better—in "The Psychotherapy of Hysteria" (1895d).

DR: We are not dealing with rigid models. I believe the fact that he sometimes uses the same words does not imply that they mean the same thing. After all, in the context of models at different levels the same word comes to form part of the structure of a more complex and more dynamic model and acquires a different meaning.

Goyo: I thought that previously it had been a matter of making the unconscious conscious. Not now. Now Freud says that making a conflict conscious is not enough to resolve it, and that something new arises, "new resistances in the ego"—resistances to the uncovering of resistances.

Arturo: This is also connected with *Inhibitions, Symptoms and Anxiety* (1926d), where he speaks of the five types of resistance. One of these, the *superego resistance,* is connected with the unconscious sense of guilt and related to the negative therapeutic reaction, which is mentioned in this paper as one of the obstacles to cure.

DR: The fifth type of resistance, the *id resistance,* is a theoretical abstraction, but it may be observed in clinical practice—in, for example, a closed circuit of communication (called *entropy* by some authors), which is repeated between the patient and the therapist.

Termination, distortions, relativity

Jean-Paul: Do the effects observed in the termination of therapeutic analysis differ from those in training analyses?

Aída: What happened with Ferenczi and his reproaches to Freud? What were they about? A failure to diagnose? A premature termination, as the analysis lasted only a short time? Was it a typical problem of an unresolved termination, or a negative therapeutic reaction? Ferenczi seems to have been very confused when he looked after, caressed, and kissed his patients.

DR: Ferenczi was then seriously confusing himself with Freud, himself with patients, and his own adult needs with his infantile needs. He was confusing love and hate, who he was, and who the other was. It is rather like the fusion of a baby with his mother, or like being in love. A poet put it much better: "One half of me is yours, the other half mine own." I would say, "but if mine, then yours, and so all yours."

Ferenczi's analysis with Freud may be an example of semantic distortion in which the decision to dismiss a patient is something that the analyst regards as a reasonable decision. However, the patient may distort it and experience it as if his therapist is rejecting him or no longer loves him.

Gerardo: Semantic distortion is the distortion that takes place in the meaning of the treatment.

Aída: In other words, what is *terminable* for the therapist may be recoded by the patient—although at more infantile, primitive, and hidden levels—into a totally different meaning.

DR: We may think this when we come to the vague and ambiguous term "natural end" used by Freud. "Natural" for what part of the patient, we wonder? For an adult part, it may represent something quite different from its meaning for an infantile or undifferentiated and symbiotic part. The parts of the mind that live at primitive levels of nondifferentiation, at levels of confusion and symbiosis, cannot understand the concept of the *natural end.* They find it incomprehensible and in some cases even transform it delusionally into an attack on their infantile needs.

Coco: That is what happened to Ferenczi with Freud at the end of his treatment.

DR: What is terminable for the therapist may not be so for the patient, who, in some parts of his mind, wishes to fulfil or to act out infantile needs that have never been resolved.

Elsa: Didn't the same thing happen with the Wolf Man's termination?

Gerardo: He may have felt well looked after by Freud, thanks to the collections of money organized to help him, and we may look from this new point of view at the fact that he concealed his recovery of his inheritance and the family jewels. It is not that he was dishonest or lying or concealing. These are *ethical* and not psychoanalytic ideas. In psychoanalytic terms, his action expresses his wish to continue being looked after in a symbiotic relationship, or one in which the infant is supported by the mother for a longer period than normal.

DR: What you say may be right. Another clinical diagnosis may even be possible in regard to the Wolf Man. But what interests me above all is *to hold on to doubts, and not to things that are cut and dried.* We should realize that in very disturbed patients there are areas involving object relations that are highly regressive, obscure, and encapsulated. These are areas that are still largely unknown to us. The best form of learning is to begin to recognize what we do not yet know.

Jean-Paul: We can create a model to represent what we do not yet know. We can imagine that the unknown is behind a wall and is not visible. Then we can explain the obstacles by additional hypotheses.

Goyo: Each model is a personal creation, but many people confuse the model with absolute, total, and unchangeable truth. The model, included in a context of higher-level hypotheses, serves for theory formation.

Arturo: So when Freud talks about the unmodifiable bedrock of biology, is that a model?

DR: Strictly speaking, it is a metaphor. But if we interpret it as a psychological model and use it as Freud does, in a psychological sense, whether as penis envy or masculine protest, it is useful to me, because it puts the question on the psychological level, and this is my limited area of psychoanalytic work.

Learning

Aída: I feel more comfortable if I have a firm theory with a solid structure that tells me what I should do.

Gerardo: If I can tolerate the idea that there are things I do not know, I feel more humble towards the patient and have a greater desire to learn.

Goyo: A third solution may be to modify one's theories, but the point is to be able to tolerate change; otherwise one is in the position the opponents of Galileo were in when he wanted to change a theory: their reply to him was that they could see no need to look through the telescope because the structure of the universe and the celestial spheres had already been completely explained by the master, Aristotle.

DR: Each of you three represents a model of the dialectical movement of learning: a person striving and wishing for an orderly, more stable and rigid theory; a person able to doubt or to have humility in the face of not knowing; and a person capable of seeking a new approach, a new theory. Each of you is expressing *different phases* of learning, through which we all pass.

It is as Sartre put it about freedom: Freedom is a process, a constant struggle, a goal which one tries to achieve. To say that one is already free, that one has total liberty, is just as rash as to say, in the practice of psychoanalysis, that one already knows everything and that there is nothing more to be learned.

Jean-Paul: To return to the matter of theory, I think that theory is one thing, whereas the clinical use that may be made of it in psychoanalysis is another.

Elsa: The explanations supplied by a theory may be very wide-ranging and useful, but a theory may be unable to explain all the patients to whom it is applied.

DR: It is impossible to explain all patients by a single theory. But some particular theory may be more applicable to the understanding of a larger number of patients.

Coco: So in practice it is not so easy to apply a single theory equally to all patients.

DR: I should say that there is a general psychoanalytic theory that serves as a foundation for the advancing of new, additional hypotheses. But the additional hypotheses to be formed for particular clinical cases must not be general ones applicable to all clinical cases.

Coco: It is not so easy. . . .

William: "If to do were as easy as to know what were good to do, chapels had been churches, and poor men's cottages princes' palaces. . . ." [*The Merchant of Venice*, Act I, Scene 2]

REFERENCES AND BIBLIOGRAPHY

Abraham, K. (1908). The psycho-sexual differences between hysteria and dementia praecox. In: *Selected Papers of Karl Abraham* (pp. 64–79), trans. D. Bryan & A. Strachey. London: Hogarth Press.

Abraham, K. (1911a). *Notes on Investigation and Treatment of Manic-Depressive States.* London: Karnac, 1979.

Abraham, K. (1911b). Notes on the psycho-analytic investigation and treatment of manic-depressive insanity and allied conditions. In: *Selected Papers of Karl Abraham* (pp. 137–156), trans. D. Bryan & A. Strachey. London: Hogarth Press.

Abraham, K. (1916). The first pregenital stage of the libido. In: *Selected Papers of Karl Abraham* (pp. 248–279), trans. D. Bryan & A. Strachey. London: Hogarth Press.

Abraham, K. (1945). *Selected Papers on Psycho-Analysis.* London: Hogarth Press.

Ahumada, J. (1990). On narcissistic identification and the shadow of the object. *International Review of Psycho-Analysis,* 17: 177–187.

Alvarez, A., & Reid, S. (1999). *Autism and Personality.* London/New York: Routledge.

Amati-Mehler, J. (1987). Il Bambino e la tecnologia. *ULISSE Enciclopedia della ricerca della scoperta, Vol. 13.* Milan: Editori Riuniti.

Amati-Mehler, J. (1992). Reflessione sul "Bambino Tecnologico". *Revista di Picoanalisi.*

239

Amati-Mehler, J. (1998). *Informazione e formazione della mente.* Lima: Peruvian Psychoanalitical Society.

Anzieu, A. (1986). Cadrages. Construction du cadre, construction du Moi. *Journal de la Psychanalyse de l'Enfant,* 2: 64–77.

Anzieu, A. (2000). Detachement, renoncement, separation. In: D. Houzel & C. Geissmann (Eds.), *L'enfant, ses parents et le psychanalyste.* Paris: Bayard.

Anzieu, D. (1974). Le moi-peau. *Nouvelle Revue de Psychanalyse,* 9: 195–208.

Anzieu, D. (1986). *A Skin for Thought.* London: Karnac.

Anzieu, D., Houzel, D., Missenard, A., Enriquez, M., Anzieu, A., Guillaumin, J., Doron, J., Lecourt, E., & Nathan, T. (1987). *Les enveloppes psychiques.* Paris: Dunod.

Avenburg, R. (1975). *El aparato psíquico y la realidad.* Buenos Aires: Nueva Visión.

Bateson, G., & Jackson, D. (1964). Some varieties of pathogenic organization. In: D. M. Rioch & E. A. Weinstein (Eds.), *Disorders of Communication, Vol. 42* (pp. 270–283). Research Publications, Association for Research in Nervous and Mental Disease. Baltimore, MD: Williams & Wilkins.

Bick, E. (1968). The experience of the skin in early object relations. *International Journal of Psychoanalysis, 49* (3): 484–486. Also in M. Harris Williams (Ed.), *Collected Papers of Martha Harris and Esther Bick.* Strath Tay: Clunie Press, 1987.

Bick, E. (1986). Further considerations on the skin in early relations. Findings from infant observations integrated into child and adult analysis. *British Journal of Psychotherapy,* 2: 292–299.

Bion, W. R. (1953). Notes on the theory of schizophrenia. *International Journal of Psychoanalysis, 35:* 113–118.

Bion, W. R. (1967). *Second Thoughts.* London: Heinemann. [Reprinted London: Karnac, 1984.]

Bion, W. R. (1984). Differentiation of the psychotic from the non-psychotic personalities. In: *Second Thoughts.* London: Karnac.

Bleger, J. (1967). *Simbiosis y ambigüedad.* Buenos Aires: Paidós.

Blum, H. (1987). Analysis terminable and interminable: A half-century retrospective. *International Journal of Psychoanalysis, 78* (1).

Bollas, C. (1990). Regression in the countertransference. In: L. B. Boyer & P. L. Giovacchini (Eds.), *Master Clinicians on Treating the Regressed Patient* (pp. 339–352). Northvale, NJ: Jason Aronson.

Bonaminio, V., & Slotkin, P. (2002). Cracking up: The work of the unconscious experience. *International Journal of Psychoanalysis, 83:* 304-309.

Borges, J. L. (1936). Los traductores de las mil y una noches. In: *Historia de la Eternidad.* Buenos Aires: Emece Editores 2005.

Borges, J. L. (2001). *Antología personal*. Buenos Aires/Barcelona: Editorial Sol 90, Biblioteca Argentina.

Boyer, L. B. (1982a). Analytic experiences in work with regressed patients. In: P. L. Giovacchini & L. B. Boyer (Eds.), *Technical Factors in the Treatment of the Severely Disturbed Patient* (pp. 65–106). New York: Jason Aronson, 1990.

Boyer, L. B. (1982b). Historical development of psychoanalytic psychotherapy of the schizophrenias: Freud's contribution. In: L. B. Boyer & P. L. Giovacchini (Eds.), *Psychoanalytic Treatment of Schizophrenic, Borderline and Characterological Disorders* (2nd revised and enlarged edition, pp. 35–70). New York: Jason Aronson.

Boyer, L. B. (1983). *The Regressed Patient*. New York: Jason Aronson.

Boyer, L. B. (1989). Countertransference and technique in working with the regressed patient: Further remarks. *International Journal of Psychoanalysis, 70*: 701–704.

Boyer, L. B. (1990a). Countertransference and technique. In: L. B. Boyer & P. L. Giovacchini (Eds.), *Master Clinicians on Treating the Regressed Patient* (pp. 303–324). Northvale, NJ: Jason Aronson.

Boyer, L. B. (1990b). Introduction. Countertransference: Brief history and clinical issues with regressed patients. In: L. B. Boyer & P. L. Giovacchini (Eds.), *Master Clinicians on Treating the Regressed Patient*. Northvale, NJ: Jason Aronson.

Boyer, L. B. (1999). *Countertransference and Regression*. Northvale, NJ: Jason Aronson.

Branik, E., & Rosenfeld-Prusak, K. (1995). Identity problems of Jewish adolescents in Germany. In: *Children, War and Persecution*. Osnabrück: Secolo Verlag.

Braudel, F. (1985). *La Méditerranée: L'espace et l'histoire*. Paris: Flammarion.

Brudny, G. (1991). *Represión primaria. Sus acepciones en la obra de Freud*. Edición Asociación Psicoanalítica Chilena, Vol. 2. Santiago: Ananke.

Cancrini, G., & Pelli, M. (1995). Lavorare "con" le famiglie e lavorare "sulle" famiglie: Alcune reflessioni tra approccio sistemico e intervento psicoeducazionale. *Rivista Interazioni, 1*: 151–158.

Corominas, J. (1998). *Psicopatología arcáica y desarrollo. Ensayo psicoanalítico*. Barcelona: Paidós.

Correale, A. (1994). Famiglia e psicosi. *Rivista Interazioni, 1*: 136–139.

de Mijolla, A. (Ed.) (2001). *Dictionnaire de la psychanalyse*. Paris: Calmann-Levy. [English edition: *International Dictionary of Psychoanalysis*. Macmillan Reference. Farmington Hills, MI: Thomson Gale, 2005.]

Dupetit, S. (1985). *La drogadicción y las drogas*. Buenos Aires: Kargieman.

Eickhoff, F. W. (1986). Identification and its vicissitudes in the context of the Nazi phenomenon. *International Journal of Psychoanalysis, 67*: 33–44.

Etchegoyen, H. (1999). *The Fundamentals of Psychoanalytic Technique* (revised edition). London: Karnac.

Fenichel, O. (1945). *The Psychoanalytic Theory of Neurosis*. New York: Norton.

Ferrari, P. (1987). Enfants présentant une problématique abandonnique. *Journal de la Psychanalyse de l'Enfant. Le transfert, 4*.

Ferrari, P. (1997). "Modèle psychanalytique de compréhension de l'autisme et des psychoses infantiles précoces." Paper presented at the International Congress of Autism, Buenos Aires.

Ferro, A. (1996). *Nella stanza d'analisi*. Milan: Raffaello Cortina Editore.

Folch, P., & Eskelinen, T. (1989). Symbolisation, jeu et transfert. *Revue Française de Psychanalyse, 6*: 1829–1842.

Freud, A. (1936). *The Ego and the Mechanisms of Defence*. New York: International Universities Press.

Freud, S. (1894a). The neuro-psychoses of defence. *S.E., 3*.

Freud, S. (1895d). *Studies on Hysteria. S.E., 2*.

Freud, S. (1898a). Sexuality in the aetiology of the neuroses. *S.E., 3*.

Freud, S. (1900a). *The Interpretation of Dreams. S.E., 5*.

Freud, S. (1905d). *Three Essays on the Theory of Sexuality. S.E., 7*.

Freud, S. (1905e). Fragment of an analysis of a case of hysteria. *S.E., 7*.

Freud, S. (1908c). On the sexual theories of children. *S.E., 9*.

Freud, S. (1909d). Notes upon a case of obsessional neurosis. *S.E., 10*.

Freud, S. (1910c). *Leonardo Da Vinci and a Memory of His Childhood. S.E., 11*.

Freud, S. (1910d). Future prospects in psycho-analytic therapy. *S.E., 11*.

Freud, S. (1911c). Psycho-analytic notes on an autobiographical account of a case of paranoia. *S.E., 12*.

Freud, S. (1912b). The dynamics of transference. *S.E., 12*.

Freud, S. (1912–13). *Totem and Taboo. S.E., 13*.

Freud, S. (1914c). On narcissism: An introduction. *S.E., 14*.

Freud, S. (1914f). Some reflections on schoolboy psychology. *S.E., 13*.

Freud, S. (1914g). Remembering, repeating and working-through. *S.E., 12*.

Freud, S. (1915c). Instincts and their vicissitudes. *S.E., 14*.

Freud, S. (1915e). The unconscious. *S.E., 14*.

Freud, S. (1917e). Mourning and melancholia. *S.E., 14*.

Freud, S. (1918b). From the history of an infantile neurosis. *S.E., 17*.

Freud, S. (1920g). *Beyond the Pleasure Principle. S.E., 18*.

Freud, S. (1921c). *Group Psychology and the Analysis of the Ego. S.E., 18*.

Freud, S. (1922b). Some neurotic mechanisms in jealousy, paranoia and homosexuality. *S.E., 18*.

Freud, S. (1923b). *The Ego and the Id. S.E., 19*.

Freud, S. (1924b). Neurosis and psychosis. *S.E., 19*.

Freud, S. (1924d). The dissolution of the Oedipus complex. *S.E., 19.*
Freud, S. (1926d). *Inhibitions, Symptoms and Anxiety. S.E., 20.*
Freud, S. (1933a). *New Introductory Lectures on Psychoanalysis. S.E., 22.*
Freud, S. (1937a). Analysis terminable and interminable. *S.E., 23.*
Freud, S. (1937d). Constructions in analysis. *S.E., 23.*
Freud, S. (1939a). *Moses and Monotheism. S.E., 23.*
Freud, S. (1940a). *An Outline of Psycho-Analysis. S.E., 23.*
Freud, S. (1940e). Splitting of the ego in the process of defence. *S.E., 23.*
Freud, S. (1950 [1892–1899]). Extracts from the Fliess papers. *S.E., 1.*
Freud, S., & Bullitt, W. C. (1967). *Thomas Woodrow Wilson: A Psychological Study.* London: Weidenfeld & Nicolson.
Freud, S., & Hawelka, E. (1974). *L'Homme aux Rats.* Paris: Presses Universitaires de France.
Garzoli, E. (1979). "La interpretación y los sueños." Symposium of the Buenos Aires Psychoanalytic Association.
Garzoli, H. (1991). "Una revisión sobre los conceptos de drogadicción y adicción de transferencia." Paper presented at the Buenos Aires Psychoanalytic Society Meeting, Buenos Aires, Argentina (March).
Geissmann, C., & Geissmann, P. (2000). Croissance d'une pensée: Psychanalyse d'une enfant autiste. In: D. Houzel & C. Geissmann (Eds.), *L'enfant, ses parents et le psychanalyste.* Paris: Bayard.
Giovacchini, P. (1990). Epilogue: Contemporary perspectives on technique. In: L. B. Boyer & P. L. Giovacchini (Eds.), *Master Clinicians on Treating the Regressed Patient* (pp. 353–381). Northvale, NJ: Jason Aronson.
Goldberg, P. (1990). The holding environment: Conscious and unconscious elements in the building of a therapeutic framework. In: L. B. Boyer & P. L. Giovacchini (Eds.), *Master Clinicians on Treating the Regressed Patient.* Northvale, NJ: Jason Aronson.
Green, A. (1977). *Le discours vivant. La conception psychanalytique de l'affect.* Paris: Presses Universitaires de France.
Green, A. (1986). *On Private Madness.* New York: International Universities Press, 1990.
Green, A. (1992). *La folie privée.* Paris: Gallimard.
Green, A. (1996). La sexualité a-t-elle un quelconque rapport avec la psychanalyse? *Revue Française de Psychanalyse, 60*: 829–848.
Green, A. (1997). *Les chaînes d'Éros.* Paris: Odile Jacob.
Grotstein, J. S. (1987). "Schizophrenia as a Disorder of Self-regulation and Interactional Regulation." Paper presented at the Boyer House Foundation Conference on The Regressed Patient, San Francisco (21 March).
Grotstein, J. S. (2000). *Who Is the Dreamer Who Dreams the Dream? A Study of Psychic Presences.* Hillsdale, NJ: Analytic Press.

Hartmann, H. (1964). *Essays on Ego Psychology.* London: Hogarth Press.

Hochmann, J. (1994). *La consolation. Essai sur le soin psychique.* Paris: Odile Jacob.

Hochmann, J. (1997). *Pour soigner l'enfant autiste.* Paris: Odile Jacob.

Houzel, D. (1988). Les angoisses d'anéantissement du nourrisson. *Psychiatrie Française,* 3: 19–27.

Houzel, D. (2000a). L'alliance thérapeutique. In: D. Houzel & C. Geissmann (Eds.), *L'enfant, ses parents et le psychanalyste.* Paris: Bayard.

Houzel, D. (2000b). Le traumatisme de la naissance. In: D. Houzel & C. Geissmann (Eds.), *L'enfant, ses parents et le psychanalyste* (pp. 447–458). Paris: Bayard.

Izzo, E. (2000). "Más allá de la interpretación" [Interpreting in the treatment with a severely disturbed patient]. Buenos Aires Symposium at the Argentinian Psychoanalytical Association (April).

Jones, E. (1962). *Sigmund Freud: Life and Work.* London: Hogarth Press.

Kernberg, O. (1965). Notes on countertransference. *Journal of the American Psychoanalytic Association, 13:* 38–56.

Kernberg, O. (1979). Technical considerations in the treatment of borderline personality organization. In: J. Le Boit & A. Capponi (Eds.), *Advances in Psychotherapy of the Borderline Patient* (pp. 269–305). New York: Jason Aronson.

Kernberg, O. (1984). *Severe Personality Disorders: Psychotherapeutic Strategies.* New Haven, CT: Yale University Press.

Kernberg, O. (1985). *Internal World and External Reality: Object Relation Theory Applied.* New York: Jason Aronson.

Kernberg, O. (1992). *Aggression in Personality Disorders and Perversions.* New Haven, CT: Yale University Press.

Klein, M. (1930). The psychotherapy of the psychoses. In: *The Writings of Melanie Klein, Vol. 1: Love, Guilt and Reparation and Other Works 1921–1945* (pp. 233–235). London: Hogarth Press, 1975. [Reprinted London: Karnac, 1992.]

Klein, M. (1935). A contribution to the psychogenesis of manic-depressive states. In: *Contributions to Psychoanalysis, 1921–1945.* London: Hogarth Press, 1968.

Klein, M. (1945). The Oedipus complex in the light of early anxieties. In: *The Writings of Melanie Klein, Vol. 1: Love, Guilt and Reparation and Other Works 1921–1945* (pp. 370–419). London: Hogarth Press, 1975. [Reprinted London: Karnac, 1992.]

Klein, M. (1968). *Contributions to Psycho-Analysis.* London: Hogarth Press.

Klein, M. (1975a). *The Writings of Melanie Klein, Vol. 1: Love, Guilt and Reparation and Other Works.* London: Hogarth Press. [Reprinted London: Karnac, 1992.]

Klein, M. (1975b). *The Writings of Melanie Klein, Vol. 3: Envy and Gratitude and Other Works*. London: Hogarth Press. [Reprinted London: Karnac, 1993.]

Klein, S. (1980). Autistic phenomena in neurotic patients. *International Journal of Psychoanalysis*, 61: 395–402.

Kliman, G. (1998) "The Cornerstone Method: In-classroom Therapy for Seriously Disturbed Preschoolers." Paper presented at the American Academy of Child and Adolescent Psychiatry, Chicago (October). [Abstract in: *Scientific Bulletin of the Children's Psychological Health Center* (www.cphc-sf.org/resources_articles_bulletin0299.shtml).]

Klimovsky, G. (1971). *El método científico en psicología y psicopatología*, ed. D. Ziziemsky. Buenos Aires: Nueva Visión.

Klimovsky, G. (1980a). Estructura y validez de las teorías científicas. In: D. Ziziemsky (Ed.), *Métodos de investigación en biología y psicopatología*. Buenos Aires: Nueva Visión.

Klimovsky, G. (1980b). Teorías científicas, estructura y validación. In: D. Ziziemsky (Ed.), *Métodos de investigación en biología y psicopatología* (pp. 59–70). Buenos Aires: Nueva Visión.

Lagache, D. (1961). La psychanalyse et la structure de la personalité. *La Psychanalyse*, 6.

Laplanche, J. (1999). *Entre séduction et inspiration. L'homme*. Paris: Presses Universitaires de France.

Laplanche, J., & Pontalis, J.-B. (1967). *The Language of Psychoanalysis*. London: Hogarth Press, 1973. [Reprinted London: Karnac, 1988.] (First published as *Vocabulaire de la psychanalyse*. Paris: Press Universitaires de France.)

Liberman, D. (1970–72). *Lingüística, interacción comunicativa y proceso psicoanalítico, Vols. 1–3*. Buenos Aires: Nueva Visión-Galerna.

Liberman, D. (1978). Affective response of the analyst to the patient's communication. *International Journal of Psychoanalysis*, 59: 335–340.

López, B. (1983). Los afectos y el narcisismo. *Psicoanálisis (APdeBa)*, 5: 26–46.

López, B. (1985). Una distorsión semántico-pragmática. El paciente del discurso ininterrumpido. *Revista de Psicoanálisis (APdeBA)*, 7: 279–300.

Mahler, M. (1968). *On Human Symbiosis and the Vicissitudes of Individuation, Vol. 1*. New York: International Universities Press.

Martini, G. (1995). Dinamiche tra gli operatori dei servizi di salute mentale e i genitori dei pazienti psicotici: Un terreno che scotta. *Rivista Interazioni*, 1: 81–94.

Marty, P., M'Uzan, M., & David, C. (1963). *L'investigation psychosomatique. Sept observations cliniques*. Paris: Presses Universitaires de France.

McDougall, J. (1990). Identification, neoneeds and neosexualities. In: L. B. Boyer & P. L. Giovacchini (Eds.), *Master Clinicians on Treating the Regressed Patient* (pp. 189–210). Northvale, NJ: Jason Aronson.

Meadows, P. (1969). *Modelos, sistemas y ciencia*. Buenos Aires: University of Buenos Aires Publications.

Meltzer, D. (1966). The relation of anal masturbation to projective identification. *International Journal of Psychoanalysis, 47*: 335–343.

Meltzer, D. (1975). Adhesive identification. *Contemporary Psychoanalysis, 11*: 289–310.

Meltzer, D. (1986). *Studies in Extended Metapsychology*. Strath Tay: Clunie Press.

Nicolò Corighiano, A., & Borgia, F. (1995). Tra l'intrapsichico e linterpersonale. La folie à deux: come ipotesi-modello di un funzionamiento interpersonale. *Rivista Interazioni, 1*: 40–51.

Ogden, T. (1986). *The Matrix of the Mind: Object Relations and the Psychoanalytic Dialogue*. Northvale, NJ: Jason Aronson.

Ogden, T. (1990). Analyzing the matrix of transference. In: L. B. Boyer & P. L. Giovacchini (Eds.), *Master Clinicians on Treating the Regressed Patient.* Northvale, NJ: Jason Aronson.

Ogden, T. (1994). *Subjects of Analysis*. Northvale, NJ: Jason Aronson.

Ogden, T. (2001). "The music of what happens" in poetry and psychoanalysis. In: *Conversations at the Frontier of Dreaming*. Northvale, NJ: Jason Aronson.

Oliner, M. M. (1988). *Cultivating Freud's Garden in France*. Northvale, NJ: Jason Aronson.

Page, I. H., & Durstan, H. (1962). Persistence of normal blood pressure after discontinuing treatment in hypertensive patients. *Circulation, 62*: 433–436.

Painceira Plot, A. (1997). *Clínica psicoanalítica a partir de la obra de Winnicott*. Buenos Aires: Lumen.

Pérez-Sánchez, M. (1986). *Observación de niños*. Barcelona: Paidós Ibérica.

Perren-Klinger, G. (1995). Psychotrauma: A change in perspective. From pathology to coping, from individual to community, from victim to survivor. In: *Children, War and Persecution*. Osnabrük: Secolo Verlag.

Pichon-Rivière, E. (1959). *Del psicoanálisis a la psicología social*. Buenos Aires: Galerna, 1972.

Popper, K. (1965). *Conjectures and Refutations: The Growth of Scientific Knowledge*. New York: Basic Books.

Quinodoz, J. M. (1989). Female homosexual patients in analysis. *International Journal of Psychoanalysis, 70*: 55–63.

Quinodoz, J. M. (1999). Dreams that turn over a page: Interrogation dreams with paradoxical regressive content. *International Journal of Psychoanalysis, 80.*

Racker, H. (1968). *Transference and Countertransference.* New York: International Universities Press.

Reid, S. (1997). *Developments in Infant Observation: The Tavistock Model.* London/New York: Routledge.

Resnik, S. (1987). *The Theatre of the Dream.* London: Tavistock.

Resnik, S. (1994). Erotizzazione e psicosi nella famiglia. *Rivista Interazioni,* 1: 73–81.

Rosembaum, B., & Sonne, H. (1986). *The Language of Psychosis.* New York: New York University Press.

Rosenfeld, D. (1975). Trastornos en la piel y el esquema corporal. Identificación proyectiva y el cuento infantil "Piel de Asno". *Revista de Psicoanálisis,* 2: 309–330.

Rosenfeld, D. (1976). *Clínica psicoanalítica. Estudios sobre drogadicción, psicosis y narcisismo.* Buenos Aires: Galerna.

Rosenfeld, D. (1980). Handling of resistances in adult patients. *International Journal of Psychoanalysis,* 61: 71–83.

Rosenfeld, D. (1984). Hypochondriasis, somatic delusion and body scheme in psychoanalytic practice. *International Journal of Psychoanalysis,* 65: 377–387.

Rosenfeld, D. (1985a). Distorsions des actes. *Nouvelle Revue de Psychanalyse,* 30: 191–199.

Rosenfeld, D. (1985b). "Identification and its vicissitudes in relation to the Nazi phenomenon." Paper presented to the International Psychoanalytical Congress, Hamburg.

Rosenfeld, D. (1986). Identification and the Nazi phenomenon. *International Journal of Psychoanalysis,* 67: 53–64.

Rosenfeld, D. (1988). *Psychoanalysis and Groups: History and Dialectics.* London: Karnac.

Rosenfeld, D. (1989). Handling of resistances in adult patients. *International Journal of Psychoanalysis,* 61: 71–83.

Rosenfeld, D. (1990a). Primitive object relations in drug addict patients. In: L. B. Boyer & P. L. Giovacchini (Eds.), *Master Clinicians on Treating the Regressed Patient.* Northvale, NJ: Jason Aronson.

Rosenfeld, D. (1990b). Psychotic body image. In: L. B. Boyer & P. L. Giovacchini (Eds.), *Master Clinicians on Treating the Regressed Patient* (pp. 165–188). Northvale, NJ: Jason Aronson. [Chapter 7, this volume]

Rosenfeld, D. (1991). Freud: An imaginary dialogue. In: J. Sandler (Ed.), *On Freud's "Analysis Terminable and Interminable"* (pp. 142–162). New Haven, CT: Yale University Press. [Chapter 8, this volume.]

Rosenfeld, D. (1992a). Psychic changes in the paternal image. *International Journal of Psychoanalysis, 73*: 757–771.

Rosenfeld, D. (1992b). *The Psychotic: Aspects of the Personality.* London: Karnac.

Rosenfeld, D. (1997). Understanding varieties of autistic encapsulation: A homage to Frances Tustin. In: J. Mitrani & T. Mitrani (Eds.), *Encounters with Autistic States: A Memorial Tribute to Frances Tustin.* Northvale, NJ: Jason Aronson.

Rosenfeld, D. (2000). Le rôle du père dans la psychose. In: D. Houzel & C. Geissmann (Eds.), *L'enfant, ses parents et le psychanalyste.* Paris: Bayard.

Rosenfeld, D. (2001a). Psychotic addiction to computer and videogames. In: P. Williams (Ed.), *A Language for Psychosis* (pp. 175–198). London: Whurr. [Chapter 4, this volume.]

Rosenfeld, D. (2001b). Toxicomanie, addiction, et transfert psychotique. In: A. de Mijolla (Ed.) *Dictionnaire de la psychanalyse.* Paris: Calmann-Levy, 2001 (English edition: *International Dictionary of Psychoanalysis.* Macmillan Reference. Farmington Hills, MI: Thomson Gale, 2005).

Rosenfeld, D. (2005). Der 11 September: Militärdiktatur und psychotische Episode. *Jahrbuch der Psychoanalyse. Trauma: Neue Entwicklungen in der Psychoanalyse, 50.* Stuttgart: Fromman-Holzboog. [Chapter 1, this volume.]

Rosenfeld, D., & Pistol, D. (1986). "Episodio psicótico y su detección precoz en la transferencia." Paper presented at the Sixteenth Latin-American Psychoanalytic Congress, Mexico City (July).

Rosenfeld, H. (1965). *Psychotic States.* London: Hogarth Press.

Rosenfeld, H. (1979). Transference psychosis in the borderline. In: J. Le Boit & A. Capponi (Eds.), *Advances in Psychotherapy of the Borderline Patient* (pp. 485–510). New York: Jason Aronson.

Rosenfeld, H. (1987). *Impasse and Interpretation.* London: Tavistock.

Sandler, A. M. (1988). Concluding discussion. In: J. Sandler (Ed.), *Projection, Identification, Projective Identification.* London: Karnac.

Sandler, J. (1991). *On Freud's "Analysis Terminable and Interminable".* London: International Psychoanalytical Association. New Haven, CT: Yale University Press.

Santamaría, A. (1978). "El paciente, la enfermedad y la muerta en psicoanálisis." Paper presented at the XIIth Latin-American Psychoanalytic Congress, Mexico City (July).

Sartre, J.-P. (1960). *Critique de la raison dialectique.* Paris: Gallimard.

Schacht, L. (1988). La planète imaginaire. *Journal de la Psychanalyse de L'enfant, 5*: 235–262.

Schilder, P. (1935). The psycho-analysis of space. *International Journal of Psychoanalysis*, 16: 274–295.

Scott, W. C. M. (1948). Embryological, neurological, and analytical implications of the body scheme. *International Journal of Psychoanalysis*, 29: 141–155.

Searles, H. (1960). *The Nonhuman Environment in Normal Development and Schizophrenia*. New York: International Universities Press.

Searles, H. (1961). The sources of anxiety in paranoid schizophrenia. *British Journal of Medical Psychology*, 34: 129–141.

Searles, H. (1979). *Countertransference and Related Subjects*. New York: International Universities Press.

Searles, H. (1986). Transference psychosis in the psychotherapy of schizophrenia. In: *Collected Papers on Schizophrenia and Related Subjects*. London: Hogarth Press/Karnac.

Searles, H. (1990). Unconscious identification. In: L. B. Boyer & P. L. Giovacchini (Eds.), *Master Clinicians on Treating the Regressed Patient* (pp. 211–226). Northvale, NJ: Jason Aronson.

Segal, H. (1950). Some aspects of the analysis of a schizophrenic. *International Journal of Psychoanalysis*, 31: 286–278.

Segal, H. (1986). *The Work of Hanna Segal*. London: Karnac.

Segal, H. (1988). *Introduction to the Work of Melanie Klein*. London: Karnac.

Segal, H. (1994). Fantasy and reality. *International Journal of Psychoanalysis*, 75 (2): 395–401.

Shakespeare, W. (1979). *The Complete Works*. Annotated. The Globe Illustrated Shakespeare. Greenwich House. New York: Crown.

Steiner, J. (1990). The defensive function of pathological organizations. In: L. B. Boyer & P. L. Giovacchini (Eds.), *Master Clinicians on Treating the Regressed Patient* (pp. 97–116). Northvale, NJ: Jason Aronson.

Steiner, J. (2006). Interpretative enactments and the analytic setting. *International Journal of Psychoanalysis*, 87: 315–320.

Thomä, H., & Kächele, H. (1988). *Lehrbuch der psychoanalytischen Therapie, Vol. 2: Praxis*. Berlin/Heidelberg: Springer-Verlag.

Tustin, F. (1972). *Autism and Child Psychosis*. London: Hogarth Press.

Tustin, F. (1981). *Autistic States in Children*. London: Routledge & Kegan Paul.

Tustin, F. (1986). *Autistic Barriers in Neurotic Patients*. London: Karnac.

Tustin, F. (1988). "To be or not to be": A study of autism. *Winnicott Studies* 3: 43–55.

Tustin, F. (1990a). Autistic encapsulation in neurotic patients. In: L. B. Boyer & P. L. Giovacchini (Eds.), *Master Clinicians on Treating the Regressed Patient*. Northvale, NJ: Jason Aronson.

Tustin, F. (1990b). *The Protective Shell in Children and Adults*. London: Karnac.

Tustin, F. (2000). L'autisme psychogénétique. In: D. Houzel & C. Geissmann (Eds.), *L'enfant, ses parents et le psychanalyste*. Paris: Bayard.

Volkan, V. (1996). *The Infantile Psychotic Self and Its Fates: Understanding Schizophrenics and Other Difficult Patients*. Northvale, NJ: Jason Aronson.

Volkan, V. (1997). *The Seed of Madness*. Madison, CT: International Universities Press.

Wallerstein, R. (1988). One psychoanalysis or many? *International Journal of Psychoanalysis, 69* (1): 5–21.

Wallerstein, R. (1993). Between chaos and petrification: A summary of the Fifth IPA Conference of Training Analysts. *International Journal of Psychoanalysis, 74*: 165–178.

Wallerstein, R. (1994). Borderline disorders: Report on the Fourth IPA Research Conference. *International Journal of Psychoanalysis, 75.*

Watzlawick, P., Beavin, J., & Jackson, D. D. (1967). *Pragmatics of Human Communication*. New York: Norton.

Williams, P. (2001). Psychotic developments in a sexually abused borderline patient. In: *A Language for Psychosis*. London/Philadelphia: Whurr.

Wilson, C. P. (1989). Family psychopathology. In: C. P. Wilson and I. L. Mintz, *Psychosomatic Symptoms: Psychodynamic Treatment of the Underlying Personality Disorder* (pp. 63–82). Northvale, NJ: Jason Aronson.

Wilson, C. P., Hogan, C. C., & Mintz, I. L. (1992). *Psychodynamic Technique in the Treatment of the Eating Disorders*. Northvale, NJ: Jason Aronson.

Winnicott, D. W. (1957). *Collected Papers: Through Paediatrics to Psycho-Analysis*. London: Tavistock.

Winnicott, D. W. (1958). Transitional objects and transitional phenomena. In: *Through Paediatrics to Psychoanalysis: Collected Papers* (pp. 229–242). London: Tavistock/Hogarth Press. [Reprinted London: Karnac Books & The Institute of Psychoanalysis, 1992.]

Winnicott, D. W. (1962). Ego integration in child development. In: *The Maturational Processes and the Facilitating Environment* (pp. 56–63). New York: International Universities Press, 1965.

Winnicott, D. W. (1969). The use of an object and relating through identifications. In: *Playing and Reality* (pp. 86–94). New York: Basic Books, 1971.

Winnicott, D. W. (1971). Le corp et le self. *Nouvelle Revue de Psychanalyse, 3*: 37–48.

Winnicott, D. W. (1992). *Collected Papers: Through Paediatrics to Psychoanalysis*. London: Tavistock/Hogarth Press. [Reprinted London: Karnac Books & The Institute of Psychoanalysis, 1992.]

INDEX

251

transference (*continued*):
in schizophrenia, 146
very primitive types of, 229
work in, 36, 75
microscopic, 75, 112
transferential interpretation, 95
transitional object, 66
transitional space, 66
creation of, 66
transsexual patients, 130
transvestites, 71
trauma(s)/traumata, 3–4, 30, 38, 40, 69
catastrophic, 66
Freud on, 220–222
traumatic episode, 35
traumatic experiences, childhood, 1
traumatic neurosis, 221
treatment, obstacles to, 223
truth, love of (Freud), 228
Tustin, F., 44, 64, 81, 143, 165, 172, 184, 185, 189
autism:
and projective identification, 25
protective function of, 30
autistic encapsulation, 80
autistic-like seeking of sensorial stimuli, 63, 139
autistic object, body as, 166
autistic omnipotence, 178
psychotic episode as "black hole", 22, 140, 166–167

ulcerative colitis, 194
unconscious, primitive, 111
unconscious dynamics, patient's, 1

verbalization, 21–22, 24
Videla, J. R., 13
video games, psychotic addiction to, xiv–xviii, 117–144
violence, xiv, 4, 9, 44, 81, 89, 99, 146, 163
"Julie", 47, 49, 62, 68, 70
"Lorenzo", 117–118, 121–126, 128, 130, 132, 139
in schizophrenic patients, 133
Volkan, V., 18, 66, 130
vomiting, 44–48, 50–52, 54–55, 68, 70, 73, 107
and disturbances of thought, 55

Wallerstein, R., 18, 54
Watzlawick, P., 36, 226
weaning, 22
Williams, P., 66
Wilson, C. P., 47, 106
Wilson, T. W., 225
Winnicott, D. W., 30, 31, 66, 69, 138, 188, 211, 213
"Wolf Man" (Freud's patient), 223, 225, 230–231, 235
working through, 79, 232
of loss of object, 35
of mourning, pathological, 35